Empire Javelin, D-Day Assault Ship

After graduating in European history from the University of East Anglia, Philip Kay-Bujak spent ten years in the Royal Anglian Regiment as a TA officer and twenty-three years teaching history and classics in the independent sector. He was a housemaster at Langley School, in Norfolk and Headmaster of Stover School, in Devon. An Associate of the Royal Historical Society, he is now retired and is a full-time writer. His previous works include *Undefeated* (2008), *The Bravest Man in The British Army* (2018), *The Life of Cicero* (2023) and *Gallia Narbonnensis*, which details the Roman invasion and occupation of what is now southern France. He lives in East Sussex.

Other books by Philip Kay-Bujak

Norfolk & Suffolk in the Great War

Attleborough: the evolution of a town

Undefeated

Around the World in 100 Years

The Bravest man in the British Army:

My Heart is in the Highlands: The Life and Work of Archibald Kay

Cicero: Lessons for Today from the Greatest Orator of the Roman Republic

Empire Javelin, D-Day Assault Ship

The British vessel that landed
the US 116th Infantry on Omaha Beach

Philip Kay-Bujak

Pen & Sword
MARITIME

First published in Great Britain in 2024 by
Pen & Sword Maritime
An imprint of Pen & Sword Books Limited
Yorkshire – Philadelphia

ISBN 978 1 39903 581 1

A CIP catalogue record for this book is
available from the British Library

Typeset by Mac Style
Printed in the UK by CPI Group (UK) Ltd, Croydon, CR0 4YY.

FSC
MIX
Paper | Supporting
responsible forestry
FSC® C013604
www.fsc.org

Pen & Sword Books Limited incorporates the imprints of After
the Battle, Atlas, Archaeology, Aviation, Discovery, Family History,
Fiction, History, Maritime, Military, Military Classics, Politics,
Select, Transport, True Crime, Air World, Frontline Publishing, Leo
Cooper, Remember When, Seaforth Publishing, The Praetorian Press,
Wharncliffe Local History, Wharncliffe Transport, Wharncliffe True
Crime and White Owl.

For a complete list of Pen & Sword titles please contact

PEN & SWORD BOOKS LIMITED
47 Church Street, Barnsley, South Yorkshire, S70 2AS, England
E-mail: enquiries@pen-and-sword.co.uk
Website: www.pen-and-sword.co.uk
or
PEN AND SWORD BOOKS
1950 Lawrence Rd, Havertown, PA 19083, USA
E-mail: uspen-and-sword@casematepublishers.com
Website: www.penandswordbooks.com

Contents

Acknowledgements

There is no voice that speaks with more authority than those who participated in the events contained in any work of history – this book on the SS *Empire Javelin* is no exception to this rule. The backbone of this book is that it is connected throughout to the real lives of real people, joined together by the evidence of their own experience and corroborated by those around them. Thus, I am indebted to many individuals and organisations who, in large or small ways, have contributed first-hand accounts of people who participated in the journey both of the soldiers of the 116th Infantry Regiment, 29th Division, and the SS *Empire Javelin* and created their own piece of history.

Without the help and support of Michael Pocock and his wonderful collection of records relating to hundreds of ships in his Maritime Quest, this book could not even have got off the drawing board. Equally all the contributors to Maritime Quest deserve my grateful thanks including Hannah Leiditch in relation to Paul Beltz, and John Coxhead. The papers of Lieutenant John Gilmour RNVR and Sub-Lieutenant James Green RN were also invaluable in understanding the journey of the SS *Empire Javelin* up to and beyond D-Day and the role of the Royal Navy in supporting the American troops landing on Omaha beach. In relation to the latter, I am indebted to Kevan Elsby who shared much of his enthusiasm and understanding about the role of the LCAs in the Omaha beach landings.

I would like to extend my thanks to Richard Markham who, in memory of his father Tommy, gave permission for many of his father's images to be used in the book and to John D. Long, Director of Education at the National D-Day Memorial Foundation for the provision of images of Bedford VA before 1941. I would like to thank Truman Adkins and Mary Kay Washington – both of whom enabled me to find out more about Lieutenant Benjamin Rives Kearfott who arrived in Company A only five days before D-Day and lost his life on 6 June 1944. Another hero of D-Day was Lieutenant Edward Marcellus Gearing and from his son Michael Gearing I was able to understand more about his father than I would ever have been able to without his help and it was Barbara Adamson of the Shenandoah County Historical Association that spanned the thousands of miles between us, as if it were nothing, and connected me both to Michael Gearing and provided a perfect copy of the photograph I needed. To Dr Bert

Bratton for his permission to use the images of war provided by Major Hazen I also extend my thanks. Both the 29th Infantry Division Association and The USS Landing Craft Infantry National Association have helped in the provision of materials through their websites as have the BBC Oral History archives and to Ohio State University who have custody over the Cornelius Ryan Archive.

In the UK, the sacrifices made by American forces on D-Day will never be forgotten thanks the dedication of the members of the Ivybridge Heritage & Archives Group in Ivybridge. Worthy of special mention are Lesley Thatcher, who never tired of my emails, and Sheila and Martin Hancox. Their dedication to preserving the past has created a wonderful resource of materials relating to the period when the 116th Infantry were resident in the town and I am very grateful to them for their willingness to help.

Finally, thank you to my family Helena, Skye and Cameron for their patience, understanding and interest during the preparation and writing of this book.

P.K-B April, 2024

Part I

The Birth of a Ship

'If, as I believe, you are convinced, Mr President, that the defeat of the Nazi and Fascist tyranny is a matter of high consequence to the people of the United States and to the Western Hemisphere, you will regard this letter not as an appeal for aid, but as a statement of the minimum action necessary to the achievement of our common purpose.'

I remain, yours very sincerely,
Winston S. Churchill

(Concluding paragraph of a fifteen-page letter sent from Winston Churchill as Prime Minister to Franklin D. Roosevelt. Written and sent on 7 December 1941 shortly after the Japanese attack on Pearl Harbor.)

In the small town of Bedford, Virginia, who would have guessed that the news that arrived by radio or newspaper on the evening of 7 December – 'a date that will live in infamy' or the morning of 8 December – would signal the start of a process that would ultimately conclude with the deaths of many of their young men in under four years' time. The Japanese attack on the American naval base of Pearl Harbor was to trigger a seismic change in the lives of millions of American men and women including every inhabitant of the town of Bedford. Indeed, some of those from the town who would lose their lives on Dog Green beach in Normandy only two and a half years later would undoubtedly have been clustered around a radio during the afternoon of Monday 8 December 1941 – whether already in uniform as part of the Virginia National Guard or sitting in a bar somewhere on the streets of Bedford.

Life moves in mysterious ways – those of us lucky enough to have had the experience of a fairly long one will understand this more than most. Few can say when or how their time will come but preparing to serve in a war accelerates and shrinks the imagination – the future seems very far away and thoughts shorten to the next few weeks or even the next few days. But the minds of the men of Company A of the 116th Infantry Regiment, 29th Division, as they rolled across the cold, wet, salty and grey English Channel, were focussed on an even shorter time frame – they wanted and prayed to survive just until mid-morning of that day.

For many of the passengers that would set sail on board the SS *Empire Javelin* in the early afternoon of 5 June 1944, the war had begun back on that Monday afternoon in December 1941 and had led them here where their life would end before 08.00 on Tuesday 6 June and before their 30th birthday. As the German troops ate their early morning breakfast defending the stretch codenamed by the allies as Omaha Beach, the American soldiers were sick to their stomachs and had been for hours on end; as the Germans drank coffee, the Americans vomited over the side of the ship – some had been doing this since they set sail in the middle of the afternoon the day before, and as the German soldiers stretched their aching early morning limbs and thought of home, the boys from the small town Bedford Virginia, a town of just three thousand souls – less the ninety or so young men on board the *Empire Javelin* – thought of nothing else except getting off the bloody boat and how to dodge the first bullets.

Chapter One

The Genesis of the *Empire Javelin*, 1939

None of this was the fault of the ship. In those dark early hours before that June day dawned, the wet, slippery and cold steel decks of the *Empire Javelin* had been built, painted and sailed across the Atlantic Ocean all in under three years for one purpose only and this was it: to carry the American troops for the invasion of Normandy across the water to France. The ship was doing what she had been built to do and was by all accounts doing it well. The men and women who had designed the ship, and those who had built it, were fast asleep in their beds on the east coast of America, or were just thinking of going to bed in California; they had no idea that their ship was in the process of fulfilling their ambitions for her. The British Royal Navy crew that was sailing her were indeed pleased with her performance. Crawling along at only a few knots, the SS *Empire Javelin* was doing as her name required – heading on a straight course to her destination just off the sand dunes of Normandy and for Dog Green Beach at the far western end of what was to become a very blood-soaked beach. But only four years before, in 1940, the idea of building the *Javelin* had not even been conceived.

The Lend–Lease deal was to be the genesis of vast building and manufacturing programmes in the United States designed to keep Britain fighting, with the ultimate hope of winning the war against Nazi Germany. But it had not been an easy deal to strike and was only agreed after a series of creeping steps forward. In the United States of America, politicians and people watched wars from a great distance. Similar to our position in the world today, as we see and hear updates from the media on the war in Ukraine, the American people were equally detached from the realities of war. It was not their homes that had been blasted to pieces by German aircraft nor their sons who had been blown apart by German artillery, and they watched as Europe suffered just as we watch and wait to see whether the war will spread.

The British government of 1939 was well aware from the start that they could not take on Germany in a face-to-face land war. The policies of appeasement and the impact of depression had combined to see the British armed forces reduced to a minimum and when war broke out in September 1939, no amount of propaganda films or House of Commons bravado could escape the conclusion that the British Navy was the only means of mounting a sustained defence of the British Isles – but even ships can be sunk.

For the time being all Britain and her Commonwealth allies could do was process the thousands of French and Polish troops and people who had escaped and were arriving daily in the ports and frantically work out how to turn the British peacetime economy into a wartime one. Meanwhile, in a re-run of 1914, the regular British forces were transferred to northern France to block any attempt to attack France north of the apparently impenetrable Maginot Line. However, the simple fact was that it would take time and a lot of money to refashion factories from making shoes into making guns, torpedoes, aircraft, tanks and they did not know how long they had to do this – but the government did know who they needed to turn to in the short term.

Since September 1939 and the outbreak of the war in Europe, the hands of Franklin D. Roosevelt, indeed the hands of every US President, had been tied by legislation that prevented the USA from providing arms and ammunition outside of the United States. In the United States, the 1930s were dominated by non-interventionism with three separate acts passing into United States law in 1935, 1936 and 1937 which, cumulatively, did what they were meant to do to keep the United States out of any wars, anywhere in the world.

> 'Our own troubles are so numerous and so difficult that we have neither the
> time or inclination to meddle in the affairs of others.'
> Congresswoman Edith Nourse Rogers

As the European situation unfolded, it was clear to Roosevelt that it would become impossible for the United States to remain totally neutral. Relations between the United States and Japan were equally strained and the forces of democracy were under attack around the globe. There were three right-wing, militaristic and aggressive nations under what was now known as the Axis with Germany, Italy and Japan seemingly determined to break the international conventions, tear up the weakening League of Nations and adopt war, both in Western Europe and in the Far East, to achieve their stated aims. There was also the slowly stirring and sinister giant of the Soviet Union with the communist dictatorship of Stalin to consider and where and when they would play their part in this new international crisis.

At the beginning of 1939 in his State of the Union address, Roosevelt reassured his party and his people:

> 'In reporting on the state of the nation, I have felt it necessary on previous
> occasions to advise the Congress of disturbance abroad and of the need of putting

our own house in order in the face of storm signals from across the seas. As this Seventy-sixth Congress opens there is need for further warning. A war which threatened to envelop the world in flames has been averted; but it has become increasingly clear that world peace is not assured.'

Franklin D. Roosevelt
4 January 1939

Roosevelt needed some wriggle room on the Neutrality Acts if he was to be able to support Britain in her fight, but any thought of a drift away from neutrality was steadfastly denied and rejected by both congress and the senate – until Germany and the Soviet Union invaded Poland in September 1939. The next step came quickly and Roosevelt suggested a compromise with a fourth Neutrality Act which he introduced late in September 1939 and the 'cash & carry' scheme began – much to the relief of the British government still led by the exhausted Neville Chamberlain who steadfastly harboured a belief that it was possible to persuade Hitler from going any further. In essence, the new Neutrality Act ended the embargo on munitions and allowed the sale of arms and military equipment to foreign powers provided they collected and transported these goods in their own merchant ships and paid for them in cash – with the effects of the Depression still fresh in everyone's mind, this meant paying in gold. The Act was agreed and signed into law by the President on 4 November and allied nations – most especially the British – were now able to purchase war materials leaving the United States still, in theory at least, neutral.

For the majority of the American people, non-intervention was still by far the most popular policy. The America First Committee and the dedication of the aviator Charles Lindburgh to peace provided a constant stream of messaging that Hitler was no threat to the United States. Britain, supported now by its Commonwealth nations such as Canada, India and Australia, had to fight hard for survival across the world – its remaining forces stretched thinly, short of supplies and ammunition and the convoys collecting arms via the cash and carry scheme were under constant threat of U-boat attacks across the Atlantic, as was all British merchant and Royal Navy shipping anywhere in the world. In the four months between September and December 1939 alone Britain lost three trawlers to mines laid in the Thames estuary; five ammunition ships, a battleship – HMS *Royal Oak* – over ninety merchant ships, an aircraft carrier – HMS *Courageous*, three destroyers and over twenty coastal trawlers to a mixture of mines and U-boat torpedoes. A shot had yet to be fired in anger at a German soldier and Britain was already running short of food and ships.

By May 1940 the British Merchant Navy had already lost over 150 ships and thousands of seamen which would take time to replace and this rate of attrition was not sustainable, but neither was the cost of military supplies in gold and the once packed vaults of the Bank of England were echoing with the sounds of emptiness. These were dark days for Britain and her allies with the so-called phoney war between October 1939 and May 1940 lulling some into a false sense of security; this was violently and rudely shattered when Hitler invaded France on 10 May 1940. The French and British fought on until 25 June and the United States watched from afar and slowly the mood began to change in Roosevelt's favour. Small town America knew that Britain was suffering and no doubt in Bedford Virginia, as in tens of thousands of other towns and cities, opinion was divided as to how the United States should react.

With the cataclysm of Dunkirk, the strategic position for Britain became desperate with the majority of the equipment both of the French army and that of the United Kingdom and her allies at that time, having been either destroyed or captured. If Hitler had decided to advance on London in the next few months, he would have been touring Buckingham Palace within days or at most two weeks despite the levels of bravery and courage that would have faced his troops. The Battle of Britain, fought by the tenacious heroes of the Royal Air Force with its complements of Czech, American, Canadian, Polish, French, New Zealand, Irish, Belgian and South African pilots – it was all about having enough pilots – gave Hitler a bloody nose but his eyes, thankfully, had never really been on invading Great Britain in the first place. His notion that Goering and the Luftwaffe could bring Britain to heel from the air was mistaken but the British cupboard was bare of everything except a stubbornness not to give in.

With the failures in France, Winston S. Churchill had replaced Neville Chamberlain as Prime Minister at the head of a wartime cabinet and he faced a serious shortage of everything – most critically destroyers. Daily communications between the Foreign & Commonwealth Office in London and the State Department in Washington had been going on since the outbreak of war the previous year and civil servants on both sides recognised what was at stake and fed through the political temperatures to their respective bosses. This issue of destroyers trumped almost every other requirement given the intensity of the Battle of the Atlantic against the U-boats and, more acutely, with the loss of seven first rate destroyers in the costly battles of Narvik in April and June 1940. Subsequent briefings from the British Chiefs of Staff had informed Churchill that:

'...we do not think we can continue the war with any chance of success' without 'full economic and financial support' from the United States.

Regardless of Churchill's optimism and desire to go down fighting with a pistol in his hand in Downing Street, the more realistic Roosevelt had known that this was the reality for some time. It was all a question of timing, as politics so often is, and Roosevelt and his closest advisors had to balance the mood of his own people, the support of his congressional and senatorial party on one side against the ability of the British to fight on and the strategic decisions of Hitler on the other.

During May 1940, a great many discussions were held between the British ambassador, the Marquess of Lothian, and the United States Department of Defence. On 15 May, Churchill himself had cabled Roosevelt stating that Britain was in dire straits and needed more assistance. A scheme had emerged by which the British would grant access and rights to the United States to airfields in Trinidad, Bermuda and Newfoundland plus access to British bases around the world – this would be of great political advantage to Roosevelt in support of any help the United States might give in the future. Expecting a reciprocal agreement, Churchill initially rejected this proposal on the grounds that there was no advantage to Britain and that he needed destroyers. Perhaps it is surprising to us how politicians traded with each other, less because that's not what politicians do, but because of the situation facing them both with threats to democracy and their own survival. Having said this, we must remember that politicians also have to sell whatever steps they take to their supporters.

In a cable to Roosevelt, Churchill asked directly for destroyers from the American fleets but, although this was rejected, Roosevelt did declare that the United States had many millions of rounds of ammunition and 'obsolescent' small arms which could be shipped to Britain. Sailing close to the wind, Roosevelt was doing what he could without incurring criticism that he could not manage or that could be critical to his own survival as President or indeed cause Germany to declare war on the United States also. But by August, and as these shipments of ammunition began to arrive – if they survived the trans-Atlantic route through the U-boats – so too did German bombers as the Battle of Britain became more intense and Roosevelt reacted to the endless stream of warning reports from his sources that Britain could not hold without greater assistance.

The convoy system running to and from the ports of Bristol, Swansea, Liverpool, the Clyde and Scapa Flow was already a complex, dangerous and exhausting process. Trying to protect shipping packed with munitions and arms either purchased with the ever-dwindling reserves of British gold or given away by Roosevelt as obsolete and surplus to requirements by the United States, made the merchant ships heavy, the convoys slow and everyone a target – including the destroyers.

Having had reassurances that access to British bases around the world would now indeed be granted to the United States, to his great credit, Roosevelt acted again and on 30 August 1940 his Secretary of State, Cordell Hull, announced agreement to loaning out these destroyers in principle and when, a few days later, American Admiral Harold Stark declared that 50 smaller destroyers of the Caldwell, Wickes and Clemson class were not vital to United States security, the deal was agreed. Although old and having been in mothballs and some with substantial defects, this was a massive step towards the ending of American neutrality in the Second World War and the destroyers were quickly given a quick overhaul and sent on their way.

Chapter Two

The Tizard Mission

By September 1940 it was clear to the United States that support for Britain was essential for the survival of democracy in Europe. A large part of that continent was now under fascist rule and news of deportations of political dissidents to labour camps and the rounding up of Jewish people into ghettos across Europe was reaching families in cities across America. Pressure was mounting in the right circles of business and politics that recognised more help and cooperation was needed and, in the same month of September 1940, Roosevelt welcomed a British mission led by Henry Tizard – a British scientist and chairman of the Aeronautical Research Committee.[1]

The intention from the British side was, on the surface at least, to garner support from the Americans to develop new technologies which, because of the all-out war effort now under way, Britain did not have the resources to exploit. James Phinney Baxter III in his Pulitzer Prize winning book *Scientists Against Time*, described the arrival of the small British delegation in this way:

'When the members of the Tizzard Mission brought one cavity magnetron to America in 1940, they carried the most valuable cargo ever brought to our shores.'[2]

No doubt the sharing of this revolutionary technology, which had applications for the development of radar, needed exploitation but just as importantly, secure handling and so there was initial reluctance on the British side – notably from Churchill who wanted everything his own way as was his nature. But Tizard was convinced that scientific collaboration would not only propel the British innovations forward and help win the war through science but also collaboration would free the hands of the Americans to move another step forward in supporting the war effort against Germany and Italy.

Tizard may have been an Oxford educated chemist but he was also a very shrewd negotiator as well as a visionary and he was able to see through and plot a way around Churchill's politically biased reservations. His very small team of talented individuals set off on 30 August to cross the Atlantic on board a Canadian liner, SS *Duchess of Richmond*, bound for Newfoundland and Halifax Harbour. Interestingly, also on board were 1,000 officers and men of the Royal

Navy who were on their way to sail back some of the first of the destroyers released by the Americans.

Over the next few days and weeks, hugely important meetings were held in 'secret' locations – the Americans, uncertain of exactly what it was the British wanted to show them – arranged for discussions in restaurants, hotels and bars but very quickly, after they picked their jaws up off the floor, they realised that they were part of one of the single most important meetings in history. Tizard and his team revealed not only the micro-waves of the cavity magnetron but also the Whittle jet propulsion engine, which the Americans discovered was far more advanced than their own project, plus the gyroscopic gun sight and the MAUD report on the feasibility of the atomic bomb.[3] The end result was that scientific cooperation between the United States and the United Kingdom entered a new phase and the initial suspicions of the Americans dissipated in the light of these amazing new developments.

Tizard and his team continued their discussions with the Americans about their exchange of secret scientific advances against a steadily depressing and serious backdrop over the remaining months of 1940. In June the Germans had almost completed the building of the extermination camp of Auschwitz-Birkenau, Churchill had given his 'Fight them on the Beaches' and 'Finest Hour' speeches in Parliament, the Soviet Union invaded Lithuania signalling their further duplicity as a potential ally, by August the Battle of Britain was at its height with tragic losses and desperation – Churchill gave his 'Never in the field of human conflict was so much owed by so many to so few' speech and by September, just as Tizard and his team were discussing travel arrangements, the war in North Africa was expanding fast further draining the British war effort. The convoys bringing crucial supplies from the United States continued to be harassed and crippled by the U-boat campaign – convoy HX 72 of 43 ships woke on the morning of 22 September to find that eleven ships had been sunk during one night, Norway had fallen and in October a further thirty-two merchant ships were sunk in two days in convoys SC 7 and HX 79. Greece fell in November and Franklin Delano Roosevelt won a third term as President of the United States on 5 November. Eleven days later the city of Coventry was bombed by 500 bombers of the Luftwaffe – 60,000 of the city's 75,000 houses were destroyed.

Two days after Roosevelt was re-elected, Winston Churchill dictated and sent a cable direct to the President. In what he later described as one of the most important letters he ever wrote, Churchill described the dire military and economic situation facing Britain and reveals that the bank is almost out of gold either in London or any holdings it may have had around the world.

Churchill told Roosevelt that they would very soon not be able to pay for any more food or weapons and:

'While we will do our utmost and shrink from no proper sacrifice to make payments across the exchange, I believe that you will agree that it would be wrong in principle and mutually disadvantageous in effect if, at the height of this struggle, Great Britain were to be devested of all saleable assets so that after victory was won with our blood, civilisation saved and time gained for the United States to be fully armed against all eventualities, we should stand stripped to the bone.'

Churchill to Roosevelt, 7 December 1940, page 14/15

Within days, Roosevelt, with a strong fresh wind of endorsement by the American people in his sails, began work on what would become, in 1941, the Lend-Lease deal.

By the start of the new year, Roosevelt felt confident enough to propose outright sale of munitions to the United Kingdom – a Gallup poll in February 1941 revealed that 54 per cent of Americans were in favour of giving aid under a Lend-Lease scheme by which the United Kingdom would receive food, oil and weapons free of charge but to be paid for after the completion of the war – the United Kingdom only repaid these loans in 2006 having also borrowed the money from the United States for this purpose. The Lend-Lease bill was signed into law by the president on 11 March, 1941 and permitted the nation to:

'...sell, transfer title to, exchange, lease, lend or otherwise dispose of, to any such government (whose defence the President deemed vital to the defence of the United States) any defence article.'

With the German invasion of the Soviet Union in June 1941, Lend-Lease was extended to Russia by November 1941 – China was also added along with France and significant number of other allies such as Mexico, Norway and Poland. The support given under Lend-Lease to the Soviet Union was so substantial that not only did the material assistance help the Russins defeat Germany on the eastern front (without which even Zhukov felt that they would not have succeeded) but it also laid the foundations of the post-war Soviet military in the new Cold War with a total of 17.5 million tons of arms and equipment shipped up to 1945, just over 5 million tons to the Soviet far east across the Pacific, 4 million tons via the South Atlantic and the Persian Gulf and the rest into Archangel in the Baltic.

Chapter Three

Lend-Lease & MARCOM

With this profound step change in support for the allies in Europe, all pretence of America neutrality was over. It had not been easy for Roosevelt but the storm clouds over Europe seemed to be heading their way and Roosevelt needed to step up 'putting his own house in order' as he had said right back in January 1939. For the United Kingdom, the Office of Lend-Lease Administration under Harry Hopkins began work almost immediately. Working through a steel executive named Edward Stettinius, the office started issuing contracts immediately to the huge armaments industry in the United States. Many large steel corporations were well established manufacturing businesses while others were created out of the mergers of smaller companies whose resources, when pooled, enabled them to bid for the huge number of new government manufacturing contracts.

One such merger had occurred just over ten years earlier between the combination of the Llewellyn Iron Works, Barker Iron Works and Union Iron Works to create the Consolidated Steel Corporation formed on 18 December 1928. These smaller companies were based on the west coast in California and Texas and had benefitted from the boom in steel requirements during and after the First World War. Consolidated Steel survived the depression years of the 1930s and, like many other American firms, went into the shipbuilding business in 1939 sensing that the market would require their services on a larger scale as in the First World War. The main yard for Consolidated Steel was the huge sprawling Orange shipyard on the banks of the Sabine River in Texas but this was not enough to cope with the contracts flooding out of Washington.

The United States Maritime Commission, or MARCOM, had been created in 1936 and was intended to oversee a new shipping programme to design and build five hundred new merchant cargo ships to replace the older vintage vessels still operating from the First World War but with the arrival of the Lend-Lease programme, MARCOM took on the major role of coordinating what was to develop as 'the largest and most successful merchant shipbuilding effort in world history'. Under the control of MARCOM, Liberty ships, Landing Ship, Tank (LSTs), Tankers, a whole range of C2, C3 and C4 ships and dozens of others were designed, constructed and launched for use either by the United States armed forces or sent overseas as part of Lend-Lease. The C1-A and the C1-B class of ships were designed before the start of hostilities in 1941 and were meant to be commercially viable ships, more expensive to build than what were to be known as Liberty Ships under Lend-Lease, the C Class was designed to be a strongly built, long lasting cargo ship and a few are still in operation even today. The C class were built with a mixture of diesel and steam engines with a central stack and several large companies made bids for the contracts and keels were already laid down before 1940.

The Consolidated Steel Corporation were one of the successful bidders to MARCOM and they began laying down the keels of the majority of the C1-B class at their Wilmington Shipyard in California and also won some the Liberty Ship contracts – these were prefabricated and quickly built ships the first of which was launched on Liberty Fleet Day on 27 September, 1941 where the first fourteen of the Lend-Lease ships were all launched across America on the same day as part of MARCOM's Emergency Shipbuilding programme. The instigator of this massive initiative was of course President Roosevelt and he was present to launch the very first Liberty Ship, the SS *Patrick Henry* at the Bethlehem Steel Yard in Maryland – his speech was recorded and played at every launch that day:

My fellow Americans:
This is a memorable day in the history of American shipbuilding – a memorable day in the emergency defence of the nation. Today, from dawn to dark, fourteen ships are being launched – on the Atlantic, on the Pacific and on the Gulf and among them is the first Liberty ship, the Patrick Henry.

While we are proud of what we are doing, this is certainly no time to be content. We must build more cargo ships and still more cargo ships – and we must speed the program until we achieve a launching each day, then two ships a day, fulfilling the building program undertaken by the Maritime Commission.

Our shipbuilding program – not only that of the Maritime Commission, but of the Navy – is one of our answers to the aggressors who would strike at our liberty.

I am speaking today not only to the shipworkers in the building yards on our Coasts, on our Great Lakes and on our Rivers – not only to the thousands who are present at today's launchings – but also to the men and women throughout the country who live far from salt water or shipbuilding.

I emphasize to all of you the simple, historic fact that throughout the period of our American life, going way back into Colonial days, commerce on the high seas and freedom of the seas has been a major reason for our prosperity and the building up of our country.

To give you one simple example: It is a matter of history that a large part of the capital which in the middle of the past century went into the building of railways and spread like a network into the new undeveloped areas across the Mississippi River, across the Plains and up into the Northwest, was money which had been made by American traders whose ships had sailed the seas to the Baltic, to the Mediterranean, to Africa and South America, and to Singapore and China itself.

Through all the years after the American Revolution your government reiterated and maintained the right of American ships to voyage hither and yon without hindrance from those who sought to keep them off the seas or drive them off the seas. As a nation we have realized that our export trade and our import trade had a definitely good effect on the life of families, not only on our Coasts but on the farms and in the cities a hundred or a thousand miles from salt water.

Since 1936, when the Congress enacted the present Merchant Marine Law, we have been rehabilitating a Merchant Marine which had fallen to a low level. Today we are continuing that program at accelerated speed.

The shipworkers of America are doing a great job. They have made a commendable record for efficiency and speed. With every new ship, they are striking a telling blow at the menace to our nation and the liberty of the free peoples of the world. They struck fourteen such blows today. They have caught the true spirit with which all this nation must be imbued if Hitler and other aggressors of his ilk are to be prevented from crushing us.

We Americans as a whole cannot listen to those few Americans who preach the gospel of fear – who say in effect that they are still in favour of freedom of the seas but who would have the United States tie up our vessels in our ports. That attitude is neither truthful nor honest.

We propose that these ships sail the seas as they are intended to. We propose, to the best of our ability, to protect them from torpedo, from shell or from bomb.

The Patrick Henry, *as one of the Liberty ships launched today renews that great patriot's stirring demand: "Give me liberty or give me death."*

There shall be no death for America, for democracy, for freedom! There must be liberty, world-wide and eternal. That is our prayer – our pledge to all mankind.'

With this speech, Roosevelt changed the direction of the war.

For Consolidated Steel, the first contracts indicated that there would be more and, despite strong competition from numerous other contenders, Consolidated Steel went on to win numerous other orders to the point where an 'emergency shipyard' was needed to cope with the demand. This new yard become known as Wilmington Shipyard in Los Angeles. At the height of production, the

Wilmington Yard employed over 12,000 workers and built hundreds of vessels for MARCOM of different shapes and sizes.

Despite all the contracts for shipping, Consolidated Steel still ranked only 29th amongst United States businesses in terms of the value of their contracts which gives some idea of the enormous scale of investment that the United States was able to make into arms and industry well beyond the reach of any other nation, or group of nations, in the world.

A year to the day after Roosevelt had received the cable from Churchill explaining that Britain was now on its knees, on 7 December 1941 Japan attacked Pearl Harbor. Churchill's plea that Britain be saved from defeat while America readied herself for the seemingly inevitable clash with Japan had been met and Britain was still fighting and now the might of America joined her.

In Wilmington, the ship yards continued to work hard during 1941 and 1942. The strategic situation was now studied in theatres of war around the world rather than just in Europe and collaboration in the fighting between Britain and her allies and the forces of the United States came ever closer – both scientifically and militarily. The arrival during 1943 of American bomber squadrons signalled that the war was turning and the offensive was now in allied hands, so too were thoughts about the liberation of Europe and 1944 was earmarked as the year by which all could be made ready for the invasion of Europe – whenever that might come. So it was that the plans for landing large numbers of troops quickly into a densely packed area required ships that could hold and embark hundreds of troops – if not thousands – in shallow water and in the summer of 1942, the Navy, Army and MARCOM looked at the C1 and C2 class with different eyes as the early stages of planning the invasion of Europe were already underway with a SHAEF joint planning staff in England.

The C1-S-AY1 variant was created out of the plan that thirteen ships of this class would be needed to land allied forces on the coast of Normandy. The hull and internal structures were already there so there was no need to reinvent the wheel and all that was required was to convert a C1 ship from carrying a cargo of food or tanks to carrying infantry – and to be able to unload them into landing craft that the ship also carried on board. Work on these adjustments to the C1 created the C1-S-AY1 variation and, given that the Consolidated Steel Corporation knew how to construct the C1, they were also given the order to build thirteen of the new variants and the order went out to the Wilmington shipyard to make preparations and the life of the ship, initially to be named *Cape Lobos*, was about to begin.

By 1943, detailed planning for the allied invasion of Europe was well advanced. In top secret meetings the location and scope of the initial landings were briefed out to a small but highly productive planning team based at Supreme

Headquarters Allied Expeditionary Forces or SHAEF. The thirteen ships that were going to form the back bone of the allied landings would be made available to Britain as soon as they were built and 'bareboat' chartered – meaning that all that was available was the ship, no fitting out, supplies or ammunition for the guns – the Royal Navy and Merchant Marine would have to do that when they received the ships from the Ministry of War Transport who would receive the ships on behalf of the British government.

The C1-S type was to be designated as a Landing Ship, Infantry or LSI (Large) and, similar to all the other ships in her class was just over 414 feet long with a beam of 60 feet and a draft of 25 feet. The total tonnage without cargo or crew was 7,177 tons which made these ships a substantial unit even before they were loaded with the men and materials that they were being designed to handle. Most of the keels were laid down during the spring and summer of 1943 with an expected launch date of either side of Christmas 1943 or into early 1944. Given that these LSIs would be sailing in enemy waters for most of their sea life, each ship was also equipped with a single 4-inch single mount gun together with a 12 pounder also in a single mount and, to deter air attack, the all essential 20mm anti-aircraft gun with twelve dotted all around the ship.

The pivotal events that led up to the passing of the Lend-Lease bill were not lost on the citizens of Bedford, Virginia. Far from being a small, remote town, Bedford is and was in the 1920s and 1930s situated at the centre of Bedford County, 800 square miles of rolling farmland, apple orchards, rivers and green fields in the west-central area of Virginia on the Piedmont Plateau. Named after John Russell, the fourth Duke of Bedford who was Britain's Secretary of State prior to the Wars of Independence, Bedford was easily accessible and traffic flowed through from all points of the compass. Because of its location, news also reached Bedford pretty quickly and this small town of 3,000 residents in the 1930s lay 180 miles southwest of Washington DC with the Smith Mountain Lake to the north and the stunning Blue Ridge Mountains, with their 4,000-metre-high peaks, watch over the town to the west.

A visit to the town today would make you feel warmly welcome, it has always been that way, friendship, support and consideration was and still are characteristics of most Virginians rightfully proud of their town, their heritage and their state. Many of the red brick high Victorian period buildings remind one of the expansions that brought construction and energy to the town in the 1880s and the young men of Bedford then would recognise many of these places as unchanged today – the town has its own historic district with 208 listed buildings in two neighbourhoods with a variety of nineteenth and twentieth century styles. Apart from the modern shops in the streets and the modern vehicles, it would not seem as though much has changed. Mind you, the

Depression affected Bedford as much as any other town in the United States and jobs had been lost, businesses had been closed and money was scarce in the early 1930s and economic poverty and social strife was the backdrop to the unfolding events in Europe.

Many of the young men who lived and worked in and around the town of Bedford lived a quiet and sensible life. Boys like Roy and Ray Stevens supported their families, got jobs when they could with Roy working on the production line at a local mill called Belding Hemmingway while Ray worked in a grocery store in the town. As twins, they had always been and would forever be close but their life before the war revolved around Bedford.

One of the many friends of the Stevens boys was Grant Yopp and he even joined the Stevens family when his own father had left home. Grant was like a half-brother to Ray and Roy and helped them work for the family income – there were after all fourteen children in all in the Stevens family and fifteen if he added himself.

Another pair of brothers were Raymond and Bedford Hoback. A one-time regular soldier, Bedford had left the army and come back home to be with his childhood sweetheart Elaine. His brother Raymond was quieter and had a love for religion – his head down often reading verses from the Bible. Raymond was making a career in the town before the war and worked for the Highways Department and for another local company called Rubatex.

The largest commercial employer in Bedford in the 1930s was Hampton Looms and Frank Draper Jnr was employed there and stood out in the company baseball team, practising in the hot summer evenings and playing with the son of the town's deputy sheriff, Elmer Wright. By all accounts, Elmer could have gone on to quite a career but for the outbreak of war given that he had signed a contract to play professionally with St Louis Browns in 1937. Another name to add to the list of baseball playing young men in the town and that was Robert Marsico – Robert worked for the Piedmont Label Company and was a talented catcher.

So many other young men were making their way through life in and around Bedford such as John Wilkes, John Schenk and Taylor Fellers who was a foreman with the Virginia Highways Department. The charming Weldon Rosazza and Leslie Abbott a hardworking and God-fearing comedian with a joke always on his lips were also comrades in arms within A Company of the 116th Rifle Regiment – the local National Guard formation.

Described as 'quiet and dependable', Nicholas Gillaspie spent his life to date on the family farm. Always smiling and polite, Nicholas was another keen baseball player but also letter writer while Clifton Lee also kept a low profile in the town simply getting on with his job working at Hampton Mills. One of seven children, John 'Jack' Reynolds also grew up on a farm in the Shenendoah Valley near Bedford, devoted to his mother and to his family. Elisha Nance was from a very respected local tobacco farming family; Earl Newcomb was a road digger and Earl Parker was madly in love with Viola Shrader – one of many beautiful young women in Bedford who also worked at Belding Hemmingway. By 1940, at the age of 26, Earl had been promoted to sergeant in the local National Guard Company. Graduating from Bedford High School, his early life was spent on a beef farm with his parents and again, like so many of the boys he knew, loved country pursuits – shooting, hunting and of course baseball. 1940 was also the year that Earl married Viola Shrader – falling in love with war imminent was so common that they went with it and just made the most of every moment together, making love, dancing when the opportunity came, laughing and doing what young people the world over do together:

'I don't know how you'd go shoot anybody,' Viola told Earl just before he left. 'If its me or them,' he shrugged, 'I guess I'll have to.'[4]

To these young men and women, to their elders and parents and grandparents and to their siblings, be they Republican of Democratic voters, President Roosevelt had already cemented his place in American history with his new deal. His first and second terms in office were primarily beset by trying to pull the bruised and damaged economy back around and then men and women of Bedford and the rest of Virginia began to notice the change. Roosevelt may not have been liked by all or even supported by all, but he was largely trusted by most to make the right decisions; his reputation as a moral man carried a strong currency in places like Bedford. When it came to responding to the war in Europe, Roosevelt already had a great deal of moral credit in the bank and Americans knew that he was trying to do the best for America first and the world second, they also knew that, if, America had to go to war, then they would only be doing it for the right reasons.

Despite coming from a wide range of socio-economic backgrounds, with differing religious affiliations and heritage, all the young men of Bedford shared three things in common. Firstly, they knew Green's Drugstore really well. Many frequented this place just for the best strawberry ice cream in the region but also as a place to hang out or drop into when they needed something. Green's was a local honeypot for the town of Bedford, some even worked there when they were younger and others tried their first efforts at setting up a date with a pretty girl. Green's was part of the passage of life. Secondly the young men of Bedford, like men all over Virginia, shared a love of family, time and place. They all shared a sense that they were part of a larger family, a community, the sort of thing that

America is very good at and Britain is very poor at – knowing and loving your neighbour, working as a community, sharing public events, celebrating happiness and sadness as a community. It was this aspect of the town of Bedford that was to cause incredible sadness in such a short space of time – a sadness that the town will never lose. Lastly, they were patriots. Due to the way in which the United States came into being with small communities bonding together to form states and states forming a nation, patriotism was part of the DNA of a young American man or woman. This sense of belonging and a need to serve to protect gave impetus to always being ready to defend the nation from attack. If one wanted to, then one could do this full time and join one of the services but there was another way – to join the National Guard and so the third aspect that all the men so far named in this chapter shared in common was that they were all members of the Virginia National Guard.

Part II

The Birth of a Regiment

'There's nothing stronger than the heart of a Volunteer.'
General James H. Doolittle
Medal of Honor

Chapter Four

Gathering Clouds Beyond the Blue Mountains

We have no real equivalent in the United Kingdom to the United States National Guard. Most nations have a policy in place for the training of a reserve army of part-time citizens who can then swell the numbers of the professional forces in time of war but the version that the United States developed since its inception as a civilian militia in the late eighteenth century is unique. Part of the distinctive character that forms the National Guard is that each unit is formed within a community region or state. Whereas in Britain, or indeed elsewhere, this is also true, it is the very strong nature of community in the United States compared to other countries that makes a National Guard unit something more than just a group of part-time reserve forces – a group of individuals serving in a unit. In the United States, the National Guard was a second home for a large percentage of the young male population, and this was especially true for the development of the National Guard after 1918.

In a social setting where communications between families of the same town or city are strong and where a sense of civic pride exists where a supportive atmosphere prevails, encouraging a sense of unity, then a National Guard unit becomes an extension of those roots and rarely is one an individual in a group of other individuals. Instead faces are already known, relationships are well established, men had come from the same schools and backgrounds and even worked in the same places. During the 1930s, this was very much the case for Company A of the 116th infantry regiment of the 91st Infantry Brigade of the 29th 'Blue & Gray' Division of the United States Army.

The 29th Division was a National Guard Infantry Division. Formed in 1917, it had seen service during the First World War and although stood down after the war, it was reconstituted as a division in 1921 and allotted the states of Maryland and Virginia as its recruiting areas and the three regiments of infantry that formed the division, along with ancillary units, were the backbone of the division – the 115th, 116th and 175th. Formed around Lynchburg, which was only some twenty-eight miles to the east of Bedford in Virginia, the 116th infantry had also had a long and proud history with battle honours, fighting for the Confederacy, going back to the US Civil War. Constituted as part of the Virginia National Guard in 1916, the 116th fought throughout the remainder of 1917 and 1918 and then, as a National Guard formation, on their return home to Camp Lee in May 1919 they were disbanded from regular service. Again, reconstituted in 1921 and assigned to the 29th Division, the 116th began recruiting again and company training locations were re-opened across Virginia. There were to be three battalions for the 116th regiment each of twelve rifle companies with a stated complement of 175 of riflemen plus two or three officers, each commanded by a Captain. For the 1st Battalion of the 116th Infantry Company A was to be based in Bedford, Company B covered Lynchburg, Company C covered from Harrisonburg in the north of Virginia and Company D covered Roanoke which was around thirty miles from Bedford and the southwest of the town. With a headquarters in Richmond, the Virginia National Guard was a proud, well run, disciplined fighting force – maybe well short of regular army standards and fitness, but proud just the same.

By 1939, each of the companies was well established with between 50 per cent and 60 per cent of the complement on roll and attendance was very good with very little 'dead wood'. This gave each company around one hundred men, give or take, and in the future, if war came, then this number would have to be made up to the official 190 by either enlisted men or transfers from other units. Training was once a week at the training hall or armoury; each company had their own locations, the battalion and regiment hosting a summer camp to get as many men together as possible. Like tens of thousands of other young men across the United States, the National Guard offered a change from the predictable monotony of rural life, plus there was a chance to earn some fresh dollars and to do something different. For many though, in the back of their minds was the idea that they were also doing their patriotic duty, supporting their country and of course the uniform was attractive to girls, but the main benefit was that they were training to be soldiers with their friends, guys they knew from in and around the town.

For the young men and older officers of Bedford, training was held in the rooms of the imposing Court House building, which had changed little since 1918. There was a great deal of marching drill, led by the platoon sergeants or company sergeant who accompanied every training event along with basic arms drill and field craft. Then it was back home late at night with a laugh and pat on the back as they dispersed and walked home after another week of bonding, joking and laughing together. The seriousness of war and the realities of command had not even touched their souls and few felt that they could even fire a shot in anger; they had no idea, despite their main attribute of morale and comradery, how far short of real training for a hardened enemy they were.

They were not hard enough, fit enough or fast enough to survive. But all that would change.

The summer of 1939 was hot, very hot and 'The Peaks of Otter Rifles' as the company was known locally – after the twin Peaks of Otter that overlooked the town – had no sooner returned to Bedford, handed in their equipment at the armoury and knocked on the door to be met by their families when news of the war that had broken out in Europe spread across the town. The autumn months through to January 1940 were spent in the same routine, but now the drills had a certain importance about them as men just like them, British and Polish, had been doing the same drill but they had not been enough to defeat the German army who had swept the Poles aside and the Russians too now seemed like an enemy of them all. The Labor Day speech of Roosevelt that contained his commitment to neutrality held a particular importance for the fathers and mothers of the men of The Peaks of Otter Rifles – here was their President committing himself to not sending their sons to war. The National Guard was a place of an increased level of seriousness, and recruitment had improved with new men enlisting – just in case. New faces included another 18 year old by the name of John Clifton, the onetime town newspaper boy, and Gordon 'Henry' White, a true farmer at heart who was most at home working in the fields alone, just doing his thing with a plough.

Company A was more than just the lead company of the 1st Battalion, it was also the lead company of the entire regiment of twelve companies and the officers and men were always ready to demonstrate this in inter-company competitions and training exercises and camps. In the 1940 Virginia National Guard Review, Company A was noted as having the following record:

> 'Regimental trophy for best all-round honor rifle company in the regiment, six out of 10 years it was awarded; indoor-rifle match 1929–30; street banner 1927,1929,1931,1932,1936; national trophy for excellence in marksmanship, 1934, 1935, and William Randolf Hearst musketry trophy 1934. Company A furnished men for the state rifle team in 1923, 1926, 1929, 1930, 1932, 1933 and 1934. It has attended 16 annual field encampments, including the Twenty-ninth Division maneuvers, Indiantown Gap, Pennsylvania, and First Army Manoeuvres, Manassas, Virginia in August 1936 and 1929 respectively.'[5]

When one considers that all this was achieved by part-time soldiers, all with jobs and commitments, one can sense that theirs was a very committed group of young men and the battalion could rely on Company A to set the standard for the regiment.

The spring and early summer months of 1940 carried on as best America could, knowing she was helping the British war effort but equally aware that Britain was losing. Radio had entered the lives of over 50 million Americans and provided almost daily news from American war correspondents such as Ed Murrow and his small team of CBS reporters, Martha Gellhorn who reported from London as the bombs dropped during the Blitz and Ernie Pyle – who drove across America thirty-five times between 1935 and 1940 telling the stories of ordinary Americans he met along the way – before he too left for Britain to report on the suffering. Although millions of Americans wished to cover their ears or put their head in the sand, these reporters and others like them painted a vivid picture to small town America of the battles the British were fighting, the shipping being sunk, the heroism of the RAF pilots and crews and, after the fall of France in June 1940, that Britain was fighting alone in Europe.

That same summer, Virginia Beach was to be the last peacetime camp for the men of the Virginia National Guard units and times were changing. Even the families noticed a more serious tone from the mouths of their boys as talk inevitably drifted towards what the future might hold. As Alex Kershaw, in his book on the Bedford Boys, elaborated:

'Senior officers in the National Guard talked ominously of mobilisation. Subtly things began to change in Company A. Officers grew more serious. Older men and those with "essential" civilian jobs left the unit.'[6]

In the month of May, Churchill had already written and sent his secure cable to Roosevelt desperately asking for more destroyers to fight the U-boat threat and top-secret discussions were going on in Washington about gaining access to British bases in return for destroyers and the next level of losing neutrality was evolving. In June and July 1940, as the men of A Company in and around Bedford prepared for their summer camp with more precision and purpose, news that the Battle of Britain was in full swing had reached the newspapers and radio and in August, as the Bedford Company unpacked their canvas tents on Virginia Beach, Sir Henry Tizard was packing his suitcases for his trip across the Atlantic to share the most vital secrets that British science could provide. At the end of August, Roosevelt announced, with the public reassurance of the Navy behind him, that America had fifty destroyers she did not need for her own defence and that they would be giving them to Great Britain for fighting the war.

No wonder then that Bedford slowly but surely felt that their predictable, controlled and safe world was coming to an end and a large part of the town was going to be affected if Roosevelt decided the time had come to mobilise the National Guard. On 8 September, while the Tizard mission was astounding their American counterparts with their scientific developments, Roosevelt's voice once more entered the homes of millions of Americans to announce that he felt a State of Emergency had to be declared whereby America needed to act faster to prepare to defend herself.

The announcement of an Office of Production Management signalled that America was stirring like the sleeping giant some of the Japanese so feared. The speech was a preliminary pill to swallow before the main medicine and in the following month it happened – in October 1940, Company A and all the eleven other companies of the 116th infantry received orders that they were to be mobilised into the standing army for a year. The shock was tempered by the fact that they were far from alone as the United States National Guard comprised eighteen infantry divisions of eighty regiments of infantry – a total of 300,034 troops which doubled the size of the United States' ground forces. Once the initial tears and fears had subsided, no one could imagine anything more than just additional training, better weapons and maybe seeing more of the country – after all, the majority of men from Bedford had never even been outside Virginia so no doubt some felt that there might be some real upside to this event. The date for reporting for active duty was fixed for Monday 3 February 1941 so there was quite some time made available by the Army Department to do what was needed for families, giving up and handing over jobs and even preparing wills or taking out life insurance – all a very far cry from the summers of previous years in the National Guard. No one would have even contemplated that fate would ultimately lead to these men of this individual Company being chosen as the front line of the entire United States Army landing on Omaha beach in a little over three and half years' time.

Chapter Five

Creating the Regiment, 1940

'The soldier is the Army. No army is better than its soldiers. The soldier is also a citizen. In fact, the highest obligation and privilege of citizenship is that of bearing arms for one's country.'

General George S. Patton Jnr

One can only wonder what was in the mind of Wallace R. Carter on 2 February 1941. One of the young men of Bedford who had so far decided against volunteering to serve in the National Guard, did exactly that – on the day before the order for mobilisation was received. Although for sure he had not heard them, maybe in his own private way he felt the words of General George S. Patton Jnr and that, as a citizen, he had a right and a duty to enlist and be there to fight for the nation if needed. Or maybe it was the steady build-up of news reports from Europe that inspired him to do something practical, or maybe he had been arguing with himself and his family for months before finally deciding this is what he was going to do. Wallace had plenty of time to wonder about the best thing to do. Working in the Bedford pool hall after school lessons had ended, Wallace was pretty good with a pool cue and at baseball – he played for the Mud Alley Wildcats, a baseball team from the poorer side of the town. Always with a cheeky smile and money in his pocket from his pool matches, Wallace was born on 31 January 1923 making him only just 18 when he enlisted in A Company and, on the day he swore the oath along with six officers and ninety-two enlisted men, Wallace had only tried his uniform on the day before.

Fort Meade was to be the divisional camp but not all the barracks were yet complete, giving the boys of Bedford and the surrounding district another two weeks to drill daily and prepare to move out. Each day that passed provided a steadily aching feeling to mothers concerned about where their sons were going but there was, as yet, no war, no fighting and nothing but training ahead which gave solace to those who recalled the days of 1917 and the departure of the American Army and the men of Bedford.

Due to depart by train on 18 February 1941, the day before their departure the town had arranged a send-off party at Bedford High School. The 17th was eight days after Churchill had given a speech to the people of Britain ending with a direct appeal to the United States to 'give us the tools and we will finish the job'. It was also five days after General Erwin Rommel arrived in North Africa to begin his attacks on the British Army in Egypt and three days after a new Japanese ambassador, Kichisburo Nomura, arrived in Washington promising President Roosevelt that he would do all he could to establish a better understanding between the two nations.[7]

The 18th saw the men wake with hangovers but the town was determined to make their send off a memorable one. Before they left the train station in the Mud Alley district of Bedford a parade was planned that would process all along Main Street. At the front the marching bands and twirling drumsticks in their sparkling uniforms, along each side of the street crowds cheered and clapped, down the centre marched Company A in their best unforms, complete with headaches and providing the music was the town's Firemen's Band.

Once through the town it was final departures and kisses with everyone – this was to be the very last moment that families would see their loved ones for some time, for many it was the final goodbye. No one knew what the future held and, as the train pulled out of the station, these would be the final images of each other to hold in their thoughts. Such is one of the costs of war.

On paper, a regiment can be many things – the inheritor of a fine reputation, regarded as fit for duty, considered to be well led, the best trained and the best in the brigade but it is not until the men are tested and at all levels under the widest range of conditions, most notably in battle, that one can say it is a front-line regiment with an A1 fighting quality. During those first few months of training, Company A got used to doing things more quickly – saluting faster, marching promptly, stripping and assembling a weapon nimbly (even blindfolded) and firing a closely grouped magazine at a target with their brand new M1 Garand rifles without thinking. Their levels of self-discipline sharpened up as did their focus on fitness and the training now seemed to have a real point.

Bedford was seven hours away to the southwest and thoughts of home crept ever more readily into their minds. There was a limit to how much active training the division could give to a citizen army, and resentment at not being needed grew. Alex Kershaw reminds us that even the *New York Times* commented on the levels of ill-discipline infecting the huge resource of manpower that was being underused but was fit for purpose. The longing for this enlisted year to come to an end in January 1942 so that the National Guard units could return to their homes, was not to last much longer as the thoughts of home were extinguished when, in August 1941, Congress extended by one additional year the term of service both for draftees and mobilised National Guardsmen.

The winter of 1941 was cold, very cold in Washington and at Fort Meade where the 116th formed part of winter manoeuvres for the whole of the 29th Division in North Carolina. Freezing cold feet and equally cold fingers wrestled with marching through snow and handling the freezing cold steel of their Garand rifles and ammunition. Through the snow they could all see their distinctive monad – the Korean symbol of eternal life as their divisional badges on their helmets and shoulders coloured half blue and half grey – indicating that the Division was composed of men whose families had fought on both sides in the Civil War only eighty or so years earlier. The young men of Bedford joked, cursed, limped and nursed their way forwards to Camp A.P. Hill where there were at least tents to protect them from the gusts of freezing cold winds. It was there on 7 December 1941 – a year to the day since Churchill had sent his fifteen-page telegram to Roosevelt telling the President that, without substantial help, Britain could not hold out – news of the Japanese attack on Pearl Harbor arrived. Ambassador Nomura had failed to reconcile the interests of the two nations as he had promised on his arrival in Washington the previous year and history has illuminated his fruitless struggle against what was destined to happen anyway. Possibly Roosevelt and his advisors knew all along that war would be the end result, hence the National Guard had been trained up to a level of readiness and held in camp with only two months of service to go – good fortune or good planning? The truth is out there. That war with Japan was inevitable has been known for some time but the debate on what Roosevelt did and did not know has rumbled on ever since.

For the men of Company A, it really did not matter who knew what, to virtually all Americans – except a small number in Washington – the Japanese attack came as a complete surprise. The loss of men was not yet apparent and would not become known for some weeks due to the carnage and destruction of six American battleships. The huddled families of Bedford sitting around their radio sets mirrored a scene that was repeated across the vastness of the United States, some reached for a school atlas to find out where Hawaii was while others, mothers mostly of over 300,000 young men and women knew full well that the National Guard was not coming home for a while yet. The timing was incredible.

Shock gave way to anger, anger gave way to a desire for vengeance and justice and both of these gave way to the reality that America was now at war and there was going to be no going home to Bedford in January 1942. But the regiment was far better trained, leaner and meaner than it had been when it arrived and the next morning, a Monday, it was fully loaded and being transported by truck in convoy back to Fort Meade. According to Alex Kershaw:

'*During the trip, the caravan stopped so that the men could stretch their legs and have a smoke. Second Lieutenant Ray Nance and several other officers gathered in a ditch below pine trees, out of the biting wind.*

A few yards from Nance, the 116th's regimental chaplain set up a portable radio and tuned it to a news station. On a carpet of pine needles, Nance and his fellow officers soon sat transfixed as they listened to President Roosevelt make what would become perhaps the most famous speech of his Presidency. Dressed in a formal morning suit, Roosevelt stood alone at the rostrum in the House of Representatives and opened a black notebook. The entire Congress then stood in unison and gave him the first joint ovation since 1932.

Roosevelt gripped the rostrum.[8]

This was not a stop en route by chance. The country had been forewarned that the President would give a speech to Congress at 12.30 on Monday 8 December and this would be broadcast by all the major news channels and the officers had decided that they would be in a position, with a radio to hear what was said. In fact, it is likely that all the other companies in the long regimental column did exactly the same and their reactions to the speech would have been the same:

'*Mr. Vice President, Mr. Speaker, Members of the Senate, and of the House of Representatives:*

Yesterday, December 7th, 1941 – a date which will live in infamy – the United States of America was suddenly and deliberately attacked by naval and air forces of the Empire of Japan.

The United States was at peace with that nation and, at the solicitation of Japan, was still in conversation with its government and its emperor looking toward the maintenance of peace in the Pacific.

Indeed, one hour after Japanese air squadrons had commenced bombing in the American island of Oahu, the Japanese ambassador to the United States and his colleague delivered to our Secretary of State a formal reply to a recent American message. And while this reply stated that it seemed useless to continue the existing diplomatic negotiations, it contained no threat or hint of war or of armed attack.

It will be recorded that the distance of Hawaii from Japan makes it obvious that the attack was deliberately planned many days or even weeks ago. During the intervening time, the Japanese government has deliberately sought to deceive the United States by false statements and expressions of hope for continued peace.

The attack yesterday on the Hawaiian islands has caused severe damage to American naval and military forces. I regret to tell you that very many American lives have been lost. In addition, American ships have been reported torpedoed on the high seas between San Francisco and Honolulu.

Yesterday, the Japanese government also launched an attack against Malaya.
Last night, Japanese forces attacked Hong Kong.
Last night, Japanese forces attacked Guam.
Last night, Japanese forces attacked the Philippine Islands.
Last night, the Japanese attacked Wake Island.
And this morning, the Japanese attacked Midway Island.

Japan has, therefore, undertaken a surprise offensive extending throughout the Pacific area. The facts of yesterday and today speak for themselves. The people of the United States have already formed their opinions and well understand the implications to the very life and safety of our nation.

As commander in chief of the Army and Navy, I have directed that all measures be taken for our defense. But always will our whole nation remember the character of the onslaught against us.

No matter how long it may take us to overcome this premeditated invasion, the American people in their righteous might will win through to absolute victory.

I believe that I interpret the will of the Congress and of the people when I assert that we will not only defend ourselves to the uttermost, but will make it very certain that this form of treachery shall never again endanger us.

Hostilities exist. There is no blinking at the fact that our people, our territory, and our interests are in grave danger.

With confidence in our armed forces, with the unbounding determination of our people, we will gain the inevitable triumph – so help us God.

I ask that the Congress declare that since the unprovoked and dastardly attack by Japan on Sunday, December 7th, 1941, a state of war has existed between the United States and the Japanese empire.'

As the column carrying the tired and thoughtful men of the 116th restarted their engines and continued northwards through that cold, grey December day taking them on to Fort Meade, Congress debated the President's request. By the time the trucks started to roll through the gates to the enormous divisional camp, Congress had stopped debating and the men from Bedford went to bed that night knowing that the United States was now at war with Japan.

Only four days later, on 11 December 1941, they were also at war with Nazi Germany and Italy. One of the many strategic mistakes made by Adolf Hitler was his unilateral declaration of war on the United States. Without any meaningful consultation with his political or military advisors, the Fuhrer, in a fit of unimaginable hubris, decided that the Americans were similar to the Russians – weak, borne down by moral depravity, led by Jewish interests and no match for the Ayrian supremacy of his military forces. The support that

Roosevelt had been giving Britain had of course rankled with him since 1939 and it is a miracle he had been able to hold his impulses as long as he had. In his decision and eighty-minute speech Hitler was tragically misguided but no senior figure either wanted to disagree with him or wanted to believe anything other than that he might be correct. For the United States, this was something of a blessing and, on the morning of 11 December, Roosevelt simply wrote a very short note to Congress asking to declare war on Germany and this was passed the same day by 3pm. For the United States, combat with Germany could be isolated to North Africa, where there was space to fight and an ally already on hand, and the Atlantic where the open addition of the United States Navy could now support the British in doubling down on the U-boat war. It was therefore possible to divert significant land forces to the war against Japan and a land war in Europe could wait – or at least start in Italy against the weaker opponent leaving Hitler to exhaust his forces to a lingering and disastrous death in Russia.

Chapter Six

First to Ship Out and First to Fight

The very first American divisions to ship out for overseas combat were from the National Guard. Leaving in September and October 1942 respectively were the 32nd and 34th Infantry Divisions who were sent west from the United States straight away to defend New Guinea and east to North Africa while a third National Guard Division – the American Division – was posted immediately to Guadalcanal to support American Marines who had been fighting the vicious Japanese assault.[9] Thereafter a very large number of regular army divisions were also sent to North Africa where it was decided that, strategically, the British needed substantial reinforcements if they were to not lose all of North Africa and crucially access to the Suez Canal and middle eastern oilfields. During November 1942, almost every available transport ship was therefore ordered to sail with the men and material of the regular army and the 1st and 2nd Armoured Divisions and the 1st, 3rd, 9th and 25th Infantry Divisions were transported in huge convoys during September to October 1942 and entered fighting in the November of 1942.

For the remainder of the National Guard Divisions and those of the regular army, strategic thinking at Army group level developed as the various theatres of war unfolded. Some divisions were ordered overseas as replacements for worn out units fighting the Japanese or the German and Italians in North Africa, while others were held in strategic reserve. But there were others, such as would happen to the 29th, that were destined for new fronts. The 3rd, 36th, 37th, 45th plus the 82nd (Airborne), were transferred in order to become part of the new Italian front landing at Salerno and Anzio in 1943. For the 29th, as they watched their fellow National Guard Divisions deploy and searched for news of their actions, the majority of 1942 was spent preparing to move and wondering in which direction they would be sent.

The new commanding officer for A Company was Captain Taylor Fellers. Along with Second Lieutenant Nance, Taylor Fellers was a local Bedford boy himself but whereas some of the enlisted men were there to occupy time, wear the uniform and have fun out of the ordinary routine of life, Fellers was a career soldier. Described by his sister Bertie Woodford, Fellers was:

'...always very serious even as a boy and had a very competitive spirit. He was all soldier – everybody thought he would go a long, long way.'
Bertie Woodford from an interview with Alex Kershaw

From a well-to-do Virginian methodist family of six children, Taylor Fellers was well aware of his familial expectations from an early age and had joined the National Guard in 1932. Fellers put pressure on himself to succeed and set himself high personal standards and the Army, or at least the National Guard, was the perfect place to carve out two careers – one as an army officer with all the prestige and respect that this brought to a man from Virginia and as family man with a successful civilian career. A National Guardsman could find himself promoted quickly for all manner of reasons and no doubt Taylor Fellers looked forward to his captaincy within five more years – but wartime promotions have no timetable, it is fitness to command that is the primary need.

Nicknamed 'Tail Feathers' by his fellow sprinters at school, he was a tall, long-legged country boy who could certainly run. Fellers was also known to be fairly tough on discipline – he was tough on himself and his men and, despite knowing most of the men socially out of uniform, they respected him, which was not an easy thing to achieve. Being able to socialise for six days of the week and then put on a uniform and suddenly transform into an officer required a delicate but clear aspect of leadership and he had showed that he knew how to handle this dual personality as he was promoted to Sergeant in 1935 after only three years in the Guard. By the late 1930s he had been accepted into his Masonic Lodge which was a sure mark of acceptance by the local establishment and that he was regarded as safe and loyal to the traditions of the local Virginian elites. Taylor Fellers was promoted to Second Lieutenant on 1 April 1939 – an ambition fulfilled.

The current company commander was Captain James Patterson, whom Taylor Fellers would shortly replace when he was promoted, and again all in short order as the unit underwent greater scrutiny in terms of its fitness for role. All of these rapid changes, as well as the fears for the future, fed into the next stage of his evolution as a gentleman from Virginia which then resulted in marriage to Naomi Newman, moving into a converted courthouse in 1940. Their marriage was not going to have long before it was going to be severely tested by the arrival of war. Nevertheless, Taylor Fellers' parents watched their son's progress with pride, as I am sure they did all their children, but they were especially proud with his promotion to Captain of the first company of the 1st Battalion of 116th Infantry Regiment.

But a unit, of whatever size, is nothing without its warrant or non-commissioned officers. There one can identify the true level of performance in any unit and Fellers was especially lucky to be able to lean on John Wilkes who was promoted as his Master Sergeant – the beating heart of the Company. Described as a straight speaking and honest, hardworking man, John Wilkes was well respected both in and out of uniform. He had joined to earn a few extra dollars a month to support his parents and siblings and was recognised for his personal toughness and self-discipline – for John Wilkes it was the army way or the highway when you were in uniform and that's just what any captain needed behind him to run the unit.

> 'I knew John long before the war,' recalled Roy Stevens. 'He used to play a lot of pool in town.... We also played poker, and he used to joke about how he was on furlough back in Bedford one time and he got into a fight with a fellow called Sam Ruff. Sam was seventy pounds lighter than John, but he just happened to hit him right. "That little fella – he broke my nose!" John would say and then laugh.'[10]

Married to Bettie before the war, she saw a milder, more sensitive side to her husband. Bettie recalled how John loved bowling and the movies – they saved the money and watched *Gone with the Wind* for four hours, spent most of their time on the farms of the area, picnicked near Smith Mountain Lake and shared never to be forgotten moments as he drove his tan wood-panelled station wagon down Main Street in Bedford.

Although it was possible for the men of A Company to get passes for furlough back home, these were usually only for two or three days at a time – there was too much going on. As 1942 moved forward, so did an increasing tempo of training for everyone and no-one was certain what the future would hold. In August orders arrived to move the division from Fort Meade to a new camp – this time to the warmer climate of Camp Blanding near Jacksonville. Until very recently, the camp had been home to the 1st Infantry Division – 'The Big Red One' who had now been ordered to England as part of their journey to North Africa – but they would meet again in 1944 after the 29th had spent a year in intensive training in England and the 1st had refitted after their losses in Africa.

The 'Blue & Gray' division was tasked with protecting the eastern seaboard from attack but in reality, this provided meaningful time for training in patrols and guard duty while Captain Taylor Fellers was one of many junior officers sent on a crash training course for two weeks. Senior commanders and staff officers also received new roles within the division or were moved on to non-combat roles outside the division to ensure that it was battle ready when the time came for the expected move overseas. Hard decisions about friends and colleagues alike had to be made and a new divisional commander, Major General Leonard

T. Gerow, was appointed, to take command on 11 October 1942 – just as the Division received orders to embark – but for where?[11] Rear echelon commanders came and went but Fellers and his young officers stayed put and he had time to make good friends with his fellow company officers in the 1st Battalion as well as spend time in command task exercises with his battalion and regimental commanders as part of the team building that was so essential for a combat role. Immersed in training, Fellers seemed to revel in the challenges given him and on more than one occasion his men sensed that he would be promoted to a new role within the regiment.

Chapter Seven

The Arcadia Conference

Many of us subscribe to the notion that our lives are set by fate, that we should not worry about the future as it has been pre-ordained for us. Others reject this notion of pre-destination and the universe acting on our lives and call it fate – that we cannot exert any control, chaos rules and any result can emerge. For a smaller group, a group that I am pleased to be a member of, it is a mixture of the two – this is called synchronicity. In a synchronic world, our lives are like a jigsaw. We can select a certain piece and place it on a board – for example by joining the National Guard. Another person selects a piece and tries to fit it into the jigsaw and it may or may not fit – if it does then our lives take another direction and so the process continues. But there can be a time when all the pieces do fit and the sum of those parts is far greater than just the jigsaw. Try to imagine for a moment a jigsaw in three dimensions where many people are adding pieces and they fit together perfectly but just one piece, or one decision by anyone and the whole design changes. This is the background to the story of the Bedford Boys. Their fate was not predestined because it had nothing to do with fate, it was synchronicity and the first pieces of the jigsaw had been laid just thirty miles from them while they were freezing at Fort Meade or in the snowy fields of North Carolina in December 1941.

Almost immediately after the attack on Pearl Harbor, British and American planners agreed on a series of top-secret meetings to be held in Washington. As the boys in A Company warmed their hands over a stove, Winston Churchill flew close by and attended nearly three weeks of secret meetings codenamed ARCADIA. Unlike the wartime conferences, which were as much for public display of unity as any decision-making relevance, Arcadia was an attempt to agree a set of secret strategic principles just between the United Kingdom and the United States. Agreement was found on such things as setting up a combined planning group to be named COSSAC to start detailed work on an invasion from March 1943, setting up a Combined Chiefs of Staff based in Washington, the appointment of a single commander for the ETO – European Theatre of Operations – limiting reinforcements being sent to the Pacific and preparing a build-up of forces in the United Kingdom and then a whole series of tactical decisions such as American bombers would be based in England and airfields constructed to receive them to begin raids on Germany as soon as practicable. However, one decision was going to matter more than most to the Bedford Boys and that was the Germany First principle – the defeat of Germany was the highest priority and, by implication, a landing in Europe was designated of vital significance.

But Arcadia had not yet affected the life of the 116th infantry or the division of which it was a key and respected part. The late summer and early autumn saw the boys from Bedford enjoy what a big city in the sun like Jacksonville could offer and furlough home to Bedford became more difficult with gasoline rationing and the 560-mile distance made it impossible to see family face to face. Letter writing or occasional telephone calls were the only ways to maintain regular contact and letters flowed to and from the boys and their families, wives and sweethearts. But fun and laughter characterises these periods of bonding between brothers in arms and Jacksonville served its purpose perfectly with its plethora of night clubs, music bars, dance halls, cafes and brothels for the unattached men of Bedford. For the married men, it was harder, for the fathers it was harder still.

On 19 August 1942 the British launched an attack on the German occupied town of Dieppe. Few Americans had a grasp of their own geography let alone that of France, but as news slowly filtered through a few weeks later, it became clear that, no matter how well the propaganda machine tried to cover up what had happened at Dieppe, something had gone terribly wrong. It was the Canadians who suffered the most and their blood was spilt illustrating the challenges of landing a military force on the coast of France. The lessons of Dieppe were to surprise, shock and, for a while, debilitate the British members of COSSAC as they meant rethinking almost every aspect of their planning if the same thing, on a much larger scale, was not to happen again. Although the men of the 29th Division paid little attention to it, their senior officers were already working out what role they might be asked to play in the coming months or years.

By October 1942, the impact of the jigsaw pieces created at Arcadia the previous December began to catch up with the 116th infantry and orders came through that they were to move again but still they did not know where. As the orders came through from the chief of staff down through the chain of command to the company commanders and their inspection parades, the news very quickly was transmitted to families, girlfriends and wives back in Bedford. Despite all the time they had had during the year, there still seemed so much to do.

New equipment arrived, new weapons were issued and everything had to be packed in the correct order for transportation. Their day of rail departure from Camp Blanding was released and it was clear that to see their loved ones before they left was going to be an impossible task and men would have to resign themselves to letters, photographs and keepsakes. But this did not apply to the women of Bedford and Alex Kershaw relates the story of Bettie Wilkes. She and her husband John had married for love, that really deep kind of love that feels like marrying a best friend as well as a lover, and she was not going to sit and wait for news that he had left – wherever he was going. Bettie decided to ask around – were there any other girls who wanted to come with her to Florida? Of course there were and Viola Parker and Elaine Coffey joined her task force and they were given time off from work to make the trip south. Viola had recently found out that she was pregnant, and so had a particular reason for ensuring she saw Earl before he left and wanted to make sure his family on the beef farm near the town also knew that she had seen him.

Excitement and anxiety surrounded the wives and fiancées as they took their tickets on board the crowded train packed with hundreds of others all making the same trips for the same reasons, people from all over America and much further still than Bedford. Verona Lipford, 16-year-old sister to A Company's Frank Draper was also on that train with her mother Viola, having been taken out of school for a whole week just to make the trip – never having had a day off for anything before. When they all eventually met in the Florida sunshine, a day of ice cream and laughter followed, each person never admitting in their face that they were counting the seconds, the minutes and the hours as they passed by edging ever closer to when they would have to be pulled apart. The agony and the ecstasy of love and dread in equal amounts in all its forms and with all its pain.

Bedford Hoback was able to spend quality time with his fiancée Elaine Coffey – they seemed a very long way from home but his previous service in Hawaii came back to help Elaine through these difficult hours and telling her not to worry. Timing their final words, getting the timing wrong and having to say them more persuasively a second or even a third time was the hardest part. For some, they just wanted to leave, it was too much, for others, well they never wanted to leave but someone had to make the break and it was left to Master Sergeant Wilkes to do what was expected of him. The men fell in, the girls, sisters, mothers, wives had one more of the strongest hugs that they could ever remember, then let go – some of them, forever.

The two train journeys that followed could not have been more different – for the women of Bedford, it was going to be a long, long emotional journey home, but for the men of Company A the train station where the rest of their unit, plus a few hundred others of the 1st Battalion of the 116th were waiting meant they were back in the army. The officers were serious, their faces white with concern that they had not forgotten anything and, unable to turn around and run back for one final kiss, they disappeared over the brow of a hill. On their train the chewing gum and bravado masked the emotional trauma that they had just been through, but for most, these were young men for whom fear holds no fear and the excitement of going to war overcame the loss of only a few minutes earlier. For the older men it was a question of holding their nerve. The train started to move, and move northwards – it was going to be New Jersey and then Europe following in the footsteps of the 1st Infantry Division a few weeks before. They still were not sure where they were headed but the Army kept them moving through the rain of New Jersey and on to Camp Kilmer – the final stop before embarkation.

The recently appointed commanding officer of the 116th was Colonel Charles Canham. Nicknamed 'Old Stoneface', Canham had been selected for the 116th for a special mission – to make his regiment battle ready and battle hardened. It is very doubtful that he knew why this was but equally likely that his soldier's mind deduced that it was for more than just coming up against the enemy. It was Canham's job to look for weakness anywhere in his infantry regiment and either fix it – or remove it.

A strict disciplinarian, Canham was a regular career soldier and this was a unit that needed more than a National Guard commander to lead it. Born in Kola, Mississippi, Charles Canham joined the Army on 23 May 1919 at the age of 18 – the same age as a large number of his men in the regiment. Seven years later, he had worked his way into and been commissioned out of West Point and spent the 1930s mostly commanding units in the Philippines before he was selected by Major General Leonard T. Gerow to command the 116th Infantry.

Colonel Canham and his regimental headquarters team oversaw every detail of what was to happen next. Every man went through the same process – the old First World War flat top helmet was now discarded and a new 'coal scuttle' helmet was issued, uniforms were changed, socks were changed, first aid kits were issued, bags were packed and repacked, the list was endless and the supply system was working perfectly, America was going to war and, as their final train brought them into Hoboken Station, Colonel Canham was there to see that the re-birth of the Regiment went smoothly.[12]

Part III

Fatal Attractions – Preparations for D-Day

'You are a soldier of the United States Army. You have embarked for distant places where the war is being fought'

President F.D. Roosevelt

September of 1942 was hectic. In the war in Europe, German forces had just begun to force their way into Stalingrad – they had no need to be there other than that it was Hitler's wish and the battle they were engaged in there would last the best part of a year. Convoys exchanged signals as they passed each other in the Atlantic swells and U-boat losses approximately equalled new U-boat commissions – the Battle of the Atlantic was currently a score draw. In North Africa, Rommel was exhausted and had been brought home for a rest; General Montgomery was busy planning for his counter offensive at El Alamein which was but a month away from the planned start; and in the Pacific, the United States Navy was still basking in the jubilation of their victory at Midway the previous June and was now rushing to support the Marines engaged in bitter fighting for the island of Guadalcanal. In late September the men of Company A, still led by their Company officers and Captain Fellers boarded ferries to take them and their extensive equipment across the Hudson River and onwards to board the massive cruise liner the *Queen Mary* which was waiting, along with her sister ship the *Queen Elizabeth* which, between them, would take 15,000 men of the 29th Infantry Division to England.

Once aboard and shown to their closely packed bunks, each man was also given a letter from the President which simply said *'You are a soldier of the United States Army. You have embarked for distant places where the war is being fought.'*

Chapter Eight

The Journey to England, 1943

The identities of military planners are, by and large, lost to history. Very like their counterparts at Bletchley Park who worked on Enigma, planning teams of both serving officers from all the services and civilian advisors, were sworn to secrecy for the rest of their lives, their movements monitored and their lives hidden from view. Similarly, the work that they were asked to do was just as vital as Enigma and also impacted on the lives of men and women – tens of thousands of men and women from a multiplicity of countries and organisations went to their deaths directly because of, or in spite of, planners such as COSSAC from March 1943 and Enigma – and only a handful of people even knew of their existence.

As the men of the 116th infantry found their way around a new country and routine, the planners of 1942 were tasked with three different operations. Firstly, to manage the build-up of Allied forces in Britain preparatory to a large-scale invasion. Secondly to draft out in detail Operation Sledgehammer – the establishment of a defensive salient on the French Cotentin peninsula to pin down German forces and then to launch a breakout into central France and thirdly Operation Roundup – in which a number of beachheads were to be seized on the coastline of northern France and breakouts launched into German occupied territory – in 1943, this last operation had a codename change to Operation Overlord.

The first of these planning decisions had already been worked out and was, by mid to late 1942, already underway. Codenamed Operation Bolero, this was the large-scale transportation of American troops to Britain, and it needed to be planned and coordinated between the respective staffs of the United States Navy and the Royal Navy, convoy routes and escort ships decided and allocated, marshalling areas established, port destinations prepared, fuel and food provided for the ships and railway routes coordinated with the British transportation system. At the end of the chain, existing camps needed to be identified or new temporary ones built. Thus, Operation Bolero, once decided and agreed upon, was activated and the men of the 116th Infantry, including of course the men of Company A from Bedford, Virginia, were responding to fresh orders that had been released by the joint staff planners. To the men and women working on military plans, it was a very impersonal exercise; numbers not individuals mattered, geography not personal circumstances and timetables not next-of-kin.

Synchronicity, or was it fate, showed its hand. Bolero was to continue well into 1943 – the numbers of men and equipment needed to tally with the final invasion plans would take almost a year to assemble, then they had to be trained and fed while they were based in the UK. But interfering with this build up was Churchill's preference for avoiding the main blow for as long as practicable. His own wartime decisions in 1914 at Antwerp, 1915 at Gallipoli and 1942 at Dieppe had all been costly failures and many thousands of men had died because of his, at times, petulance and rashness in pushing for offensive operations which were doomed to fail. With Dieppe, Churchill had many reasons to wish to divert away from opening a second front until all was in place and so the Bolero timetable became disrupted as smaller scale landings were made in North Africa with Operation Torch in November 1942, Operation Husky which were the landings on Sicily in July 1943 and Operation Avalanche in November 1943. The combined effect of these was to bleed resources from Bolero and it would take longer for the 29th Division to receive fellow divisions into its area of training exercises.

The strategic imperative was the invasion of Europe and the destruction of Germany but Churchill and Roosevelt could see that Stalin was doing a pretty good job of that on his own. American support was flooding into the far eastern ports of Russia and every day thousands of tonnes of equipment arrived in Vladivostok. After 1945, rather similar to 1917, the Americans were to rue just how helpful they had been as over a third of the Russian military was equipped with American machinery and weapons. But Stalin was acutely aware that the longer the war went on with his taking the brunt, that Russia too was wearing itself out – a subtle sub plot of Stalin's two partners.

The journey on the *Queen Mary* had been a mixed experience. Anticipation and adrenalin on one level, frustration and shock on the other. The anticipation of the journey affected all the men of Company A. Whether from Bedford VA or from New Jersey, Delaware or Boston everyone was prone to sea sickness and for 99 per cent of the men they were about to find that out. This was their first time on a ship and certainly their first time at sea and to cope with this number of officers and men the ship was divided into three decks – Red, White and Blue with each person being given a coloured button for his area on the ship – movement between areas was not allowed. There was the usual hustling and bustling trying to find their section on the ship and then stow their weapon and sizeable kit back on a bunk bed that was one of six high. Refitted in Boston in January 1942, the *Queen Mary* had been stripped of most of her luxury and was now just a large, carpet- and door-less mass of white and grey metal to house 10,000 souls instead of the maximum of 3,000 she was built for. Her hull was painted grey for Atlantic Ocean camouflage and she soon acquired the nickname of the 'Grey Ghost'. Five double-mounted 40mm cannon were fixed into newly constructed mounts around the ship and six three-inch guns but her main weapon was designed to be speed: *The Queen* could achieve 30 knots if required when a U-boat at best could run at 7 knots below the surface. In the eight months between January to August 1942, the U-boats had sunk 609 allied ships – both Merchant and Royal Navy and, because of her propaganda value, Hitler had put a bounty on the *Mary* of $250,000 for the U-boat crew that sank her.[13]

After claiming a bunk, hopefully a top one to avoid the flow of sea sick puke and stench of those above raining down onto one's bunk, it was time to reconnoitre the ship – but no – the ship's Captain Illingworth ordered everyone to remain below decks until they were out to sea. The *Mary* began to pull away from her berth and men became gradually aware of whether they were going to become victims of sea sickness or not. For John Schenk, the first large rolling of the Mary told him all he needed to know – this was going to be the longest seven days of his young life so far.

During the summer months of the 'GI Shuttle' a rotation system allowed two men to share a bunk with fifteen thousand on board with half sleeping outside on the top deck for two days and the other half in the bunk. But by the time the Bedford Boys were on board, it was too cold so it was in the holds only with time on top very limited because of the weight all moving around at the same time. The frustrations of a below deck journey caused tempers to flair and fights broke out, the dark claustrophobia of the eighteen inch clearance between bunks was made worse by the smell – there were no showers for the enlisted men for a week and the sick filled rancid air mixed with heavy cigarette smoke and the heavy rolling of the ship and the lack of ventilation – not wishing to give their position away at night with a light or an open window – was a horrible test of willpower to get through it for everyone on board.

The huge former first-class dining hall was the mess hall which worked all day to provide twelve sittings with huge heaving queues around the rolling corridors as the ship reached the mid-Atlantic. For officers, stewards were provided to serve their food and the commanding general with his staff sat at the same tables across the voyage. If you couldn't face eating then there was always gambling hidden away down in the numerous corridors and toilet blocks. On board *Queen Mary*, alcohol was banned and she was a 'dry' ship although how well that was enforced, we can only guess. Gambling too was banned but the divisional MPs really had little chance to stop it – well-rehearsed lookouts and alarm systems were in place and the officers played in the evenings behind closed doors.

To break the monotony of the seven-day passage there were lifeboat drills – even though there were nowhere near enough boats for the number of people on board – and watching gunnery practice or attending a religious service with the chaplains. 20 year old Wallace Carter was one of Company A's most enthusiastic gamblers and he was able to pass the hours playing 'Snake Eyes' with his dice and he needed far less room to play dice than with his trusty pool cue – plus there was not enough room to swing a cat let alone play for the Mud Alley Wildcats. Sergeant Earl Parker lay on his bunk and thought of Viola and wondered how the pregnancy was going – thinking about her every day kept him going. Captain Taylor Fellers spent a lot of his time in briefing meetings with his battalion commander and getting his sergeants together checking on the men, the routines and getting ready for disembarkation. Together with her sister ship the *Queen Elizabeth*, these two great liners showed the world what was coming – but where and when was still top secret. Churchill summed up the work these two ships did in this way:

'Built for the arts of peace and to link the Old world with the New, the Queens challenged the fury of Hitlerism in the Battle of the Atlantic. Without their aid, the day of final victory must unquestionably have been postponed.'[14]

Captain Fellers could relate to the problems of the journey and no doubt did his best to keep up the spirits of his Company with his fellow officers. Commanding B Company was Captain Ettore Vincent Zappacosta. The youngest of three children in an Italian family, Ettore was from Philadelphia, Pennsylvania and had been posted to the 116th to lead Company B from within the 116th. Always wanting to be a soldier, Ettore had joined the regular army in August 1934 and served for three years reaching the rank of corporal before discharge in 1937. Building a career as a draftsman, Ettore immediately re-enlisted at the outbreak of war in Europe and was selected for officer training and was commissioned on the day of Pearl Harbor – 7 December 1941 – and was promoted to captain and commander of B Company, 1st Battalion, 116th in 1942. Fellers and Zappacosta worked well together – from hugely different social backgrounds, Zappacosta had regular army service behind him which fitted him well for those times when a National Guard officer needed help. Zappacosta was also well regarded by his men for his personality, high standards and determination – he was exactly where he wanted to be in life. Later on in their service in the UK, Fellers could relate to Captain Berthier Botts Hawks III. From Elizabeth County Virginia, his father was the manager of a coal company and Berthier was also a regular soldier having enlisted on 14 June 1938 and was commissioned in February 1941. On the *Queen Mary* Berthier Hawks was a lieutenant in C Company but later in 1942 he was given command as captain of Company C and would train and fight alongside Captain Fellers through the period up to and beyond D-Day. The last infantry company commanding officer for the 1st Battalion was Captain Walter Otis Schilling. Aged 34 at the time of the crossing, but 36 by D-Day, Captain Schilling was from Roanoke, Virginia and, like Fellers, had joined the National Guard in 1929 as a career outside of his work as an electrician in a silk mill. By 1931 he was married to Marie Equi and Walter was promoted Lieutenant on 7 April 1938. Being part of the National Guard for Virginia and in the same battalion, both Schilling and Fellers knew each other well and no doubt had a healthy rivalry as they led and made their companies what they were. Neither would have got this far if they were not considered as good as any regular officer and, with something to prove, they were often seen as better than the entitled superiority of the regular army officer corps.

The United States Army had undergone many internal changes as it moved from a peacetime construct into a wartime one. The size and shape of divisions were adjusted as was the strength of the infantry battalion with cuts in manpower and heavy weapons to reduce the drag of non-combat personnel and to increase mobility and firepower at platoon level. All these changes were drip-fed into the training and structure of the units and the officers and men of the 116th, like every other battalion, had to change their shape. The usual four infantry companies were fixed at a total of 180 men each and the battalion HQ was also now refitted as a smaller but capable fighting company of 130 men. These together with an anti-tank unit of 31 created a battalion strength of some 818 men and 32 officers.

At the time of embarkation, the four company commanders of the 1st Battalion were Captain Schilling alongside Fellers, Hawks and Zappacosta, their combined strength of nearly 850 men – soon to be filled up with replacements to bring them up to full strength and the whole commanded by Lieutenant Colonel John Metcalfe.[15] They were on their way.

The *Curacoa* Incident – a portent of what was to come

With the journey nearly over, some of the now two hundred strong men of Company A, 116th infantry, were up on the decks – with their lifejackets on as was standard for every passenger – even the commanding general. It was 2 October 1942, a grey, misty day and the men had been at sea now for seven days and they were due at their destination, wherever that was, the next day. Every day the crew and those on deck kept a vigilant watch for either a submarine periscope or even worse the white swirling track of a torpedo. German radio boasted many times that the *Queen Mary* had been sunk to try to trick the captain into giving away his position with a morse signal to the contrary, and today they were nearly successful.

Keeping up with a thirty-knot cruise liner was just not possible for any Royal Naval vessel. They would run out of fuel trying to complete the whole journey so Royal Navy protection came in tag teams of destroyers and cruisers at either end of the voyage and, now close to entering British waters, had welcomed the light cruiser HMS *Curacoa* (D41) at 09.00 that morning, sent to provide anti-aircraft protection while the *Mary* passed the north coast of Ireland. On the top decks that morning, the thousands of officers and troops milling around on what was 'a fine and clear day with a moderate north-westerly wind' had good reason to feel positive. They had almost completed their voyage without any U-boat attack and now they had a strong Royal Navy escort. The *Curacoa* waited for the *Mary* to arrive and then started her parallel voyage eastwards some ten miles away and over the next few hours set course to come closer to the *Mary* as she continued her zig-zag course. Both ships were aware of the nature of the deflections as they had signalled that it was 'No.8' and the *Mary* had been following this for many hours to deter U-boat tracking. At over eighty-thousand tons, the *Mary* took a long time to turn and she was holding a speed of 28 knots to the 25 at top speed of the *Curacoa* – a far lighter ship at just over 4,000 tonnes which meant that at some point the *Mary* would draw level and then pull away. When that point came, the *Curacao* should have been well apart and signalling good luck.

The huge liner was on a mean course of 131 degrees – therefore steadily zig zagging southeastwards. By 13.30 hours later that day they were indeed almost level and had drawn close at about one mile running to the south of *Mary* and planned to slip astern of her as she passed by. Rather like two cars exchanging lanes, it was all about timing. The relatively small gap between the ships was reasonable as any effective air defence of *Mary* required the Royal Navy ship to be at close range; *Curacao* was, however, edging ever closer to the angled course of the *Mary*. Both captains seemed certain that the other would move away as they closed but instead the officer of the watch on the *Mary*, seemingly unaware of just what was developing, made his next planned course change towards the *Curacao* and *Curacao*, the ship that could more easily turn, failed to see *Mary* now heading straight towards her and instead of steadily slipping astern of her, she was directly in the path of her enormous steel bows. At 14.10 the troops of the 29th Division, including men of Company A, were taking in the fresh air in gulps waving to the crew of the Royal Navy ship when *Mary* began her next bearing and watched the slow train crash unfold over the next few minutes, surely the *Curacao* would move away to starboard? But, as her wreck illustrates, her course was unchanged and, as eye witnesses testified at the time, her wake was dead straight like a torpedo track as the huge liner of 80,000 tonnes bore down on her. Suddenly, two minutes later at 14.12, the *Curacao* had edged right under Queen *Mary*'s starboard bow and then the noise of tearing steel and shrieks of the crews on both ships blasted through as the *Mary* slightly shuddered, and like a bad dream, she cut the Curacao in two pieces as if she was a paper model. Troops on each side of the *Mary* had the same view – smoke, screams and the sight of men in the water as the *Mary*'s engines thundered over them. Corporal Bob Slaughter was one of those on the top deck taking in some of the rare sunshine and ran to the railings to look over the side. In an interview with Alex Kershaw, he recalled:

'My first thought was that we had been torpedoed…I saw the Curacao's stern going down one side of the Mary, and the bow down the other – cut right in two. The Curacao's crow's nest was parallel to the water, and there was a sailor in there still doing semaphore signals. His eyes looked enormous – he was so frightened. All we could do was throw life-jackets. I remember thinking: "God, here we are, haven't even got overseas, and we've killed all these British sailors.'[16]

The troops on each side of the *Mary* saw half a ship steadily rolling and going under and, at nearly thirty knots, it was only about twenty seconds before the whole incident was behind the *Mary* who, as their captain knew only too well, could not stop to help pick up survivors.

One can only try to imagine the terror and suffering that befell the crew of the *Curacao* – 330 of whom lost their lives – but also the impact this had on the soldiers on board the *Mary*. Seeing drowning sailors astern of them as they thundered undeterred on their way caused hundreds to shout and scream at the crew and the captain on the bridge of the *Mary* and for hours afterward the *Mary* was a sombre and melancholy ship – was this a portent of bad luck for them all?

All the officers of the division were called below to a meeting with the *Mary*'s captain. Hundreds of officers of all ranks from Second Lieutenant to Major General stood and listened to the solemn and restrained words of Captain Illingworth. This disaster, terrible as it was, must not be spoken about. It would only provide propaganda fodder to Lord Haw Haw on German radio broadcasts and deflate morale in the United Kingdom. He and they must do all they can to impress this on both the crew and the men of the 29th Division.

The next day, 3 October 1942, arriving into the Western Isles, the men of the 116th infantry were able to marvel at the purple and hazed mountains of Arran on their left and, as they edged up the ever-narrowing Firth of Clyde towards Greenock, the officers and men of the division knew they were all having their first, and for many, only sight of Scotland. Turning eastwards, *Mary* slowed to 5 knots and, with a huge dent in her bow, she slowly came to a stop just away from the port, dropped her anchors and cut her engines. The journey was over to the relief of thousands. Now it was time to smarten up, sharpen up and get off the ship and onto dry land.

The weather had changed and Scotland welcomed the boys from Virginia with a howling wind and cutting rain as they were taken off in companies by short ferry rides to the dockside where they lined up before marching to the station. It was a cloudy day with an atmosphere of gloom to match and they still had no idea where they were going. Captain Fellers had run out of excuses to keep their minds on the job in hand. As they boarded another train, they needed to know – was it North Africa or the south coast of England? After what seemed like an endless journey crammed into small carriages, the men of A Company were waiting for clearance through yet another station. Their troop transport at least had windows out of which they could see the landscape change from mist covered mountains into mist covered fields and their compasses told them they were heading due south.

The journey south was a chance to see England for the first time. Smoke from thousands of family homes, chimneys belching from factories in the north – Glasgow, Carlisle, the Lake District, Liverpool and Oxford – and then, stopping in smaller stations, meeting their first English people. It was always difficult to work out exactly where they were. Station signs had been taken down a long time ago but the landscape told the farming boys something, cows and sheep were replaced by long flat fields recently ploughed after the August harvest. Church spires gave way to cathedral ones and building materials moved from red brick to limestone – all signs that they were moving south. Worn down by three years of war, thin and ragged, very few able-bodied men – there were girls everywhere, lots of girls and it was time to remember their phrase books and practise their whistling. Blue uniformed women of the Red Cross manned every station delivering thousands of cups of tea and biscuits through the windows of the trains and exchanging welcome greetings and names. A hundred whistles broke out when a particularly tight uniform came into view and laughter had returned to the tired and glum faces of Captain Fellers' company.

Suddenly awoken by the sounds of air raid sirens. No-one had ever heard one before but they quickly worked out what it meant and the Luftwaffe was up close and personal, maybe looking for their train. Later that night, after a long sleep and over 400 miles in one day, their troop train came to a stop and this time their sergeants had been told to wake them up, gather their gear and, at last, get off that train. For now, their journey was over. Tired, hungry, homesick and confused, it was 4 October 1942 and they had arrived in Salisbury – the home of the British Army.

The 116th completed the last part of their journey and, with their trusty kit bags over one shoulder and their rifle over their other, they marched into Tidworth Barracks just to the north of Salisbury and only ten miles from Stonehenge. It was a cold comfort welcome. Late in the evening, the long columns of men made their way from their assembly area as train after train arrived and disgorged its human cargo. Cars arrived to transport Major General Gerow and his senior commanders while the battalions organised themselves and set off in long straggling columns down poorly lit roads through the cold English countryside – it seemed more like a different planet than a different country. The sergeants did what sergeants do and barked at the men to keep in step and wake up their act and as they passed through the gates, they met their first British soldiers welcoming the 'Yanks' to Tidworth. All they could do that night was fill a well-used cloth bag with straw to make a mattress or palliasse and slump down on a rickety wooden bunk, and sleep. It was to become home for the next six months.

Chapter Nine

Your Life in the Hands of a Stranger

'Soldiers can sometimes make decisions that are smarter than the orders they've been given.'

Orson Scott Card

While the men of Company A, together with the other four companies, B,C,D and Headquarters of the 1st Battalion, 116th Infantry worked out how they were going to use Tidworth Camp and planned out their company, battalion and regimental routines and training programmes, the men and women in London that would determine their destiny in this life, kept planning.

During March 1943, the long anticipated COSSAC (Chief of Staff Supreme Allied Commander) meetings began in earnest and took over the responsibility for formulating the invasion of France. Based at Norfolk House on St James's Square in London, the building had already been home to the planners of the November 1942 Operation Torch landings in North Africa and many of the same people would now use their experience in co-ordinating a beach assault to plan for the invasion of Europe. With the knowledge they had gained from the failure at Dieppe and the success in North Africa, confidence was high that the very best people were working on this next operation. Indeed, Torch had been a multi beach landing with three large landing areas and this had necessitated large scale support from the air and sea which was exactly what would be required in France – once the sites had been chosen.

Before General Dwight D. Eisenhower, at the end of 1943, was chosen to lead the entire armed forces for the European assault, Lieutenant General Frederick Morgan was selected to lead COSSAC as Chief of Staff and he was given three tasks. Firstly, to keep planning a series of diversionary operations to keep the German intelligence structures off balance and uncertain – there was to be no thread that allowed the Germans to make any conclusions ahead of schedule. Secondly, Morgan was required to plan for the unexpected but possible collapse of Germany ahead of the invasion. Intelligence sources were aware of the tremendous strain of fighting on the Eastern Front and that there were serious plans by the German resistance within the Wehrmacht to remove

Hitler. Lastly, Morgan was asked to come up with the plans for an amphibious assault on France.

The decision to attack France was made at the Quadrant Conference in Quebec in August 1943 and May 1944 had been selected as the key month so this gave the planners under a year to gather every aspect, they could think of together into one plan. Why the 29th Division was selected for a key role is unknown but at some point, back in Washington, someone, a total stranger to the men of Company A, indeed unknown to the whole division of fifteen-thousand men, at an anonymous meeting suggested the 29th, along with the 1st Division, as the two infantry divisions earmarked for the American section of the invasion beaches. Why was it not the 34th or the 37th or any number of other divisions – a question that was going to be asked tens of thousands of times in early 1944 but, for now at least, no one knew what their role was going to be.

The conceptualisation of death is what military planners do. In reaching their conclusions that will determine the life or death of the men asked to carry out their mission, planners must try to conceptualise how their plans will unfold. Assessing the strength of the enemy, what his possible responses might be and how quickly they could reinforce were all important, but how to get men and equipment onto a beach and off it again with minimum casualties against a defended coastline was a far greater challenge. Nothing on this scale had ever been tried before and, so far, the planners had seen one success and one unmitigated disaster. Churchill, for once sensitive to the disasters he had personally ordered in the past, counselled caution and, ironically, warned his allies that a premature attack could see the beaches of France 'choked with the bodies of the flower of American and British manhood'. Failure in the past had been tactical but, in this operation, failure would extend the war for certain and possibly even lose it. But time was pressing and Hitler was fast developing his secret weapons and was well advanced in nuclear testing, another two years of war and he would be able to wipe out all opposition. Morgan was also acutely aware of the reputation of 'planners' as he said in a meeting with his staff in 1943:

> *'The term planning staff has come to have a most sinister meaning. It implies the production of nothing but paper. What we must contrive to do somehow is to produce not only paper but action.'*[17]

Morgan was going to press hard on his staff to come up with short-term diversionary operations as he had been ordered. As for the area for invasion, Morgan had come up with three possible landing areas – the Pas de Calais and the Picardy coast, the Bay of the Seine and finally the Calvados region of Normandy between the city of Caen and the Cotentin Peninsula – despite the lack of a port, the wide broad beaches of Normandy were chosen and the fate of the 29th Division took another turn. It was to be some time before Captain Tayor Fellers and Company A, his tough battalion commander Lieutenant Colonel John Metcalfe, the equally resilient regimental commander Colonel Charles 'Stoneface' Canham and the divisional commander Major General Leonard Gerow had any notion of where or what Normandy was but for now it was all about training and selection.

Gerow's Burpees

The 29th was a good division but to survive an assault on Europe, and that is what they expected to be a part of, they had to be the best division in the American Army. Since the outbreak of war, and certainly since December 1941, each component part of the division had been ramping up their physical training and the result of this was a steadily increasing percentage of men and officers could not sustain what was needed. Even before the men from Bedford had left on the *Mary*, they had left behind former comrades in arms who had either failed basic fitness tests, been gently moved on to administrative posts or simply told they would not be combat material. This process began on a whole new level in Salisbury. Gerow was plain speaking and his appointment in October 1942 was meant to take the 29th from a National Guard unit to one that could compare with the best of the regular army.

Gerow's training programme included the 'burp-up' exercises. In the late 1930s Royal H. Burpee was working on his PhD in applied physiology at Columbia University. His hope was to qualify as a teacher and he spent his spare time as director of a YMCA hostel in New York City where he witnessed the poor physical state of so many young men. In his published theses, Burpee was able to identify nearly 300 measures of fitness measured from *Age* to *Wrestling* and pioneered the notion of an individual, rather than the group, training programme. The pressing need for the Army to evaluate just how fit its soldiers were, saw the Burpee programme adopted and they selected ten exercises to test fitness against the ability of the soldier based around the burpee – the now world-famous squat, push back and jump – and measured heart rates and how quickly it returns to normal.

Those who passed received extra pay each month as an incentive and also wore the Expert Infantryman's Badge – those who failed were moved to a non-combat unit. The programme started almost immediately and was a shock to officers and men alike – the November and December 1942 drizzle and cold mornings did not help and the American troops had to get used to a lot less sunshine in Britain, all of which added to an air of despondency in Company A and it was down to Fellers and his officers to try to keep morale up while they all trained together as he wrote to his mother on 27 March 1943:

'I am beginning to think it is hard to beat a Bedford boy for a soldier. Out of less than a hundred we left there with I would say about a dozen have made officers and several more will be soon. They are good practical officers too with a year or more of regular non-commissioned service behind them. I am truly proud to be commanding my old hometown outfit and just hope I can carry them right on through and bring them all home.'[18]

Training continued into a warmer spring and by May 1943, with new recruits bringing the strength of Company A up to its full complement of 200, there was a far more optimistic atmosphere in the old Victorian barracks of Tidworth. The wars in the Pacific and North Africa had taken a turn for the better and, in the Atlantic, 'Black May' had seen the sinking of forty-one German submarines in a single month – the secret of Enigma would not be known for decades after the war had ended, but it was doing its work only 100 miles from Tidworth in Bletchley Park. Unbeknownst to the Americans of the 29th Division, the men and women at Bletchley Park were also closely monitoring German intelligence briefings to see if they had identified or guessed where the Allied landings were to take place. One of the many new recruits was PTE Donald McCarthy who was allocated to Headquarters Company of the 1st Battalion of the 116th:

'From day one with the 116th in Ivybridge training on the moors would consume every waking hour from 5am to 5pm, except Sundays. Every third day we would dig in, set up camp and bed down in this inhospitable swampy moor, anticipating live artillery and mortar fire.'[19]

Morgan, true to his word about producing action, on 2 May authorised Operation Mincemeat which had been launched with the dropping of 'Major Martin' off the coast of Spain carrying papers to indicate planning for an invasion of Greece and Sardinia as the main route into Germany. This was just one of those diversionary operations that Morgan oversaw to confuse the Germans. On the 13th came news that the Germans and Italians had surrendered in North Africa although most notably withdrawn to carry out other duties was Field Marshal Erwin Rommel. Another came on 16 May with Operation Chastise – better known to history as the Dambusters Raid. In another element of synchronicity, Rommel was rested and then despatched to plan the defences of the French coast to protect it from invasion and, as the 29th Division was given its new movement orders from COSSAC, Rommel arrived in France.

Chapter Ten

The Birth of the *Empire Javelin*, 1943

'If the women in the factories stopped work for twenty minutes, the allies would lose the war.'

Joseph Joffre

The requirement for a fleet of specially designed and adjusted Landing Ship Infantry (Large) ships was one of the earliest decisions to be made by COSSAC. Given the lightning speed and resources of the American ship building firms, it was a straight forward process of drafting out and tendering for the contract for eleven such ships. Based on the existing and successful C1 B designs, the Consolidated Steel Corporation immediately submitted their plans which included stripping away much of the deck designs to allow for space on the top decks for troops to disembark and placing the rubber lifeboats on the sides of the ship giving the LSIs (L) their very distinctive look.

Like moving all the pieces of blue sky together on a jigsaw, one of the first of the new designs, the C1-S-AY1 type, was laid down in May 1943 at the Wilmington dockyards in California. Just as Company A of the 116th infantry was preparing to move to their final training location, so the ship that was going to take them to France was now being built – and in another example of synchronicity, the two of them would meet twelve months later in May of the following year.

Initially all the ships in this new class were named after Capes and the *Empire Javelin* was actually commissioned and set to be launched as the SS *Cape Lobos*. As the drawing offices hummed to typewriters, shouts, banging doors and sirens, the holds of *Cape Lobos* were welded in place, the dockyard workers knew that these were going to be special ships, ships that would take their American brothers onto the coasts of occupied Europe. Who knew whether a brother, son or daughter would sail on them – with 10,000 or more male and female shipyard workers, there was more than a fair chance that the ships they were building would be carrying men or women that they knew. Thus, all eleven ships were built not only fast, but well.

By the time they got to the upper decks, the new designs displayed their exact purpose and the huge steel davits, which could hold a new design of landing craft, were screwed and welded in place all over the SS *Cape Lobos*. Each pair of davits had to be able to carry an empty landing craft weighing nine tonnes and then, with a length of over 42 feet and an infantry platoon of 36 armed men and a crew of four, slowly release the boat into the water. This meant that Company A, and every other company of the 116th Infantry, would need six boats to take it ashore. Then there would be the battalion Headquarters Company and further back in the chain, the regimental Headquarters. Some LSI (L) were able to carry a whole flotilla of twelve boats, but it was usual for there to be two or even three LSIs gathered together to land a complete formation – in the event the *Empire Javelin* would carry 18 LCAs.

As work in the shipyard in California continued into the summer, there were more changes of personnel in the 29th. The rate of attrition had slowed as the various units weeded out the men who were not physically going to be able to carry on and there were of course numerous injuries. Company A was spurred on by Captain Fellers and his officers such as Ray Nance and his two other young Lieutenants:

'And Company A began to earn the praise of battalion commanders: Captain Fellers was shaping a first-class fighting force. On average, the men were seven pounds heavier – most of it muscle – than when they had left America. Their chest sizes had increased by and inch at least and their self-confidence had soared.'[20]

More changes to personnel came while the division was training at Tidworth but this time at the top. The divisional commander Major General Leonard Gerow was promoted to V Corps commander on 17 July. This gave Gerow command over two fine infantry divisions – the 29th and the 1st – and he went on to play a key role in planning for D-Day including every detail of the landings on Omaha beach which would fall to Vth Corps – although the codeword OMAHA was as yet still top secret. A new divisional commander arrived in the shape of two-star Major General Charles Gerhardt who caught up with his officers and men in Devon before the end of July 1943.

By June 1943, the 116th Infantry had already moved from Tidworth southwards into the West Country where over 1,250,000 men were now in the advanced stages of training. Meanwhile in Wilmington, California, the SS *Cape Lobos* was almost complete. With the Lend-Lease programme in full swing, American industrial might was now at its peak of production and it had taken only three months of full-scale effort to get SS *Cape Lobos* looking like a ship. New steam turbine engines were built and transported to Wilmington and the specialised davits to lower fully loaded landing craft were fitted to accommodate up to sixteen boats. The SS *Cape Lobos* could accommodate 1,400 men plus their equipment if she was totally full. On 25 October 1943 she was launched into the dockyard and sailed out into the eastern Pacific and by January 1944 she was taken over the Atlantic by a skeleton crew and was escorted on her way with four other similar landing ships to the United Kingdom, with Plymouth as her destination.

Lend-Lease had done its job. It had not been easy to get to this point where brand new ships were constructed and sent, on loan, to American allies for the war effort. In fact, by the time SS *Cape Lobos* was launched, lend-lease transfers of materials to the combined forces of the allies had reached $1.5 billion a month. By 31 December 1944, total direct lend-lease had reached $35, 382,646,000 made up of 54 per cent in fighting equipment and ships, 21 per cent in aviation gasoline and metals, 13 per cent in foods and 12 per cent was the cost of creating new factories in the United States and building airfields in the United Kingdom.[21]

The SS *Cape Lobos* arrived in Plymouth in early February 1944 to be handed over to the Ministry of War Transport and thereafter over to the Royal Navy and re-registered as part of the Blue Star Line which was responsible for her administration and which also handled two other Empire ships – the *Empire Castle* and the *Empire Strength* which the company went on the purchase after the war.

The large landing ships needed an expert Merchant Navy crew for what was actually a converted merchant ship and so the SS *Cape Lobos* was given a crew of just over two hundred merchant seamen and a complement of Royal Navy officers and crews to man the landing craft – as they would be the ones coming under fire – with four per LCA. Once moored up in Plymouth, the *Empire Javelin* ran up the Red Ensign to indicate that she was a Merchant Navy vessel. The ship was also given a new name – this was part of the 'Empire' Class of eleven ships and she became *Empire Javelin*. The *Javelin* was also given a new IMO (International Maritime Organization) identification number of 169774 and a call sign of MYMQ. The crew of merchant seaman and Royal Navy seamen joined her almost straight away as they had been waiting in Plymouth for her arrival and one officer particularly keen to meet their new ship was Sub-Lieutenant George 'Jimmy' Green – the second in command of the 551st Flotilla.

The Landing Craft

Who could have known that the design of a landing craft could and would have such a bearing on the outcome of D-Day – especially for the men ordained by the planners to land on Omaha beach. Back in 1938 there was even a Landing Craft Committee charged with updating the small number of such boats that existed and which they thought would only be used by the Royal Marines in specific circumstances. Various designs were submitted by manufacturers to deal with the specific requirements of being under ten tonnes in weight, able to carry thirty-two men (the standard size of a platoon at that time) and land them in eighteen inches of water. The plans submitted by J. I. Thornycroft Ltd. produced a strong but shallow boat that fulfilled all of these needs but had one issue: the amount of time it would take 32 men to leave the boat through the narrow doors at the front. Thornycroft widened the doors a little allowing two men in full equipment to exit the boat at the same time – this was the advance the committee was looking for and, with the additional advantage of also having relatively quiet engines – for a Marine landing, likely to be covert – this was the clinching element, and they received a contract to start producing their LCA (2) variant. The element of men's lives being impacted by others takes on a whole new meaning in this respect as these very same designs were those carried forward when, in wartime conditions, the Landing Craft (2) variant was automatically chosen for the D-Day landings. The improved landing doors exit meant that all thirty-two could now exit in around 2–3 minutes, instead of the 3–4, but on Omaha beach, in full daylight view of German machine gunners with their MG42 machine guns each firing 1,800 rounds a minute, three minutes was going to feel like an eternity. Do the simple mathematics and a single gun aimed at a single point would unload nearly 5,000 rounds in three minutes, even if reduced by pauses and changing out hot barrels, the rate of fire versus the time for heavily laden men to exit a pair of doors and disaster was going to be the only result – unless mitigating factors could substantially reduce the rate of fire. It was in terms of the landing ramps or 'doors' that the Thornycroft differed markedly from the famous American 'Higgins' boats.

Steering was on the starboard side at the front protected by steel plates and was done by the coxswain of the boat, while on the port side there was also a slit opening for a Bren gun, hence the need for a gunner. The front armour plate doors were lowered by a simple pulley system by another seaman and this strong little craft, constructed of a mahogany hull to reduce weight, was powered by twin Ford V8 engines with a crewman engineer at the back under the decking to man the engines giving a total crew of four per boat.

Total production of this variant reached 1,929 and, as D-Day approached, various British firms were producing this boat at a rate of sixty per month. So many survived the war that you can often see the hulls of the LCA (2) now used as houseboats across the UK.

In Plymouth, the *Empire Javelin* took her allocation of eighteen LCAs on board in February 1944 and, as Jimmy Green explained:

'551 Flotilla was based in HMS Ceres, an old cruiser permanently anchored in Plymouth Sound to protect the dockyard from German raids. The Luftwaffe flattened the centre of Plymouth in 1940 and 1941, but the dockyard was virtually untouched. The German air raids ceased in 1941 so life on board HMS Ceres was peaceful. Our 18 LCAs were moored close to Ceres and we were able to carry out exercises and use dockyard facilities to bring our craft up to operational standards. We also managed to play an occasional game of football against local opposition.

We were really awaiting the arrival of SS Empire Javelin (our mother ship) recently built in the USA and converted to a Landing Ship Infantry (Large). It was manned by a Merchant Navy crew and had davits equipped to hoist our LCAs on board. The Javelin spent a few days in Plymouth where we worked out operational procedures for hoisting and lowering the LCAs with mixed RN and MN crews.[22]

With 551 in large black lettering on a white background pinned to the tower of the ship, *Empire Javelin* was allotted to the landing areas and, although the crews did not know where or when they would be needed, they were aware that they were to have a pivotal role in what was being planned for some point that year. Helpfully, the landing craft that were hoisted on board, were also individually numbered so that historians and researchers can occasionally identify an LCA belonging to the *Javelin* in action photographs of the beaches. A total of 448 LCAs would be used along the entire length of the invasion beaches but for *Empire Javelin*, eighteen plus two variants would be used.[23] From the 1944 Force 'O' LCA allocation book we can see that the 561st Flotilla's eighteen LCAs were numbered:

724	910	1066
730	911	1067
832	922	1068
839	924	1069
853	1012	1075
879	1063	1076

In addition, and to really overcrowd the top decks of the *Javelin*, two further craft were added and these were what the Americans referred to as 'Higgins Boats' after their designer Andrew J. Higgins. In actual fact these were personnel carriers or LCPs – Landing Craft Personnel. Far less structurally sound than the LCA, the LCPs were for the movement of second wave formations and headquarters units. In the case of the *Empire Javelin*, these boats were there to carry Lieutenant Colonel Metcalfe and the men of the Headquarters company that were also going to be on board. The men of Company A, B, C and D were numbered in LCP (L) 20 to 115.

To deal with the complexity of filling eighteen landing craft creating three formations of six boats each filled with front line infantry, lowering them safely down the sides of the ship in what might be hostile weather as well as hostile attention from the Germans, a great deal of training was needed and this was completed away from prying eyes in the lochs and inlets of the Western Isles in Scotland between February and May 1944. These four months were a vital time not just for the *Empire Javelin* but also her crew and the crews of all the other ten Empire ships that had now arrived and were quietly and unobtrusively doing the same thing.

The Master of the *Empire Javelin* was Captain McLean and he ordered the anchors to be dropped in a solitary corner of the Holy Loch which was just north of Dunoon and on the way into the Clyde and Glasgow Docks. Protected by a submarine boom which was anchored just off the town, the *Empire Javelin* was able to work her crews of various types so that every day they went through in every detail the job they were being asked to do at some point.

Even without 1,200 armed infantrymen, the ship was a busy one. The two main eye witness accounts tell us that Sub-Lieutenant Jimmy Green was the Royal Navy lieutenant responsible for the sixty sub-lieutenants and Naval ratings who manned the eighteen LCAs and that of Lieutenant John Gilmour was the Gunnery Officer in charge of the eighty Royal Navy gunners who manned the anti-aircraft guns situated all over the ship. But we also know that there were 250 merchant seamen to man the ship and the davits for the landing craft so the working-up crews numbered nearly 400 men.

Chapter Eleven

COSSAC's Final Plan –
Operation OVERLORD

*'You get your ass on the beach. I'll be there waiting for you and I'll tell you what
to do. There ain't anything in this plan that is going to go right.'*
*Colonel Pual R. Goode, from a pre-invasion briefing to the 175th Infantry
Regiment, 29th Infantry Division landing parallel to the 116th Infantry.*

Let me be clear, by the autumn of 1943, the COSSAC planners knew
exactly where the brand-new SS *Empire Javelin* would be needed.
Indeed, by September 1943, the plans for Operation OVERLORD had
been constructed down to the finest detail and hundreds of planning meetings,
thousands of communications and dozens of high-level oversight committees
had created a master plan that had selected Normandy as the landing area
and dictated that there would be a joint assault to include American, British,
Canadian, French and Polish troops in the first few days of establishing a series
of beach heads. The flow of new intelligence came in daily and was distributed
to the various MI sections 5, 6, 8 and so on and the intelligence staff of men
and numerous women in the intelligence branches analysed and assessed every
detail, adjusted what they knew and passed on their advice accordingly. The
staff of Bletchley Park did the same, looking for anything that may indicate
that the Germans had got wind of the landing site or discussions on troop
movements in Normandy.

Before concerning themselves about what happened after D-Day however,
the units had to be selected for the opening assaults and the hand of fate, or
the synchronicity of having a former commander of the 29th Division as part
of the planning process, determined that Company A of the 1st Battalion of
the 116th Infantry Regiment, 29th Division would be the first American feet
to set foot on German occupied France – the Bedford Boys.

In December 1943, pressure from Stalin was such that Roosevelt and Churchill
could resist his demands no longer and they committed to opening the second
front in the summer of 1944. Roosevelt, having delayed and pondered his selection
of an overall commander announced that General Dwight D. Eisenhower was
to be appointed Supreme Allied Commander (Europe) and to Eisenhower

would fall a place in history that few would have cherished – the decision on when to launch the invasion of Europe would be his alone.

Eisenhower felt that the original plan was too narrow-fronted and extended the beaches from three to five – this was partially to stretch the German defensive formations more thinly, but also to ensure that all the allied forces could play a part in the opening of the second front. The Americans would attack the beaches to the west of the Normandy coastline codenamed UTAH and OMAHA, while the British and Canadians would attack GOLD, JUNO and SWORD – in addition, three airborne divisions would be landed to secure the west and eastern flanks of the Normandy beaches. The US Navy and Royal Navy would undertake Operation NEPTUNE which was the mammoth task of both ferrying the largest seaborne force in history across the English Channel and protecting it thereafter – also providing minesweeping to create safe corridors, and massive naval gunfire ahead of the landing forces to hopefully destroy enemy opposition. The Royal Air Force and United States Army Air Force (USAAF) would conduct air raids for months in advance disrupting deep supply lines to German forces in Normandy and providing air cover for the duration of the landings.

The five main beaches were then sub-divided into sectors each with the Red, White, Green codes for the naval designations of port, amidships and starboard. This left OMAHA with ten sectors and, of these, it was the 116th Infantry Regiment that were tasked with taking the westernmost four beaches of CHARLIE (along with two companies of Rangers on the extreme right flank), DOG GREEN (allocated to the 1st Battalion of company A to F) and then DOG WHITE and DOG RED. The 2nd Battalion attacked the next set of beaches to their left and the 3rd Battalion of the regiment would arrive in the second wave at H+30. Each battalion was composed of three rifle companies, plus a fourth support company and a headquarters company giving each battalion five companies. The Headquarters company for the 1st Battalion, and therefore Company A – D, would be led by Lieutenant Colonel Metcalfe, subsequently the 3rd Battalion would land and then the regimental headquarters of the 116th and Colonel Canham would hopefully land on a cleared and held beach.

The plan dictated that 'Force O' would cross the English Channel from a variety of different ports on the English coast in order to arrive in their designated place off OMAHA beach at or around 01.00 on the invasion day. In advance of them and all through the night, large flotillas of heroic minesweepers would be clearing the sea in front of the beaches of German mines. Once formed up, the men would be woken (if they were asleep) at 04.00 and loading and disembarkation would begin. Once the USAAF had carried out a saturation bombing of the German positions both the day before and just before the landings began, and churned up the sandy beaches to provide additional cover, at 05.10 the escorting warships of Force 'O' would then provide ongoing salvoes over the heads of the advancing landing craft, further destroying the German defences on the cliffs overlooking OMAHA. The commander of Force 'O' was Rear Admiral John Hall, another Virginia man and a senior and experienced commander, who had already voiced some concerns over the scale of the naval bombardment of OMAHA, in that he felt it was both too light and too short – he was tragically to be proven correct.

To give a final added punch to the landings, all along OMAHA, the infantry would also be supported by two tank battalions – for DOG GREEN beach this would be the tanks 743rd Tank Battalion. They would proceed ahead of the infantry landing craft and land at H-10 – ten minutes before the infantry were due to land which was set for 06.31, or H+1. The tank formation was planned to be similar for all the beaches, in so far as it was a tank landing all along the length of OMAHA that would draw the initial fire of the German positions – or those that were left after the aerial and naval bombardments. The tanks were transported on specially designed LCTs (Landing Craft Tank) and were to be released into the water some 6,000 yards out from the beach and then make their way onto shore. For DOG GREEN beach this meant that sixteen DD (Duplex Drive) Mark IV Sherman tanks would 'swim' in eleven minutes in front of their landing craft and have had ten minutes engaging the Germans before they themselves landed – this would have given Captain Fellers and his company a great feeling of reassurance.[24]

Vierville-sur-Mer

For every sector of the main invasion beaches a target route off the beach was identified as the key objective. Known as 'draws' or 'cuts' these were well worn pathways through the long grass on hot breezy days used by the local French population to access the beach for their summer picnics, walks with the dog and peacetime playdays but on 6 June 1944 they were to become vital arteries for men to kill each other or to save lives and win a battle. On Dog Green and leading up and over the sandy cliffs and bluffs to the village of Vierville-sur-Mer, the men of Company A, and those coming after them, were briefed to seize and use route D-1 to mount the bluffs and attack the German positions in the rear.

The anonymous planners of COSSAC envisioned a scene where, at H+1, six LCAs from the *Empire Javelin*, numbered 1021 through to 1026, would arrive at DOG GREEN beach and open their doors onto a shingle beach. Each would be carrying 30–35 fully armed, tired, anxious, sick and already partially exhausted men but at least they would be on dryish land. What was left of the German defenders would be disorientated and trying to avoid the fire of the sixteen tanks on the beach in front of them. The beach should have lots of cover with shell and bomb holes everywhere from the preliminary bombardments and, once out of the shallow water and shingle, the men of the super fit and super trained Company A and Captain Fellers would be able to get up the short run of sand and then shingle beach, in between the obstacles set up by the Germans, up to a small two-foot-high sea wall. Once over that and through the rusty barbed wire, it was then a dash over a slowly rising sandy beach to the base of the bluffs in places and cliffs in others. In all, it would be less than a 400 metre effort to get from the doors of the LCAs to the safety of the bluffs.

Somewhere on a wooden desk of one of the numerous floors of the COSSAC building in St James's Square in London, maybe with a mug of tea and biscuits on a wooden tray on top of numerous maps of the French coastline of OMAHA beach, the male and female members of the uniformed planning staff decided that the landings would be going so well at that point, that it would be safe to land combat engineers next to start clearing the obstacles for later waves of troops to land. So, it was decided that, exactly two minutes after Company A had landed on Dog Green, another five LCAs would open their doors. Another LCI (L) the LCAs 1045 and 1046 would land men of Company C of the 2nd Ranger Battalion commanded by Captain Ralph E. Goranson, closely followed by LCAs 1047, 1048 and 1049 from *Empire Javelin* with combat engineers from the Special Engineer Task Force. In the minds of the anonymous planners, the defenders would be under so much pressure from the infantry now overwhelming their positions, fire from the tanks and naval gunfire, that the engineers should be able to operate relatively freely in their work.

The final phases for the 1st Battalion of the 116th Infantry would involve another landing at H+30 of Company B, led by the close colleague of Captain Fellers, Captain Ettore Zappacosta, closely followed by Company D at H+40 commanded by Captain Schilling and then Company C, commanded by Captain Berthier B. Hawks lands at H+50 putting the entire 1st Battalion of the 116th, including the battalion headquarters with Lieutenant Colonel Metcalfe and his battalion Executive Officer (XO) Major Dallas on Dog Green beach in under an hour of the first attack – they had also travelled on the *Empire Javelin* that night.

This was a densely packed and detailed plan. The one time brilliant and foresighted Field Marshal of the German Imperial Army, Count Helmuth von Moltke the Elder once said '*No plan survives contact with the enemy*' and like all plans, a great deal of Operation OVERLORD would evaporate into thin air the moment the LCAs were launched into the cold, salty and heaving waters off the coast of Normandy – but for now everything depended on the time that the assault was made. COSSAC had devoted very many hours and numerous experts towards working out what the best time of day, in terms of the tides, would deal with the gradient and type of beach to minimise casualties, but also give the best chances of seeing and thus destroying the enemy defences in front of them. The timing also had to allow for darkness to get thousands of ships over the Channel without being discovered and to reveal themselves just as they delivered their attack. Dawn was not enough, it had to be precisely the right dawn.

The fundamental principle – the tides of Normandy

Intelligence gathering throughout 1942 and 1943 had indicated a great deal about the beaches that were being considered for the landings and the information received about OMAHA had been provided by over thirty covert missions by Captain Logan Scott-Bowden of the British Royal Engineers. The 1st US Army Commander of the landing force for the UTAH and OMAHA beaches was General Omar Bradley. Bradley had the VII Corps landing on UTAH led by the US 4th Division and the 29th and 1st Divisions of V Corps (commanded by Gerow) landing on OMAHA. When, in January 1944, Bradley voiced concern especially over the beaches at OMAHA it was to Scott-Bowden that he turned. Numerous sand samples of various depths all the way in to the shingle beach and beyond had been gathered at great risk over many months by night operations from midget submarines and Scott-Bowden is recorded as saying to Bradley:

'Sir, I hope you don't mind me saying it, but this beach is a very formidable proposition indeed and there are bound to be tremendous casualties.'

When Bradley answered with 'I know, my boy, I know,' he was speaking as one only too aware of the dangers the depth of the beaches presented. It was the distance from the gravel that the LCAs would drop their ramps and the support would have to stand off shore that would determine the levels of casualties every bit as much as what was left of the German defences after the various bombardments. The key issue was how to deal with the obstacles that Rommel had distributed along the shoreline in relation to the depth of the water and therefore the tide. If the obstacles were to be seen ahead of the boats, then this would mean landing the troops when the tide was fully out and thus exposing the infantry to a longer period of gunfire from the German defences. If Bradley wanted the men dropped as close to shore as possible then this would mean landing when the tide was in – thus exposing the bottom of all the LCAs to the mines on top of Rommel's 'asparagus' – telegraph poles driven deeply into the ground and topped with mines.

To provide their plans with the greatest chance of success, the COSSAC planners needed good weather, low winds and low waves. This led them to a summer landing to give them the best odds for these types of weather conditions. To give the three divisions of airborne infantry (the largest ever dropped in one operation), the best chance of success, the planners also needed a full moon the night of the assault so that they could be certain of their drop zones. Finally, they needed a low tide just before dawn to allow the armada of ships to cross at night without being seen by enemy reconnaissance aircraft or patrol boats and then be able to appear just before dawn to be able to identify their targets visually. With these considerations in mind, 5, 6, 7 June 1944 were selected as the optimum dates.

Tide times were one of the most hidden secrets of the war. Britain had recognised how important these were right back in 1940 when the prospect of a German invasion was very real and so this information had been cleared from all the beaches, handbooks and travel guides. The same was true of Normandy and the allies made use of 'tide machines' which had been designed thirty years earlier and into these mechanical computers, around thirty variables such as past water levels, harbour schedules and the position and phase of the moon were inserted in order to predict the tidal range on the Normandy beaches. At OMAHA the difference in tidal heights was crucial because it averaged over twenty feet – a huge range between low and high tide – imagine letting your troops out in twenty feet of water – with all their boots, helmets and equipment, they would simply all drown. The planners also needed to know about the bathymetry – the shape of the sea bed under the tidal ranges to ascertain if there were sand bars upon which landing craft or even the large transports like *Empire Javelin* could founder. One other vital aspect of the tides was that the allies had to start the landings on a flooding tide – just after low tide and where the water was rising back to the beach. This was crucial. OVERLORD rested upon successive waves of troops arriving at set intervals – this meant that the commanders of the landing craft had to be able to get in, unload and get out again before the next wave arrived. If they became beached on the gravel because the tide was going out then carnage would ensue. Thus, the ideal time was just after low tide and when the water was starting to rise about one foot per hour. No-one expected the infantry still to be on the beach after an hour with the water rising around them and units of combat engineers could land with the infantry in order to blow up and clear the obstacles which would be clearly visible as they all moved up the open beach. That was the theory – what about the reality?

Chapter Twelve

The German Preparations

'Battles are won by slaughter and manoeuvre. The greater the general, the more he contributes in manoeuvre, the less he demands in slaughter.'

Winston S. Churchill

The allies were not the only ones preparing for an invasion and all the chess pieces in this puzzle of synchronicity were now about to be in play – there was just one piece left and this was a German Field Marshal. During November 1943, the 29th Division had moved to Devon to develop and intensify their training, the *Empire Javelin* was in Scotland working with her Merchant and Royal Navy crews on making sure they could get the landing craft into the water quickly and safely, the anonymous planners had determined what the future would be for them all and in Berlin, Hitler assessed the strategic position at the end of 1943 and where best to place Field Marshal Erwin Rommel.

Rommel

Now recovered from exhaustion in North Africa, Rommel could have been sent to Italy, where he would continue to face off with his recent adversary Montgomery and the Americans. Hitler was perhaps a little disappointed in Rommel's strategic view of the war and sensed that in Italy, he would advise withdrawal and concentration. Hitler may have been a poor strategist and military commander, but he was an astute political animal with a keen nose for personality changes and, in an unusual stroke of military good judgement, instead selected Albert Kesselring as commander of German forces in Italy and pondered what do with his spare chess piece. 'Smiling Albert' was to turn out to be a most able adversary in the battle for Italy. Hitler could see no role for Rommel on the eastern front where German forces were engaged in a titanic and merciless struggle against Soviet Russia – Rommel, incorrectly sensing he had a 'special relationship' with Hitler – had begun to criticise the direction of the war. Rommel was an offensive commander not a defensive one and he was inspirational – there were going to be few offensives in Russia – but even though perhaps burnt out emotionally and on the edge of depression, he still had a key role to play. So instead of a field command, on 4 November 1943, Rommel was chosen by Hitler as General Inspector of the Western Defences.

Hitler had become increasingly concerned about the allied plans for invasion. He needed to buy time in the east for the further development of his special weapons and especially the atomic bomb, he also still controlled huge swathes of Europe – if he could defeat the allied landings, wherever and whenever they came, then he would have bought breathing space to defeat Russia. But where and when would the invasion come and how would it best be defeated?

In essence, those units and officers that were not Nazi fanatics or members of a top formation – or in the SS – were not needed on the eastern front. The eastern front was different from anything else the German soldier had been asked to do and, by late 1943, it needed officers willing to die to protect Germany from the Bolshevik hordes. This meant the west, specifically France, was home to units either unfit to fight a war of attrition and movement or unable to continue in the east and in need of refitting. But the times were changing and instead of a rest home for German troops, the arrival of Rommel took it right back into the front lines again as an active front and Rommel was given a staff that befitted an Army Group commander and the power to travel, examine and plan a strategy to improve defences and create an 'Atlantic Wall' for the Reich. This appointment was to have a dramatic impact on the plans for OVERLORD and indeed the more detailed plans for the invasion of OMAHA beach – it was also going to be crucial to the future fortunes of Company A of the 116th Infantry and the *Empire Javelin* who was going to deliver them to the sandy beaches of France. Churchill was, for once, correct. In the plan that the 116th Infantry were going to be ordered to follow, there was no room for manoeuvre, everything worked as long as the enemy in front of them had been disrupted, destroyed or disorientated – if not then slaughter would be the end result.

'The battle is fought and decided by the quartermasters long before the shooting begins.'

Field Marshal Erwin Rommel

Rommel was acutely aware of the war material resources of the United States. He had seen American equipment in every British unit fighting in North Africa and he knew that every soldier landing in Normandy would be resourced by the best resourced military quartermasters in history. There was no end to the military potential of the United States and no matter how hard Albert Speer and the German armaments industry worked and produced new equipment, it would only ever be a fraction of what America could bring to the front lines against him. Rommel was, by now, convinced that the war was lost and his demeanour with his staff officers testifies to his depression and sadness that Hitler was going to destroy Germany and that there was little that he could do about it – except agonise over whether to support the resistance movement within the Wehrmacht.

Perhaps to rid himself of these heavy pressures or possibly in a naïve belief that the war could still be won if a second front in France could be defeated, Rommel threw himself into this next task. The *Fuhrerauftrag* or special commission from the Fuhrer, gave Rommel a new zest: perhaps the Fuhrer was right and the special weapons plus increases in armament production could indeed win the war in the east, if only the allies were held in the west. To this end, Rommel was convinced that any invasion had to be defeated on the beaches themselves but a static battle was anathema to the commander in the west at that time. Field Marshal Gerd von Rundstedt was an orthodox Prussian icon of the Wehrmacht, who found flexibility in command decisions difficult and held nothing but contempt for Hitler – the 'Bohemian Corporal' as he called him in private. For von Rundstedt, drawing the enemy into France and then encircling them with mobile formations was the preferred strategy.

During December 1943 and January 1944, as the Bedford Boys trained with Company A and as the whole 29th Division practised amphibious landings in Devon, Rommel and his entourage of loyal and devoted staff officers, inspected every beach, interrogated the officers and men of these static positions and formulated new ideas for coastal defences. As David Fraser wrote in his outstanding biography of Rommel:

> 'Wherever he went he preached the same doctrine. The enemy must be defeated in the coastal sector. He must be defeated soon after, or even before, struggling ashore. The main battle line must be the beach. This meant that the coastal defences must be enormously strengthened. Coastal artillery was never adequate or adequately protected, but there must be a huge effort made in mining and fortification, and everywhere he went Rommel laid down in detail, galvanised, explained, inspired.'[25]

The arrival of Rommel in northern France was to have a profound impact on the fortunes of the OVERLORD plan and the allied invasion forces and none more so than on OMAHA beach. Together with his excellent engineer commander, General Meise, Rommel issued orders in a constant stream with staff officers making urgent demands for millions of mines both for the beach obstacles and inland breakout areas, hundreds of thousands of telegraph poles to create four lines of underwater beach obstacles on the open beaches where an enemy might choose to land and millions of tonnes of concrete for expanded *Widerstandsnests* or Resistance Nests on beach fronts where little had been done for months. Rommel worked his command officers to their knees and, formally fairly idle officers such as General von Salmuth:

> '...expostulated vigorously with Rommel on one of the latter's return visits, saying that the Army Group Commanders requirements made such physical demands on the troops (civil labour being limited) that they would be good for nothing when the invasion itself came. Rommel reacted at his most violent and voices were raised.'[26]

Fritz Ziegalmann and the 352nd Infantry Division

Between December 1943 and May 1944, the fortifications of the French coastline were dramatically improved but so also was the quality of the German troops – specifically the arrival in the area of OMAHA of the 352nd Infantry Division. Although by June 1944, the 352nd was still well short of being fully trained and equipped, it was well on the way to both.

Shortly after the war and as a prisoner of war in the United States, Oberstleutnant (Lieutenant Colonel) Fritz Ziegalmann sat down to start writing his memoirs. Captured by the American forces, Ziegalmann was one of thousands of experienced Wehrmacht officers who had been swept up by Hitler's demand in September 1943 for ten new infantry divisions for the Eastern Front in 1943 and sent to staff one of these new divisions being raised in double-quick time. Fate, or synchronicity, would have it that, on 5 December 1943 – just as the men of the 1st Battalion, 116th Infantry were wondering how to organise Christmas parties for the children of Ivybridge in Devon, Ziegalmann was sent to the 352nd (352ID) forming around St Lô in Normandy, just south of what were to become the landing beaches at OMAHA. Part of the 7th Army, which was tasked with defending the long stretch of coastline, 315ID was composed of the remnants of 321ID which had been destroyed in Russia and then a mixture of young recruits taken from Germany who had never been in uniform before and a few companies of 'Hiwi's' – Russian volunteers. The division was commanded by Lieutenant General Dietrich Kraiss – a career officer in the First World War and the Reichswehr who had been decorated with the Knights Cross for his service in Russia. Kraiss was no Nazi enthusiast, he was a practical soldier and, perhaps because of his lack of political enthusiasm, he had been overlooked for further promotion and given command of the 352nd to get it into shape as best he could. Kraiss would die of his wounds in August 1944 defending St Lo.

In November 1943, the 352nd was created as a new 'Type 44' division – smaller than earlier divisional structures but to be better armed and, by the time that Ziegalmann arrived, 352ID already had two fully formed infantry regiments in place – the 914th and 916th.

> '...there were no clear orders. It was generally assumed that we could count on being sent to the Eastern Front after the 1st March 1944. So training for the 352ID focussed on Eastern Front combat operations.'[27]

Further on in Ziegalmann's memoirs, and as if to echo what Rommel had said about wars being won by quartermasters, he comments:

> 'The building process itself went very slowly, especially procurement. Since I had been, from October 1942 to March 1943, Chief Quartermaster for the Army High Command and at this time intimate with procurement issues, it fell to me to provide equipment to outfit the now forming 352ID.
>
> For example, live-fire training school was not possible until the end of February, because the delivery of gun sights and sight mounting-plates was not possible before mid-February. By March, each soldier had thrown just two hand-grenades and had only three live-fire training exercises. The training of auxiliary drivers (French civilian truck drivers) was not possible until the 1st May, because of fuel shortages....the replacements, mostly teenagers, were physically unfit for all but limited military duty, because of food shortages in Germany.'[28]

Local partisan and French intelligence gathering exercises were constantly active and, despite the efforts of the Gestapo and SD, the Germans were acutely aware that leaks of information to the allies were a daily event. However, in St James's Square where daily intelligence reports were updated and any developments along the Normandy coast were collated and passed through to senior commanders, this new German division-sized formation had gone unnoticed. Thus, as the men of Company A of the 116th started to conclude their final, gruelling and long training programme, a new German division was growing in strength and organisation and Zeigalmann noted that, although still below full combat strength, 'By the 1st March 1944, the 352ID reached adequate strength and was fully equipped'. At this moment it would have been quite expected that the division would now be sent transport orders to move to the Eastern Front but on 15 March, OKW, the High Command of the German Wehrmacht, decided that the 352ID should stay where they were and reinforce the very under strength and static 716ID which was currently stretched out very thinly guarding nearly 100 km of coastline.

Kraiss

By May, the Normandy coastline had been subdivided to accommodate the extra reinforcements of the Grenadier Regiments of the 352nd. The divisional commander, Lieutenant General Dietrich Krais plus his senior commanders had deployed Grenadier Regiment 916 into space now vacated by the men of the 716th who had been relocated further east towards Bayeux and what would be the British beaches. The men of the 352nd had put in a great deal more effort on reinforcing the coastline than the foreign conscripts of the 716th.

Despite disagreements with OKW and von Rundstedt, Rommel's express orders were always that the invasion had to be defeated on the beaches and, if at all possible, even in the water. The war in the east was and would continue to drain Germany of her remaining manpower while the resources of the United States were incalculable as German cities were experiencing day and night bombing raids from both the Royal Air Force and the United States Army Air Forces. While commanders above him such as Von Rundstedt and Hitler continued to plan for a war or movement using the Panzer Divisions held in reserve near Caen, Rommel pushed his officers to stress to their men that the enemy must be stopped on the sand – or lose the war. Thus, under the command of Oberst Ernst Goth, the men of the 916th not only added far more beach obstacles to the beach areas in front of Vierville-sur-Mer but also acted with alacrity and sound experience by restocking with large stockpiles of ammunition all the relevant strong points, erecting more barbed wire fencing and sighting their guns in pre-calculated range firing exercises. Under the direction of Rommel, the Main Line of Resistance (MLR) was therefore not hidden in forests inland but was right there on the cliffs of OMAHA. Had the 716th still been in position on their own when the 116th Infantry landed, it was likely that the Poles and Russian conscripts would have surrendered very quickly to get out of German uniform – but they had been relocated to face the British and did indeed collapse quickly.

For OMAHA, however, the new, young and enthusiastic recruits such as Unteroffizier Henrik Naube plus experienced officers and men who had survived the Eastern Front were in position instead. Naube was allocated to a position in front of Vierville-sur-Mere and was therefore facing directly towards the landing area of Company A and Captain Fellers and his men. After the war, Naube was interviewed for his recollections of his experiences in Normandy. Asked about Rommel he recalled that he had not met him personally, but he had seen him close up:

> '...he was a very energetic and active man; he walked very briskly and spoke rapidly. I did not have any direct dialogue with him, but he came to our position

and spoke with our officer. He asked very factual questions about the amount of ammunition we had in the post, how old the weapons were, what we knew of the design of Allied ships and so on. He was quite a short man, but had a very powerful presence, although, as with all famous leaders, how much of this was due to our expectations and preconceptions, it is difficult to say.[29]

The main combat positions now being inspected by Rommel and his staff, manned by the 916th Regiment of the 352nd Division, were *Widerstandsnester* or resistance nests. As Lieutenant General Kraiss displayed elements of his 352nd Division to Rommel, they inspected the nests. With a ten to twenty men unit, these tended to rely on sand bag and light concrete protection with a clear view of the beaches and were supported by far stronger *Stutzpunkt* or strong points with concrete bunkers and protected routes to a cluster of firing positions manned by a platoon or company of 200 men. Deeper behind the beaches came the *Verteidigungbereich* or a Defence Complex of two companies plus mortars. The main weapons in all of these included the Mauser rifle – accurate but slow to fire and the most powerful machine guns anywhere in the world at that time – the MG34 and 'Hitler's Zipper' the MG42 – amazing rates of fire and accuracy. Firing 7.92 calibre bullets just like the Mauser rifle for ease of ammunition supply, these were formidable weapons and the rate of fire in an experienced hand was around 1,200 rounds per minute compared for example to the British Bren gun which, at best, could manage 400. The rate of fire was such that there was only one way to advance against an MG42 and that was to wait and pray until the hot barrels had to be changed out – this gave a ten second window to move forward but in most German resistance nests, two teams of MG42 gunners worked together so that when one was changing barrels, the other was firing. It was therefore a terrifying prospect for any frontal attack against such weapons. On the morning of 6 June 1944, it was the men of Company 5 of the 916th Grenadier-Regiment that were on duty manning the resistance positions in front of the village Vierville-sur-Mer and along DOG GREEN beach.

Dotted around the nests were 'Tobruks' which were small two-man concrete machine gun emplacements with a cupola on the top allowing for a small steel rail to be embedded in the concrete for the MG34 or 42 to fix to and, like a small train-set, the gun could be easily set to fire in an arc, intersecting with similar positions nearby. Occasionally there were static tank turrets taken from old French tanks in 1940 or from disabled German Panzers – fixed in concrete and manned by former mobile tank crews who had been taken out of the front line. Nothing, especially men, was wasted.

'Our panzer had a field of fire onto the seafront and the beach, and we would fire onto the seafront and the beach and the intention was that we would fire on any enemy that tried to come up off the beach, as they came up over the dunes at that point. The purpose was to keep the enemy pinned down on the beach at that point, preventing him moving inland. In that sense, we were the main line of defence, after the machine guns and artillery that were positioned to fire along the beach itself.'

Gefreiter (Private First Class) Gustav Winter. 726th Infantry Regiment,
716th Static Infantry Division, OMAHA beach[30]

According to Henrik Naube, his *Widerstandsnest* sat and looked at the sea every day with little or no change. The sea was often grey and choppy, interspersed with flecks of white horses as they peered through their viewing scopes and binoculars. Occasionally during May 1944 there were spells of beautiful bright sunshine as they cleaned their weapons and test fired their machine guns to ensure that they had the ranges set exactly right for the point where low tide stopped – almost to the foot their bullets hit the exact spot that they waited to see the water and sand zip up into the air. Bright white tracer bullets were fixed in the machine gun belts of the MG42s every five rounds so they could watch them fizz through the air and hit the ground 400 metres away in under a second. What Naube and his fellow Grenadiers did not know was that COSSAC in London had decided that the landing craft would actually be unloading even closer to their positions on a flooding tide which would mean, depending on the sand banks under the water, that the men would be jumping into water at least up to their waist, or even deeper and having to wade pitifully slowly into the beach.

Describing his resistance nest, Naube explained that:

'This was an area of about thirty metres width and ten metres depth, set on top of some cliffs beside one of the ravines that led down to the beach wall. The point had a trench across its width, and several running to the rear, in jagged lines. Inside, these trenches were faced with concrete and had wooden floors with drainage points. Outside, there was a raised concrete parapet about one metre high, in which there were two firing points, which were vertical slits. There were two machine gun points at either end aiming through these points. It was about 300 metres down from the cliff to the nearest part of the sea wall, and there was a long, uninterrupted line of fire along the beach to the northwest [this would likely make him a member of WN71]. *The guns were MG42 types which were extremely powerful.'*[31]

The French intelligence systems were unable to get close enough to the beaches to provide detailed assessments of the defences, but low-level aerial reconnaissance and the night raids by commandos gave enough information to the planners to be able to tell General Gerow of the 29th Infantry Division and his own staff teams that there were likely to be a number of such resistance nests all along OMAHA beach. There were in fact five that could directly fire onto DOG GREEN beach and these were numbered from west to east WN73, WN72, WN71, WN70 and WN68. A visit to Normandy and this stretch of coastline today shows many of the remains of these defences and either side of the Vierville Draw and exit D1, one can see that the machine guns nests were positioned to fire across the beach not down towards the sea – on DOG GREEN it would be WN71 and WN72 that sat like rooks on a chess board defying anyone to try to make it up the beach let alone get up to the 'draw' and on into the village of Vierville-sur-Mer

Another thing that strikes you as you walk up the beach from the low tide mark is just how far invading troops would have to go before they reached the sea wall. Surrounded by huge wooden posts and then sharp angled tank traps, these would be the only cover from the masses of tracers and full head bullets pouring down. The sand is claggy from the tide that has only recently left and it is hard enough to walk up this beach let alone run with full equipment and ammunition and the closer they got to the sea wall the more fire they were exposed to as the enfilade fire would rake across from both left and right. The troops of Company 5 and Oberleutnant Hahn must have felt pretty confident that anything landing in front of them could be destroyed. The morale of the Germans was solid, far from defeatist and indeed the impact of one inspirational man had energised an entire front line. Rommel's words were repeated over and over again by officers at all levels and, whether they believed they could win or not, they believed that his strategy was right, as Henrik Naube explained:

'We were to keep a constant lookout, of course, and make regular reports by cable line to our officer's post, which was about one kilometre behind us. In case of an attack, we were told specifically to hold our fire until any enemy troops were 400 metres from the edge of the beach; although the MG42 could fire effectively beyond 2,000 metres, this instruction was to ensure that we had the largest possible target area on each attacking soldier. We were told to fire at their chests when their torsos were above water, that is to say when they reached the shallows and were wading.'[32]

These fire and control orders were designed to make sure that the allied soldiers landing in front of these resistance nests were killed and not wounded. The rate of fire of the MG42, plus the very shortened range meant that any target would be hit by multiple rounds at the same moment as the bullets would saturate such a small area.

'We were trained constantly on the importance of our task. If the allies were allowed to gain a foothold in our sector, however slender, their huge material resources would allow them to build it up and threaten the whole of France. This in turn would give them a puppet state to use in order to harass and blockade Germany itself. The concept of the allies actually invading Germany seemed unimaginable at the time, it must be said.'

Although in reality the Germans were stretched far too thinly across France and the strategic response that Hitler favoured was unclear, to the ordinary German soldiers of the Normandy coastline, they felt that they were the first line of defence for France – not Germany. This was a psychological ploy clearly propagated by the Wehrmacht so as not to alarm and panic their troops about the reality that faced Germany as Henrik Naube further states:

'Our officers sought to educate us very thoroughly on this matter. They emphasised that if an attempted landing could be defeated by us on the shoreline, and thrown back, it would take years for the Western Allies to recover, allowing us to consolidate a defensive line against the Soviets in the East. Its effect on Western public opinion might even force the English out of the war altogether; that idea was constantly emphasised. All in all, we were fully aware of the great burden of responsibility resting on us, as the first line of defence against attack.'[33]

Both the German and Soviet armed forces were part of the political resources of the state and, as such, came under the influence of political thinking hence in the Russian army every unit had its own political officer whose job it was to motivate the soldier to fight for his country, both politically and emotionally. In the German army, the former Imperial Army no longer existed as an entity – some of the senior and older officers may have cut their teeth in the old professional army which was non-political – but under the Nazis they had had to either learn to become 'Nazified' or see the political ends of their actions or acquiesce. It was because Hitler mistrusted his non-political army officer corps that the SS was founded – a politically and racially charged fighting force dedicated to achieving political and racial aims. The gestapo and SD were also interested in trapping or rooting out army officers who were anti-Nazi and anti the politicisation of the armed forces. But as we can see here in this extract from Henrik Naube's memoirs, the younger officers of the Wehrmacht were already politicised and they saw it as their task to educate their soldiers into the aims and objectives of the Nazi war machine to further incentivise them into fighting harder against the enemy.

The 'forgotten' artillery

There was one other aspect of the German defensive planning that seems to have been overlooked both at the time and by history and that was the presence of German artillery. The divisional plans saw artillery used in two main ways. Firstly, as a long-range weapon to sink the ships of the invasion and secondly as a shorter-range tool to destroy infantry. To achieve these two tactical effects the Germans had already built large emplacements inland to house their largest 150mm guns. The Merville Battery stands out as one of these most memorable sites in Normandy and even today exudes potentiality to deal out death. The site had been well chosen and the design and protection of the fortress was impressive – it would be down to British parachute troops to try to neutralise this. Similar large gun emplacements were at Point du Hoc – just to the right of the DOG GREEN beach as Fellers and his company would land and this would be given to the Rangers as their objective. But the second German objective was to be fulfilled by having the accurate and devastating 88mm gun in various emplacements along the beach and these were not given any special treatment. Not that the planners were aware of exactly how many there were or where they were, the hope and expectation was that the air bombardment and Naval gunfire prior to the landings would deal with these. Post-war narratives focussed on the arrival of the 352nd and saw the problems on OMAHA as an infantry v infantry engagement but in fact the German artillery was there, close and dangerous, right on the beach and able to fire directly at landing craft heading for the beach and on groups of men clustered on the beach. Even Bletchley Park and 'Ultra' had not intercepted or translated that heavier artillery was now in place. The French resistance had not been able to get close enough to identify where they were and constant aerial photography told the intelligence services of the RAF a lot but not everything.

As a result, the infantry defending OMAHA beach could inflict great damage on any allied attack but the fire support they could draw on from their artillery units was formidable and has been overlooked. The events of the early morning on 6 June clearly indicate that close range German artillery took out whole landing craft before they could even reach the beach plus artillery strikes onto the beach were to kill many more – and yet these positions were not even on the list of targets for the American infantry as they were unaware of their existence.

'The assault troops could do nothing about the rain of artillery shells until either the observation posts were captured or the Germans ran out of ammunition, which they did around lunchtime on 6th June.'

The Observation Post

Additionally, captured maps after the invasion reveal that the German gunners had had plenty of time to mark their ranges and could very quickly bring heavy gunfire down onto pre-coordinated targets:

'The artillery troops manning two 88mm guns in my bunker regularly fired shells along the beach to ensure their ranging was accurate. Their orders were to fire on craft approaching from the sea, prioritising boats which had not yet hit an obstacle or any that had touched the beach itself. They could also fire along the esplanade behind the sea wall if any attackers managed to climb over that wall into the town.'

Pte. (Soldat) Marten Eineg
716th Static Infantry Division[34]

The divided opinion of how best to defeat the allies at the strategic level – that is between Rommel and his aim to defeat them on their approach to the beaches and Von Rundstedt's plan to encircle them once they had landed – was replicated down the chain of command. As the 916th Grenadier Regiment took over positions vacated by the 716th and trained and consolidated their resistance nests along OMAHA beach, Rommel had informed Kraiss that he was not pleased that only one Grenadier Regiment was manning the coast and he ordered Kraiss to move up the rest of his division to ensure that the allies did not get off the beach. In the event, Kraiss did not comply as the military historian Wiliamson Murray explained in his 2006 article:

'Of the ten infantry and five artillery battalions that Kraiss had available, he placed only one artillery battalion and two infantry battalions along the OMAHA beach sector. This decision makes even less sense when one realises that he deployed two-thirds of his force in reserve or in position to defend the western sector of his responsibility – where no amphibious landing could possibly take place.......Had Kraiss followed Rommel's instructions, it is likely that the OMAHA beach landing would have failed – with considerable consequences for the Allies' ability to link together the British and American beaches.'[35]

The reasoning behind Kraiss's decision remains one of the areas of ongoing debate amongst historians still searching for the model explanation of events on OMAHA but certainly, although the men of the 116th were to meet a far fiercer resistance on OMAHA than they had been led to believe, it clearly could have been even worse.

At the same time as the German infantry and artillerymen surveyed the horizon, the men of the 116th Infantry Regiment in Devon trained to kill them. The American and British forces did not have anywhere near the same level of political education or motivation – instead they were expected, as part of a professional standing army, to receive orders and carry them out. There was no underlay of political and emotional pressure on them, simply an expectation that they would carry out the orders they were given. This is not to suggest that one soldier was better equipped emotionally to die than another; it is simply a measure of the level of courage and loyalty that a human being can show to the orders of another. Had the planners in St James's Square been aware of the orders to the basic German soldier on when and how to fire his gun to achieve the maximum deaths amongst the enemy, then would they have stuck to the same plan? Would 'Dutch' Cota have won his argument? Would the training expected of the men of the 116th infantry have been the same? All theoretical questions long after the event and as full of uncertainty as the planners were then. As matters stood by May 1944, both sides had their minds set on carrying out their orders.

Within COSSAC, the hope was that the combined effect of the air force bombing raids prior to the landings plus the heavy shellfire from the ships would neutralise anything that opposed the landings. Indeed, Lieutenant Colonel Ziegalmann's memoirs even pointed out that:

> 'It became evident that Rommel's authority was not enough to complete the construction of concrete fortifications. The availability of cement and dealing with four independent construction authorities were decisive issues. Air Force workers, Navy, Organisation Todt (the prime construction contractor) and our own 'Fortress Engineers' worked side by side often duplicating the work. Once again over-organisation proved to be a menace.
>
> Almost half of the battle installations were out-moded and, at most, poorly reinforced. In the Division's sector alone, analysis showed that only 15 per cent of the cement fortifications were bomb resistant, 45 per cent were shrapnel proof. Uneven distribution of building material was the order of the day.'[36]

With this primary source material, it is clear that all the air force had to do was drop its bombs accurately and few if any of these *Wilderstandsnester* would have survived to face Captain Fellers and the men of Bedford Virginia as they stormed from their landing craft at H-Hour. In fact, had the COSSAC planners seen for themselves what was facing the men of the 116th, they would have felt it essential that the aerial bombardment worked as it would seem impossible for any infantry unit to get off this part of the beach.

All of these concerns and priorities on both sides were at the tactical level – local to the fighting and vital in the first few hours to success or failure. It was however on the strategic level that Germany would have the best opportunity to defeat the invasion and the choices made after the first day would decide the fate of the war. Sadly, none of this would concern nearly 3,000 American troops who would not live to see 7 June 1944.

The Cota Plan

'Cota's determination and personal courage clearly made a difference in the early hours of the beach assault. But his ability to to bring order out of chaos owed as much, if not more, to his ability to visualise beforehand the difficulties he faced and to prepare himself and his soldiers to overcome them.'
McGeorge, Major. S.C., 'Seeing the Battlefield: Brigadier General Norman D. Cota's "Bastard Brigade" at Omaha Beach' Combat Leadership (2004)

It was not just the COSSAC planners that were wrestling with the challenges of the invasion, how to make it succeed and how to avoid catastrophic casualties. Well before any planning for OVERLORD began, Brigadier General Norman D. 'Dutch' Cota was considered to be one of America's most experienced amphibious warfare officers especially so given that, during 1941, Cota had been responsible for the training of the US 1st Division in amphibious landing techniques on the East Coast of America as part of their preparations for landing in North Africa. Cota was selected as Chief of Staff for the 1st Division in their landing at Arzew on the coast of Algeria in 1942 and he was able to study at first hand both the effects of his training and the problems of large-scale amphibious landings.

By May 1943, Cota had been assigned to Combined Operations Headquarters (COHQ) which was a subset of COSSAC and Cota became an integral part of the training regimes that were to govern the lives of the men of the 116th infantry as they trained in the south-west of England for the second half of 1943 and on into 1944. From the outset however, Cota had made a name for himself for being in the circumspect wing of COHQ in so far as Cota advised against a daylight landing. Amongst 'Dutch' Cota's recommendations were that the standard US infantry division be reorganised and trimmed down to reflect the needs of an amphibious landing – an overall reduction of some 2,000 to reduce the number of LCAs required and to avoid confusion on the beach. Another change he suggested was that each infantry division have its own 'Ranger-type' battalion in each regiment which would provide a powerful specialist unit to deal with the types of obstacles and resistance that ordinary infantry were not equipped to deal with. Finally, and most controversially, Cota was clear that any landing should be under cover of darkness and consist of only one or two divisions at most. Cota was concerned that the scale of the invasion plans in OVERLORD magnified the potential for confusion and losses and if, and it was a serious if, the Germans responded in certain ways to the invasion, the whole enterprise could be jeopardised. Despite his vigorous attempts to persuade planners at COSSAC of his opinions, Cota was ignored and essentially told to pipe down and work with the plans as they had been devised.

Not all of Cota's resistance was wasted however. At divisional level, Cota did influence the training of the 29th Division to the extent that Major General Gerhardt insisted on tough cycles of physical training to include scaling cliffs, fire and movement across open beaches and exposure to manic live firing exercises with both machine guns and artillery to simulate the chaos of the beach landing that could be experienced by the troops – if the German gun positions remained active after the opening bombardments. All officers from divisional level down through regimental and battalion took part in beach landing exercises and three large scale practice runs at regimental levels with supporting gunfire and landing craft were planned for the late spring of 1944 off the Devon coast.

On both sides of the English Channel then, preparations for the invasion of Europe were being made. Both sides tried to hide their activities from the other with deception plans – the Germans created false defensive fortifications for the daily reconnaissance flights to photograph and report while the Allies were heavily in debt to Operation FORTITUDE – the large-scale deception plan to hide the direction of the invasion. It was 'R' Force led by Colonel David Strangeways who reported to Montgomery that the initial approach was inept and too small in scale and recommended that a far wider and more imaginative plan was conceived and the entire scale of the deception plans was enlarged – but would it be enough?

Part IV

Final Preparations for the Assault on Europe

Chapter Thirteen

Forever in Ivybridge, Devon 1943–44

'I want to go again to the moors,
To follow their winding trails.
To stand again on their lonely slopes
In the cold and the wind and the gales
Oh, I'll go out on the moors again,
But mind me and mark me well,
I'll carry enough explosives,
To blow the place to hell!'

An anonymous American soldier

Back in May 1943, at around the same time as the keel of the *Cape Lobos* was being laid down in Wilmington, California and as Brigadier General 'Duch' Cota was arriving in his new post at Combined Operations Headquarters in London, the staff of the 29th Infantry Division received orders to move to the south-west of England.

From Tidworth Barracks, last letters had been penned and posted to friends and family back in Bedford, Virginia and Private First Class Nick Gillaspie maintained his determination to keep communicating with the folks back home, sending letters not just to family but also neighbours and friends – always keeping the beat positive and humorous despite the longing to be home and alive.

Letters were also now being sent to places outside Bedford as the recent months had seen the ongoing weeding of the regiments and new men had been allocated to Company A. One such new arrival was Private First Class John Barnes. One of the few from Company A that survived the first morning on OMAHA, writing after the war John commented:

'By February '44 I had joined the 1st Battalion (116th) barracked on the edge of Dartmoor in the little village of Ivybridge in England. The men of A Company came over two years earlier, after being federal troops from the National Guard. They were all in the Guard together from one town in Virginia, a town named Bedford. I felt a bit out of things as a New Yorker. They all knew each other as old friends from home and I felt lonelier than I had ever felt before in my life.'[37]

Apart from the obvious cohesiveness and close family feeling of the men from Bedford, John Barnes relates more tellingly:

> 'My feelings didn't improve as the southern boys were bragging that their outfit was slated to be the assault unit in the landings to start the second front in France. They had been training a long time and they were ready. I wasn't.'[38]

Private First Class Barnes was one of nearly 200 replacements sent in total to the 116th infantry regiment – so many had failed to cope with the rigorous physical, and no doubt in some cases emotional, demands of training that suitably strong and athletic young conscripts were posted overseas to report to Colonel Canham's unit. Since leaving the United States, the three battalions of the 116th Infantry had removed nearly 50 per cent of the men that had started out from the initial enlistment back in January 1942 and the majority of the new arrivals had been drafted. They came from all over the United States. Although posterity has seen their names overshadowed by the collective sorrow of the number of Bedford boys killed on 6 June, there were many others that served in Company A whose names deserve equal recognition by posterity.

Operation BOLERO was the fanciful name given to the exercise whereby almost two million men earmarked for various parts of the OVERLORD invasion plans would be moved around the United Kingdom like the French composer Ravel's most famous composition – clearly the benefits of a classical and no doubt private education were not lost on at least one of the planners at COSSAC. Over a period of six days, the men of the 116th transported themselves and their equipment southwards from Tidworth marching over 160 miles of roads and lanes before they arrived at a small, quiet and reserved village south of the great hills and rocks of Dartmoor named Ivybridge.

Devon had always been a quiet county – famous for cream teas, light brown cows, sheep, the hills and granite of Dartmoor National Park and the beautiful south coast beaches and resorts of Exmouth and Torquay. But during 1943 and 1944, the whole of the south-west, especially Devon, became home to hundreds of small barrack units for nearly one million US troops scheduled for one or other phases of the invasion of France. The small Devon roads thronged to brown and green jeeps, petrol fumes, noise, traffic jams and trucks of the United States Army and the lives of thousands of local inhabitants changed – some forever.

Ivybridge was and still is an unassuming little town, quietly getting on with life in south Devon. To the north lie the 370 square miles of Dartmoor. Always windy, often wet and naturally barren, Dartmoor was to become like a second home to the men of the 29th Division. Here they carried out exhausting forced marches, night exercises, live firing on the ranges at Okehampton in the north

WESTERN PIPE & STEEL COMPANY
SAN PEDRO, CALIFORNIA.

VERTICAL

CONSOLIDATED STEEL CORP, LTD.,
WILMINGTON, CALIFORNIA.

The Wilmington Emergency Dockyard in Los Angeles with side-by-side dry docks and the landing bay where the *SS Cape Lobos* was built.

Having joined the Merchant Navy, the *Empire Javelin* was painted in camouflage and her British designed LCAs, seen here hanging from her davits, were also painted with the wavy blue side camouflage.

Company A, 116th Infantry sitting for their National Guard photograph in 1940. Note W.A. Fellers in the back row. First row: F.L. Pollard, H.E. Holland, C.H. Perry, H.B. Hargis, H.J. Faribault, I.L. Rosazza, A.L. Inge, J.W. Mitchell, G.H. Hargis, W.H. Wilkes. Second row: C.W. Fizer, J.W. Watson, M.E. Poindexter, W.P. Hurt, R.O. Stevens, L.M. Bowyer, J.J. Saunders, Jr., C.E. Danner, J.A. Mitchell, J.L. Lancaster, A.M. Thurman. Third row: G.E. Overstreet, H.E. Wilkes, W.D. Cundiff, B.L. Williams, W.A. Fellers, C.B. Morgan, J.L. Wilkes, S. Pierce, L.C. Abbott, R.A. Noel, R.E. Stanley, L.C. Robertson. (*From the Commonwealth of Virginia National Guard Historical & Pictorial Review, 1940*)

The Bedford Firemen's Band leading the parade down Main Street with the ninety men of Company A just visible marching behind on 17 February 1941. (*Courtesy of The National D-Day Memorial*)

President Franklin D. Roosevelt making one of the most pivotal speeches in human history and asking Congress to declare war on the Empire of Japan, 8 December 1941.

Master Sergeant John Wilkes, a tough, reliable and loyal 'right arm' to Captain Fellers who kept discipline and morale at the right temperature and who would be killed alongside his company commander early on 6 June 1944.

This image was taken for the 1940 National Guard Review. Although a reserve officer, Taylor Fellers was already marked out as an excellent infantry officer and was dedicated to his role in the Virginia National Guard.

The newly promoted and married Captain Taylor Fellers and his new wife Naomi Newman pictured in 1940. (*Courtesy of the National D-Day Memorial*)

Raymond and Bedford Hoback pictured with their family prior to departure for what would be the last time. To the right John Samuel Hoback always felt that they would see service and not return.

Private First Class Nicholas Napolean Gillaspie – letter writer and killed in the first wave on Dog Green beach. Rests in the American Cemetery in Normandy.

Colonel (later Major General) Charles D.W. Caneham was appointed commanding officer of the 116th Infantry Regiment before it sailed to England to prepare it for the first assault on D-Day. One private recalled 'I got the hell out of there and moved forward. I was more afraid of Colonel Caneham than I was of the Germans.' (*Courtesy Cornelius Ryan Archives, University of Ohio*)

The Thornycroft design was excellent for covert Commando operations, but was also allocated to the *Empire Javelin* for the massed assault on Omaha beach. A totally different exit strategy was needed in order to get off this LCA than the American 'Higgins' Boat.

Officers and men of the 551st Landing Craft Flotilla commanded by Sub-Lieutenant James Green RN. (*Courtesy of Michael Pocock*)

This rare photograph of the SS *Empire Javelin* shows the ship and crew exercising in Holy Loch in Scotland. The endless daily practice carried on for months in preparation for D-Day.

The coastal waters off Normandy are still littered with the carcasses of the Sherman tanks of Company B, 743rd Tank Battalion. The heavy swell on the morning of 6 June saw them swamped and sink like stones to the bottom.

The memorial to the men of the 116th Infantry who became part of the town of Ivybridge, Devon. (*Courtesy Ivybridge Heritage & Archives Group*)

Reporting to General Kraiss and pictured here with his dog in the spring of 1944, Oberstleutnant Zeigalmann was responsible for staff matters of the 352nd Infantry Division.

Field Marshal Rommel and his entourage inspect the defences somewhere in Normandy. Topped with mines, these obstacles were below water at high tide.

Taken by an allied reconnaissance aircraft on 6 May 1944, one can see just how wide the beaches were at low tide on the Normandy coastline.

This image of the sea wall on Dog Green Beach was taken only a few days after D-Day. This was the objective for Company A and Captain Fellers but very few of his company of 230 men made it anywhere near this place of limited cover from machine gun fire. (*Courtesy of Normandy Bunkers*)

Staff Sergeant John Burwell Schenck – married to Ivylyn on 24 August 1942. Killed in the first wave on Dog Green beach. Rests in the American Cemetery in Normandy.

Staff Sergeant Earl Lloyd Parker never did meet his daughter Danny. His body was never recovered, and he is listed on the Tablets of the Missing at the American Cemetery in Normandy.

This group picture was taken of men of Company A at Uphill Camp in 1943. (*Courtesy of Tommy Markham*)

The Christmas party of 1943 was for the children of Ivybridge at Uphill Camp. Boxes of sweets and chocolate were provided by the soldiers – luxuries from the USA.

Lieutenant Benjamin Rives Kearfott was transferred into Company A only five days before D-Day as one of a number of additional officers that helped to boost the strength of Company A by nearly thirty men. Was there new information that prompted this late draft of extra men? Lieutenant Kearfott rests in the American Cemetery in Normandy. (*Courtesy of Mary Kay Washington*)

Taken on 5 June somewhere on the south coast. Given the likely time of day, these American infantrymen are possibly from the 116th as they were among the first to board that day – given that they would be landing first in Normandy.

On board the American command ship USS *Charles Caroll*, this photographer gets help putting on his life preserver. His face mirrors the growing anxiety that the landings were on.

Captain Robert Ware volunteered to serve and found himself as one of the medical officers for the 116th infantry. Ware further volunteered to land in the very first wave and was shot between the eyes as the ramp on his landing craft was lowered.

Lieutenant Edward Gearing was a born leader. He was the only officer from Company A that survived the initial landings and went on to earn the Distinguished Service Cross on the beaches on 6 June. He sadly died very young. (*Courtesy of Shenandoah County Library Archives, USA*)

Second Lieutenant John Clements was transferred to Company A as he was highly thought of in training. Married just prior to embarkation for England, he was killed trying to attack one of the two bunkers on Dog Green beach.

Higgins landing craft in line astern in an exercise before moving forward into line abreast for the assault phase. This is how the scene would have been on the morning of 6 June but with far rougher seas.

These notes were written later on the cliffs of Dog Green beach by Lieutenant Gearing, '… had no time to go back. Saw 1st Lt Ray Nance Exec Off A Co 116th. Shot through the foot. "What's happened to A Co." "As far as I know the officers are dead and everyone else is too." A Off 170–150 casualties.' (*C. Ryan Archive, Ohio University*)

Whilst clearing the houses and farmhouses later in the day, Gearing recorded, 'Table was set for breakfast bread, butter, milk (big pitcher) set for 12 people platters of bacon, eggs. Looks like they were just about to eat breakfast.' (*C. Ryan Archive, Ohio University*)

The German MG 42 and its crew of four men was the most lethal infantry weapon of the Second World War. The rate of fire was murderous and the only chance to survive was when the barrels were changed through overheating – about a ten second pause.

As the tide came in that morning of 6 June, so did the bodies of the men of Company A, B and D – washed up from 400 meters off shore having been killed at low tide.

Lieutenant John Gilmour RNVR Gunnery Officer on board the *Empire Javelin*. (*Courtesy of Michael Pocock and Maritime Quest*)

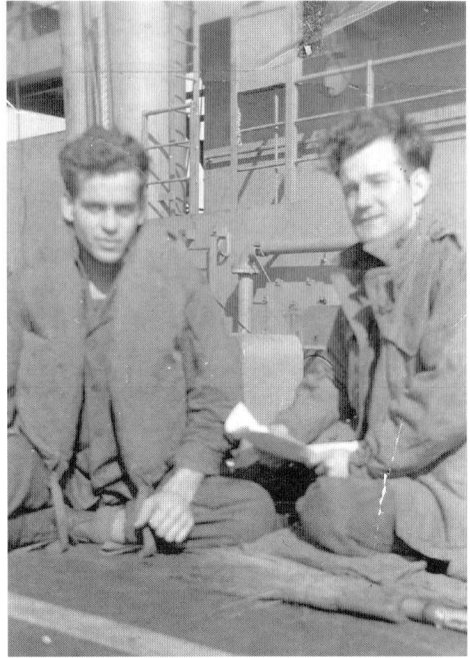

Private First Class Robert Guyser (left) and Private First Class Peter Golden sitting on board the *Empire Javelin* on 28 December 1944. A few hours later, after the *Empire Javelin* had sunk, Guyser was one of those reported missing. (*Courtesy of Lili Marlene Golden*)

One of the rare photographs taken from the *L'Escarmouche* by Paul Beltz of the *Empire Javelin* sinking after the second explosion. (*Courtesy of Hannah Leiditch in memory of Paul Beltz*)

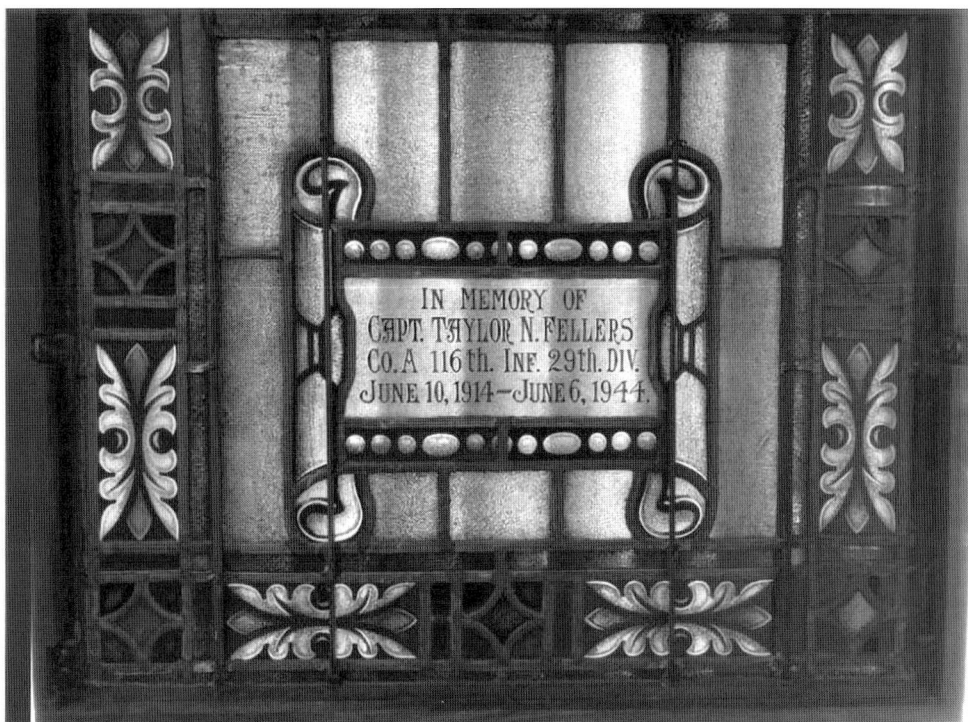

This memorial window once sat in Nazareth Methodist Church in Cifax, VA. Dedicated on 10 June 1945 by the family of Taylor Fellers, it is now in the care of the National D-Day Memorial in Bedford. (*Courtesy of the National D-Day Memorial*)

The final resting place of the *Empire Javelin*.

The grave of Lieutenant Colonel John Alfred Metcalfe Jr. Commanding the 1st Battalion, 116th Infantry, Metcalfe was instrumental in training and inspiring his five companies for D-Day. Surviving 6 June 1944, he was wounded in action on 29 June and he died of his wounds on 15 July 1944. He is buried at the Cambridge American Cemetery & Memorial, England.

Captain Ettore Zappacosta, commanding officer of Company B, 116th Infantry whose landing craft followed shortly after those of Company A and suffered immediate and heavy casualties. His body was one of the many that were buried in the temporary graves above Omaha beach and was subsequently exhumed and returned to the United States of America and now rests in the Holy Cross Cemetery in Yeadon, Pennsylvania.

Captain Walter Otis Schilling. A National Guardsman since April 1929, Schilling was regarded fondly by the men of Company D. Having trained so hard over fifteen years to serve in combat, he did not even reach the beach on D-Day as he was killed by an 88mm shell hitting the front of his landing craft. He rests in the American Cemetery in Normandy.

As a member of the 15th Army Headquarters, Paul Beltz was on board the SS *Empire Javelin* on her final journey, and it is thanks to his quick thinking with his camera that we have the final photographs of the ship before she sank. (*Courtesy of Hannah Leidich*)

and survival training. 'You couldn't stay dry. Water would always seep into everything. You'd lie down on your bed sheet and before long the water would come through. It was horrible', recalled Allen Huddleston. In an interview with Alex Kershaw for his book *The Bedford Boys*, Roy Stevens recalled that one evening on Dartmoor Captain Fellers had walked along and kicked out the tent pegs knocking down tents with men still inside – because they were not in a straight line.

The commanding General Gerhardt ensured that his men were going to be the best trained National Guard unit in the whole Army – Gerhardt was not there to be popular, he was there to do his job well and, within the division, the fearsome Colonel Canham wanted the men of the 116th Infantry Regiment to be the best disciplined and fittest of the three Regiments (alongside the 115th and 175th) and within the 116th, Lieutenant Colonel Metcalfe wanted the 1st Battalion to be the most effective fighting force of all three battalions. Finally, within the 1st Battalion, Captain Taylor Fellers wanted Company A to be the best company of the battalion. Many men had already been weeded out and replacements sent in – quite a number from New York and at the start of 1944, the 116th Infantry Regiment consisted of 166 officers, five warrant officers and 3,100 enlisted men split across all formations including the three infantry battalions. (according to Schildt p. 126–130). As D-Day approached, around thirty additional men would be transferred into Company A in anticipation of higher-than-expected casualties. Quite how this affected the existing officers and men is unknown but it cannot have done much for their confidence. Equally difficult was blending new young officers into the unit at the last moment.

To the south of Ivybridge, it was a thirty-minute run to reach the south coast of England. No white cliffs here, just long sandy beaches exactly like OMAHA. It was a tricky journey down to the coast on narrow winding Devon roads, plenty of fenders bashed each other as large trucks attempted to make the roads wider only to find a 'Devon Hedge' under the bushes – an old granite wall overgrown with ivy and blackthorn and these roads were not going to get any wider. Once at the beaches then it was amphibious training, landing and fighting on sand, learning how hard it is to run 400m on sand and, for large numbers of men, learning how to swim.

The imaginatively named Uphill Camp, which became home for the Bedford Boys of Company A, sat on the rise of a small hill to the north of the main Exeter Road that ran due west sloping downhill into the small town of Ivybridge. Unlike the majority of similar army camps, Uphill Camp was almost in the centre of the town and was a one-minute walk to the first of numerous public houses that very soon began to welcome the officers and men (though not in the same pubs of course) of the 116th. It was this close proximity that gave

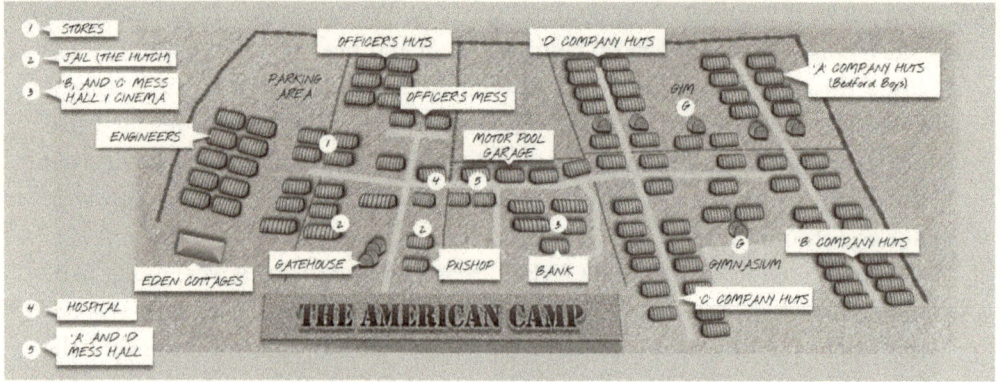

Plan of the 1st Battalion accommodation at Uphill Camp in Ivybridge, Devon c.1943.

the residents of the town and the men of the 116th plenty of opportunity to meet, make friends and create memories, indeed we have a singularly unique insight into the life of Company A specifically because of the many memories recorded by the town's active and professional History Society. So much of the social history of this period is not recorded specifically because the troops were kept well away from civilian communities.

Uphill Camp housed the entire 1st Battalion of the 116th Infantry and the close confines of what was a very tight area no doubt lent itself to all the aspects of team building needed to make this a very close unit. With numerous lieutenants, the five Company Captains (A, B, C, D and HQ) plus a few majors and the battalion commander Lieutenant Colonel Metcalfe all in the same small area, there was little chance of escaping the watchful eye of discipline – although there was an officers' mess on site for meetings during the day and duty officers overnight, the officers took over Stowford House which was just on the northern edge of town and was a beautiful eighteenth century house with large circular bay windows and must have felt like a five star hotel after the mix of really basic accommodation they had faced since their arrival in Britain.

As for the camp, a journey to the site today informs the visitor that the camp has now been built upon, all except for the corner of the field that once housed the green half-circular Nissen huts of Company A – left as a memorial to the men that slept, sweated and played here for over a year during 1943 and 1944. In a corner an oak bench seat, carved with the names of those who fell welcomes you to sit and ponder for a while, allowing your imagination to picture scenes of marching men, drilling sergeants, engines of vehicles starting up, shouts of instructors and cooks as well as the smell of beans, aftershave on nights out, baseball matches and laughter coming back after a visit to the local pubs.

Local evidence tells us that the arrival of the Americans was quite a shock. The secrecy surrounding the entire invasion build up was such that no-one had even consulted the local councils – only the landowners; then one morning a construction battalion with dozens of lorries rolled down Exeter Road and turned up onto Uphill and started building a camp. The children from the next-door school loved meeting these new soldiers with a strange uniform and accent and watched in amazement as hut after hut was erected in April 1943 until it was like a second village had been built within 200 yards of the centre of the village. Seamlessly the construction unit left and the trucks of the 116th arrived. Some officers arrived by train which stopped in the town station and again, the faces of the local townspeople were agog. They were clearly Americans but what were they doing here and how long would they be staying?

Once the first three weeks were completed, then the men were given passes to exit the main gate on the Exeter Road, turn right and, within one hundred yards, enter The Sportsman's Public House and here they met the landlady for the first time, Mrs Vera Luckham. Years later Vera recalled:

'The first contingent of the 116ᵗʰ Infantry marched here from Tidworth and were kept in camp for three weeks. The first night they had leave, they poured into the Sportsman's Arms, which was the nearest pub. We had built up a good supply of spirits, as things had been very quiet. In a few minutes it was bedlam. The Yanks started on Applejack as they called Cider and then went on to whiskey. As the first lot moved on, others came and I wondered what would happen if they drank the pub dry.'[39]

Others in the town felt that they had been 'invaded'.

'At first the local folk, being true Devonian and reserved, were hesitant and nervous as these strange men in unaccustomed uniforms flooded the streets and pubs during the evenings. They were overwhelmed with the rapidity of it all; but gradually, the friendliness and open-hearted camaraderie of the visitors overcame the initial fear, and a true Devonian welcome was extended.'[40]

It did not take long for the men of Bedford to take advantage of the 'true Devonian welcome' and before the first Christmas of 1943–1944 a few of the more gallant and adventurous men of Company A had extended more than the hand of friendship towards the women of the town. Corporal Weldon 'Tony' Rosazza had all the charm and good looks of a Hollywood film star, his good looks accompanied by sparkling eyes and his clean-cut uniform made his ambition of meeting genuine English girls so much easier and he was considered a very popular catch amongst the young ladies of Ivybridge. So too was Private First Class John Daniel Clifton – once a paperboy in Bedford, Clifton was now very much the hero in uniform. Tall and lean Clifton soon struck a steady relationship with a young lady from the town and, before he left Ivybridge, became engaged – and the guys staged a huge party for him and his new fiancée at the Sportsman's Arms.

Even Captain Taylor Fellers found solace and comfort amongst the female company that they had missed for so long. He had been married but not experienced a married life, loved but then torn away from his love and now here he was in a foreign country, thousands of miles away from home. No doubt Fellers was far from being the only officer that went through the same experiences. Sergeant Roy Stevens, a survivor of Company A, would recall after the war that on the long route marches – which could be over twenty miles in full packs – he would often push the pace along at the front with Captain Fellers and, in man-to-man conversation when the rank dropped away, Fellers admitted that his marriage was already failing. Quoted in Alex Kershaw's book, Roy Stevens recalled:

> 'Fellers and his wife had fallen out. Before we went overseas, I'd heard through the grapevine that they were about to separate. He called her the blonde bomber but otherwise never said too much about her – he'd just go out at night and have a ball.'[41]

The story continues that Captain Fellers become platonically friendly with a widow who lived on one of the many farms close to the town, a Mrs Lunscomb who apparently adopted Captain Fellers and a few other officers, entertaining them to tea and meals at the farmhouse. As Alex Kershaw relates:

> 'Within a year, Sergeant Clyde Powers would be considering marriage to a sweet natured 'rose' named Pam Roberts whom he met in Plymouth; Sergeant Roy Stevens would be dating a chirpy Liverpudlian, Mickey Muriel Peake; and company clerk Pride Wingfield would be seeing Doreen, Mickey's cousin. They shared cigarettes, taught their girls to jive and jitterbug and tried to forget the war. The next dance, the next pub, the next forty-eight-hour pass were all that mattered.'[42]

But not all the Bedford Boys went out on the local town, across to an evening at nearby Plymouth or up to London and the sights of the big city. For Earl Parker all his thoughts, as those of any new father would be, were of home and his wife and the daughter he had not yet met. According to Alex Kershaw, Earl had been so utterly convinced that the new baby would be a boy, he had agreed a name with Viola – Danny – and so Danny it was and she was as beautiful a baby as any proud dad could wish for.

Life in and around Ivybridge was a buzz with the Americans in town, in fact the whole of Devon was buzzing and humming with vehicles, equipment parks, roadside traffic and the smell of engine oils. Around Ivybridge alone, there were nearly 4,000 troops. Earmarked as Marshalling Area L1, along with 1,500 men crammed into Uphill Camp, there were battalions in tents near Cornwood and another 1,500 at Delamore House. There was no mixing of black and white units. Being from Virginia, the cordiality extended to the British population by the men of the 116th was not often if ever extended to the 'coloured units'. As one local resident recalled 'White and coloured Americans were camped separately and much to the surprise of local people relations between them were not cordial.'

In 1943 Noel was only 9 years old, he was one of the local paperboys in the town and for nearly two years, he visited Uphill Camp every day. Allowed through the main gates on the Exeter Road, Noel brought in newspapers for dozens of men – one recalled after the war that all they could see of him when he arrived was a head and two legs underneath a huge bag stuffed with the *Stars & Stripes* and then lots of editions of the *Daily Mirror* – apparently popular due to the comic strip 'Jane' who seemed to have trouble keeping her clothes on most days. Even Winston Churchill described 'Jane' as 'Britain's secret weapon'.

Like many of the children in the town, Noel had good reasons to love the American boys not least because of their banter and interesting voices but also because they provided him with sweets and a new experience – gum and candy. Noel knew many of the men by name and even rode his bike following the convoys when they went up onto Dartmoor for their arduous training exercises, having a privileged view that Adolf Hitler would have paid a great deal to have himself. Christmas 1943–1944 was an especially happy time for them all as local families were invited into the camp and a Christmas party was hosted by the officers and men of the 1st Battalion for the children. With so many fathers away on active service,' *it was nice to have the men around, they were kind and gallant and acted like temporary fathers for us children.'*

But not all was good news. Around the towns it was inevitable that the tensions and drowning of depressed spirits would result in drunkenness and, even with the iron discipline of their commanding officers in their blood, men lost control and exploded into ferocious, violent fights. 'Punch ups' between black and white American troops resulted in certain pubs being earmarked for one colour only but even between themselves, emotions boiled over – the wheels of years of training to fight being greased by whiskey and cider. One particular evening is recalled even now by the elderly residents of the town who were just young children when 'the battle' broke out. Four passing New Zealanders apparently tried to get into The Kings Arms for a drink and discovered that there was a dance going on and wanted to join the happy crowds – but this was an invitation only event and even other soldiers were not allowed in as the whole thing was being paid for by a group of grateful soldiers 'for the local hospitality they had received' – read that as you may. Vera Luckham continues the story:

> 'It was when the New Zealand soldiers were protesting about being refused admission that the blacks slipped in and the real shemozzle started. The noise was terrible. My husband Frank, who was a Captain in the Royal Engineers, was away and I only dared look out the window. Urgent messages were sent to the camps to come and stop it before anyone was killed and jeeps full of soldiers came from all directions. Men were fighting all over the place and it was like the Keystone Cops with everyone getting in each other's way. It wasn't long before D-Day and I think the Americans were all keyed-up and just let go…. it was all hushed up afterwards.'[43]

Paperboy Noel recalls the MPs arriving and taking off the caps of men fighting outside pubs before bashing them on the heads with their long white sticks before taking them in their jeeps and throwing them into 'the hutch' which was a small shed on the barracks used as a jail. Watching through the fence one morning, Noel still remembers the shock of seeing the door opened and inside them men were still laying one on top of the other exactly as they had been thrown in the night before. Interestingly, Noel noticed that it was always white MPs that went out to arrest the black troops and vice versa. Sergeant John Slaughter from Company D recalled after the war that matters over girlfriends could become really serious between the white and black units and there were even some stabbings on the roads outside the public houses in the town. Slaughter also remembered that one of the platoon sergeants from the mortar platoon was caught leaving the camp with a sub-machine gun 'heading for town and intending to clean the place out' such was the level of animosity between the men of Virginia and their black infantry counterparts and a hidden aspect of the many similar events with more than one million soldiers concentrated in a foreign land knowing that the end of their own lives might not be so far in the future.

Lieutenant Ray Nance who, although badly wounded, would survive D-Day recalled to Alex Kershaw that it was seeing white girls from the town going out with black GIs was the thing that really upset the boys from Southern Virginia. 'The men were not used to seeing that, and couldn't get used to it, although I'm sure they could if they had tried.' The war had upset traditional and historical social norms and this was felt most acutely between white and black American troops who brought their animosities and expectations with them, creating conflict within a conflict.

Fighting around the pubs of Ivybridge was a scene replicated all around the south-west as the adrenalin of men waiting to fight and knowing they might die, mixed with the emotion of being far from home and missing family and loved ones to create a heady cocktail of charged energy – but it was not all alcohol induced explosives and neither was it an 'All-American' affair. The local police reports for Ivybridge and the surrounding area during this period also make interesting reading and there were numerous road accidents on the small roads with drivers of very large trucks for example:

'A Jeep driven by PFC Harry Stone of B Company, 116th Infantry, 1st Battalion, 29th Division, US Forces, Uphill Camp, Ivybridge was involved in an accident in Ivybridge, October 1943.'

'A 13 ton US Army wrecker vehicle towing an amphibious Duck towards Plymouth driven by Colin MacNeven of 546th Ordnance Company, A.P.O. 122, the Duck became adrift and hit Ernest Edwards of North Filham sustaining slight injuries. July 1944'

PFC Channie J. Hall 1st Battalion, 116th Infantry, 5th Company, 29th Division, US Forces, Uphill Camp, Ivybridge was involved in an accident while driving a US truck. October, 1944.'

But more serious offences were also recorded that indicated that local light-fingered individuals were also at work:

'Sgt. G. Campbell, aged 31, of C Comp., 116th Infantry, 1st Battalion, 29th Div. US Forces, Uphill Camp reported to the Ivybridge Police that a US Army raincoat, US Army torch, Zippo cigarette lighter and gloves were stolen from the Kings Arms Hotel, Ivybridge. February 1944.

1st Lt. A.S.Anderson reported to Ivybridge Police that a pair of leather shoes and eight packets of US cigarettes were stolen from hut 26 at Uphill, Ivybridge. February 1944.'

A better example of local creativity in cementing US – UK economic relations came with this report dated October 1943:

'E. Richards of C Company, 392 Engineers G.S. US Forces, Stowford House, was court martialled at Dartington for disposing of two 5-gallon US Army G.I. petrol containing 10 (US) gallons of petrol. Sentenced to confinement with

hard labour for six months and forfeits two thirds of his pay for six months. (Local man fined £5 for receiving this petrol).[44]

Given that Stowford House was home to dozens of the officers of the 116th Infantry, E. Richards was dealt with particularly harshly as he was trying to steal and sell petrol from under their very noses.

Perhaps one of the more confusing and concerning incidents noted by the local news and police reports was the case of Private First Class L. Franklin. In April 1944, just as the office and Nissen hut calendars were ticking off their final days towards the inevitability of D-Day, Franklin burst into an orderly room and fired 16 shots before he was overpowered. The report states that he was court martialled for wounding and endangering life – if men were killed then the US Army hushed this event up. Franklin was sentenced to a dishonourable discharge and sent to military prison for 5 years hard labour. Whatever the background, the whole of Uphill Camp and especially Company B commanded by Captain Zappacosta must have been severely rattled by this event where one of their own seems to have lost his reason just a few weeks before D-Day itself. With no more information to base any sort of assessment upon we have to leave matters there – it could have been pre-battle stress but just as easily it may have been a personal matter between himself and those in the Orderly Room.

Even long after the men of the 116th had left Uphill Camp, most of them never to return, the camp continued to provide the local police with plenty to do and in January 1945, Ada F. Lowe, a London munitions worker aged 20 of Kensington London, was arrested for 'unlawfully trespassing on government property at Uphill Camp, Ivybridge.' Poor Ada no doubt met one of the new members of the camp in London and took the five-hour train journey to Devon to be smuggled into the camp but was discovered – she spent three months in a local prison.

The final push towards excellence – 'Uncle Charlie'

Major General Charles Gerhardt – or 'Uncle Charlie' as the men called him – was a tough commander and determined to drive the fighting quality of the division. His arrival meant that training continued throughout the fall of 1943 and into the spring of 1944. It was Gerhardt that ordered all officers to shave every day – in cold water in the field if necessary; he ordered all vehicles to be polished and forbade anyone from standing close to him. It was said that Gerhardt commanded three divisions – one in the field, one in the hospital and one in the cemetery. Many infantrymen of the 29th Division were killed in training across the south west – especially on Dartmoor and in the practice beach landings just prior to D-Day.

'Our training was rough, we never had nothing easy. We would get up and run four miles in twenty minutes and this was before breakfast. We would have to run two or three-mile obstacle courses with some of the damnedest obstacles that anyone could think of. Sometimes we thought the Devil had thought up some of those obstacle courses. Golly no-one, but no-one realised how horrible our training was. We would take two or three thirty-mile hikes a week......I can't describe it.'[45]

As the men of the *Empire Javelin* practised their gunnery drills in Scotland and worked out how to get the LCAs full and as quickly as possible into the water, the men of both groups recognised that the training was becoming more serious and their nervousness rivalled their excitement in preparing for what was to come – wherever it was.

In Devon, Private First Class John Barnes was allocated the platoon now led by Second Lieutenant John Bernard Clements Jr. Fairly new to A Company himself, Clements was a 29-year-old product of Yonkers, NY. A graduate of Oswego State College, he also received a BS degree from Buffalo State and was a school principal before enlisting in the United States Army in May, 1942. Clements married the former Miss Ferraro of Yonkers when he was a private and retained quite a lot of character within his modest frame which led to him being commissioned in May 1943 and posted to the elite Company A of the 116th which was a measure of how well he was regarded. New to Uphill Camp and to A Company himself, Second Lieutenant Clements had to rapidly get used to the rigours of training and blend in with a company of men partly from one town and partly from everywhere else.

The shock of arriving at a front-line combat unit in the middle of intensive training was quite a challenge. Another of the many new recruits to make his way from the USA to Devon was Private Donald McCarthy who joined Headquarters Company at Uphill Camp in the late summer of 1943 and he recalled how:

'From day one with the 116th in Ivybridge training on the moors would consume every waking hour from 5am to 5pm, except Sundays. Every third day we would dig in, set up camp and bed down in this inhospitable swampy moor, anticipating live artillery and mortar fire.'

PTE Donald McCarthy
Headquarters Company
1st Battalion, 116th Infantry[46]

As the men specialised in landing from an imaginary boat onto a sandy beach where, fanning out in three single rows that the British landing craft would require, they dived face-first into sand and wriggled their way up a beach they expected to be full of shell holes in which to shelter from the enemy gunfire. At this stage they had no idea that, in actual fact, the timing of OVERLORD meant that they would be landing in water – and water of an unknown depth – nor did the training mention anything about the moving sandbanks which may ground the flat-bottomed landing craft well short of the beach and in deep water ravines in front of them.

The men were trained to expect to be able to exit onto a beach in an orderly fashion with wire cutters and rows of men tasked with specific jobs. Dummy pill-boxes were built so that the infantrymen could practise being part of a final assault team, scrambling to their target, through the expected potholes on the beach from preliminary bombardments and then head on throwing live charges at the 'pillbox' shouting 'FIRE IN THE HOLE' and waiting for the whole thing to erupt. According to Private First Class Barnes:

> 'We practised this routine every day, over and over. Each man knew his job. We worked together in ways that was very different to the basic training in the United States. We took the drills very seriously and the officers made it more serious when they began to set up groups of sharp-shooters to fire freely at us in our dry runs. One time, one of the boys set off a charge that had a short fuse and it blew up in his face. I was glad I didn't see him, thank God. They said he still had his helmet strap down below his chin and after that, we never wore our helmet straps buckled, except for parades and guard duty.'[47]

One of the platoon sergeants in D Company was Sergeant John R. Slaughter. Himself only aged 19, John knew all the men in his company and many of the sergeants of Company A too and they were all camped in Uphill Camp. He recalled many aspects of these final months of training up on Dartmoor:

> 'It was the end of winter (1943–44) and the windswept moors were a foreboding place to train. There were no trees and the mushy, spongelike soil was constantly under clouds, fog and cold, misty rain. The battalion spent much of the time training and sleeping out on those God-forsaken hillsides.
>
> 'We were in the initial stages of amphibious training. Endurance and strength tests called 'burp-up' exercises were given to monitor physical fitness. Those who passed earned the Expert Infantryman's Badge and an extra $5 in the monthly pay check. Failing to qualify meant transfer to a non-combat outfit.
>
> 'Some of the criteria for the Expert Infantryman's Badge was running 100 yards in twelve seconds with army shoes and clothing, doing thirty-five push-

ups and ten chin-ups, running an obstacle course within the prescribed time and qualifying on the pistol, rifle and machine-gun ranges. It really was not that difficult, and the officers allowed some cheating so that some of the men could pass. Despite this, a few could not pass and were transferred.'[48]

What part did the design of the British LCA play in the landings on Dog Green?

What the men must have realised early on in their assault training was that they were not using the popular Higgins Boats – the United States version of the standard landing craft – but the heavier, longer and better protected British Land Craft designed by Thornycroft. This was a better boat to handle in the water and was a better boat all round, but it had the major design issue of men having to flow out in three individual files – centre followed by left and then right. Steven Spielberg made the wonderful *Saving Private Ryan* presumably in the belief that all landing craft were the same, however, a glance at any image of the *Empire Javelin* will show that this was not the case. The impact for the men of the 116th was going to be profound. It took two to three minutes to get off this landing craft – perfect for Royal Marines landing on undefended shores and in the dark for their covert operations – totally inappropriate for a massed attack on a heavily defended beach.

In early spring, as the final phases of training commenced, the entire 1st Battalion was moved, temporarily, to an area just north of a stretch of quiet, Devonian sandy beach named Slapton Sands. It was selected because it was close to Ivybridge and resembled OMAHA beach in so far as it had a gently sloping sandy area followed by shingle. 'Moved' is possibly not technically correct as the entire battalion was marched, day and night south towards Slapton in driving rain and cold, sleeping out at night in soaking wet clothes. Before reaching the beach itself, an area of salty marshland had to be crossed.

Joining Captain Taylor Fellers (Company A), Captain Ettore V. Zappacosta (Company B) and Captain Berthier B. Hawks (Company C) was Sergeant John Slaughter's Company Commander, Captain Walter O. Schilling. Captain Schilling set a ferocious standard for the men of his Company as Sgt Slaughter recalled:

'One of the men in my squad, PFC Joseph Alvalio from Brooklyn was only recently drafted and hadn't fully embraced the system. When he crossed the lake he lost a $6 machine-gun water can in the murky water. On learning of this mishap, Captain Schilling, the company commander, screamed at me: "Slaughter, what in the hell's the matter with your squad! Bust him to private! He pays for the water can and he's going to learn to take care of the equipment." Each day

for a week I had to oversee Alvolio's punishment, which was a two-mile run up a mountainous path to a swimming pool where he had to wade through the cold water, fully clothed and with all his equipment. The pool had a skim of ice over it and on the first day Alvolio slid into the water and went straight to the bottom. He was a poor swimmer and I had to pull him out of the water.[49]

Another member of Company D recalled that, like Captain Taylor Fellers, Captain Schilling had been in the Virginia National Guard before the war and so had kept himself fit – it was the new drafts that really struggled with the intensity of training. Schilling was a 34-year-old chain smoker of Lucky Strike cigarettes and together with one of his lieutenants, Lieutenant Morse, he created a team in Company D where men felt the company was their replacement family. Schilling made them complete incessant weapons training and drills so it would be second nature to them and they could assemble and clean their weapons with their eyes shut – during those 'rest' periods when they were not doing physical training.

Captain Fellers did his best, in his languid Virginian drawl, to keep the camaraderie alive that had served the unit so well for so long – but it could not have been at all easy. The Bedford Boys had been together now more intensely than any family, they had been training for eighteen months, they were as fit as any butcher's dog and they now needed a mission – and soon. Fellers wrote to his parents that the men still ruminated about home and what they missed but that the arrival of the replacements – especially the 'northern boys' from New York had rekindled the US Civil War all over again and gentle needle with tongue in cheek banter was welcome – even though it took some weeks before the Bedford Boys would let the new guys feel part of their family of men.

Without Master Sergeant John Wilkes, Captain Fellers would have struggled to maintain high levels of discipline and commitment. Wilkes had put on twenty pounds of pure muscle and looked like a brick wall with legs as he marched towards new recruits – he was virtually unstoppable. His unique way of training new recruits to snap to attention with their heels tightly together, was to spit a wad of his freshly chewed tobacco in the gaps between their legs – as no one wanted to clean that off, his methods worked perfectly. He answered to Captain Fellers alone and between them goes the credit for keeping the units tight, fit and ferocious but there were still occasions when the men just lost grip on their own discipline – Alex Kershaw relates how Sergeants Bedford Hoback and Jack Powers (one of the most admired men in the outfit) had their three stripes removed for breaches of discipline. Possibly, after so long, the point of why they were there was being lost, the intensity of training undermined their determination – or possibly just emotional exhaustion from the endless waiting to know what was going to happen to them. When we recall the incident concerning Private First Class Franklin and his sixteen shot murder attempt in the April of 1944, then D-Day could now not come soon enough or more nerves of men pushed to the limit would shatter and burst.

The final big exercise for the 1st Battalion at Uphill Camp came in March 1944. The whole unit marched, in full combat kit to the station at Ivybridge where they took a six-hour train journey to the Braunton Assault Training Area in North Devon. Twelve days of beach exercises followed where the men of Company A saw many signs that they were going into action soon. Apart from seeing senior commanders in Devon, there was an increased tempo of training and new exercises – their officers too showed all the signs of increased tension as they became focussed on fighting not drilling.

The Company had now been divided into the boat teams in which they would hit the beach. Each platoon had thirty men and each man was given a specific role whether it be four men to a machine gun, five men with explosive Bangalore torpedoes (designed in Bangalore, India by a Captain McClintock of the Royal Engineers in 1912), or one of five riflemen to give cover fire. There were also two officers, another four manning a 60mm mortar plus all the associated radios, mortar shells in cases, personal equipment and rifles, personal packs and ammunition, the mortar plate, machine gun and tripod – all of this had to be carried into a boat and from there into battle – under fire. Up in Braunton, this training was all done on land with wooden silhouettes of boat dimensions and distances worked out in yards, but training at sea and from landing craft was coming next.

Together At Last: April-May 1944

In May 1944, the SS *Empire Javelin* received orders to sail south – she was to make her way down the west coast of Scotland and England, round Land's End and drop anchor in Weymouth Harbour in Dorset, about 100 miles from Uphill Camp and the 116th. It truly was a 'combined arms' operation with men of the Merchant Navy handling the ship and officers and ratings of the Royal Navy manning the ship's guns and the landing craft. At this late stage, no one in the 116th had even heard the name of the ship they were about to join – but she was not far away now and waiting for them for the final practice runs.

As the ship sailed southwards with her eighteen LCAs on board to finally meet the men she had been built to carry, to the north of Ivybridge, a small grass airfield had been cut into the fields and an airstrip for light aircraft was available. Often the men of the 116th and Uphill Camp would march there to play baseball or even host play days for the local children – it was the children that kept many of the men sane in these final weeks of preparation. But Hanger Down, as it was known, was also used for small unit training such as platoon and company level. The grass airstrip saw numerous senior officers landed there in small aircraft such as the 0-57 Grasshopper and the famous Piper Cub. In April 1944, as groups of infantrymen were being put through their close combat drills yet again, they saw a small group of senior officers standing on the hills overlooking them. Pausing to take in their breath and focus their eyes, they saw General Eisenhower himself together with all the senior officers of the American Vth Army and, if further evidence were needed that the training period was at long last coming to an end, in May 1944 Colonel Canham was seen escorting General Montgomery ('Monty' was not promoted to Field Marshal until September, 1944) over Hanger Down and then on to one of the final briefings before D-Day itself.

At the end of March, the men of the 1st Battalion were back, exhausted in Uphill Camp and were told that now they were finally leaving. Huts were to be cleared of everything except the stoves and bunks, ready for their new occupants. The smell of bonfires of discarded blankets and sheets and old uniforms covered the town and all leave was cancelled. But two weeks later, in early April, the battalion was still in Ivybridge, notes were passed through fences and relationships continued somehow. Letters home were also stopped as the units went into strict isolation. However, on 16 April 1944, Company A, B, C, D and HQ donned their smartest parade uniforms – their kit and combat outfits, weapons and equipment were placed on a convoy of trucks. The trucks went east towards Weymouth and the men went west, marching through the town for the last time.

In the town there was relief from some, but the overriding sentiment was sadness. Despite being confined to barracks, the whole town knew when the men were leaving and were ready as the parade formed up inside the fences of Uphill Camp and then, to the noise of music, trumpets and drums, marched out into the Exeter Road, formed right and down the hill – past The Sportsman's Pub for the last time, past the Kings Arms, down the High Street and past the police station on, on to the station.

'When the people turned out for our early-hour departure, some of them, especially the new brides, had tears streaming down their faces. As they lined the streets, hanging out of windows, waving and cheering, how did they know we were finally going to war when we didn't know for sure ourselves?

We left Ivybridge and the townspeople, who had at first despised us, were out in droves lining the streets and some of them were waving out of their windows to us. We had marched out many times but this time they knew this was it. They really did learn to like us and we liked them as well. The economy boomed while we were there and many of us became friends.'

Staff Sergeant William Lewis, Company HQ,
1st Bn, 116th Infantry[50]

The senior and middle ranking officers also said their final goodbyes to the people who had looked after them over the past year. The staff at Stowford House would go back into the very cold and empty rooms which for over a year had played host to noise, cigarette smoke, laughter, shouting, breakfasts, the smell of cologne and American accents from all over the United States. Mrs Lunscomb would never have the pleasure of hosting Captain Taylor Fellers again for dinner or any of his compatriots and local taxi drivers would no longer enjoy all the new runs to and from the train station as men went up to London on 48-hour passes. A skeleton team of men had stayed at Uphill Camp but it was empty now, a ghost town and when the train pulled out of Ivybridge station for the last time, those waving hands and shouts of 'good luck' and 'I love you' would remain an image in the minds of hundreds, on both sides, for the rest of their lives.

On 17 April, the battalion arrived into a sealed camp near Weymouth and all leave was now over and communications in and out of the camp strictly limited. Company A personalities now had new responsibilities – John Schenk was in charge of communications, Ray Stevens led the mortar team and Master Sergeant John Wilkes moved around with Captain Fellers encouraging the men, some with their worried faces now beginning to show and really missing news from home.

After all the political events of the past four years, the travelling around the world, discussions, training and waiting, endless waiting, the *Empire Javelin* was now in Portland Harbour and she was waiting for the very men that she had been built for twelve months earlier. Sailing through Lyme Bay and onto Slapton Sands, the men of the 1st Battalion practised hard over two-day exercises, learning how to enter their LCA, what it felt like being lowered into the water – no scramble nets for them – the merchant seamen felt the strains and the weight and worked against the clock on a strict timetable to get the battalion into the water and they felt what it was like motoring towards the beach with their Royal Navy crew. Friendships were struck up, happy banter accompanied their joint missions and then live rounds started fizzing over their heads, landing on the beaches and the smell of diesel fumes from the boat mixed with the smell of vomit from those being sea sick and the cordite blowing on the wind and they knew this was close to the real thing.

'Assistant flamethrower George Roach was in Master Sergeant John Wilkes's boat team. Fifty years later, he would vividly recall the procedure for storming a beach:

'As the boat would land at the beach, the ramp was dropped. The lieutenant would be the first one off the boat, usually followed by four or five riflemen who would be in a position to fan out, followed by Bangalore torpedo people and wire cutters, then the flame thrower and his assistant, then the demolition team which carried charges of TNT, then second in command, in [my boat], Sergeant Wilkes....The Bangalore torpedo people would run up to where the barbed wire was, throw a pole charge across the barbed wire, explode it so that the riflemen could then follow on and fire at the pillbox which was usually situated at a distance from us, and then the flame thrower would active his flame thrower at the embrasure and then the pole charge people would come up and lay their TT packages against the embrasure and blow a hole in it.'[51]

Operation Tiger and The Battle of Lyme Bay, April, 1944

'Man, Slapton Sands was tough.'
Roy Stevens Company A, 116th Infantry

Part of the final larger scale exercises using landing craft began in the autumn of 1943 and continued right through 1944. Similar to the beaches at UTAH and OMAHA, Slapton Sands was designated as the amphibious practice area and 3,000 local residents were forcibly relocated before large scale operations began. Before long, almost every unit of the 29th Division would have practised all the various aspects of the amphibious landing to come and both Force U for UTAH and Force O for OMAHA would learn how to marshal their landing ships, embark, disembark, attack the beaches and fight on sloping sand and shingle against an enemy that had been either killed or disorientated by heavy bombing from the air, shelling from Naval ships and constant tank gunfire from the beaches.

Exercise Tiger was one of the larger formation drills to be conducted and included nine LSTs – Landing Ship Tank – which happened to contain nearly 30,000 US troops and over their heads and on the beaches a live fire exercise was also planned. The first phase, scheduled to last from 22 to 25 April, saw the convoys and supporting ships leave and pass through Lyme Bay and was completed satisfactorily. But the second phase concerning the landings saw two major disasters.

On 26 April, the 1st Battalion completed their final practice landing in Exercise Fabius 1. The crew of the *Empire Javelin* welcomed the men on board, the men filed up the wooden gang planks with all their equipment as they knew how to do, they entered their boats, the Merchant Navy crews got them down the side of the *Empire Javelin* without a hitch and the Royal Navy crews took them into the beach in formations of six boats wide across in line – with RN Sub-Lieutenant Jimmy Green chatting away to Captain Taylor Fellers as if they had known each other for years. This was just a Battalion-sized landing for the units that had been earmarked to be the first to land on OMAHA and Dog Green.

The exercise went well, Captain Fellers in his debrief did not need them to change anything – except 'get out of the damned boats quicker' – they were as trained, fit and ready to go as they possibly could be. Each company in the 116th looked to be the best and in the recruitment of new officers, only the best of the new young officers in the 29th Division were posted to them.

Fellers had been born on 10 June 1914 and was now 33 and looking forward to his birthday, while his other officers in Company A were all much younger. First Lieutenant Ray Nance, who had been with Fellers from the earliest days in Bedford, was now 28 and had stayed the course and was a reliable and respected platoon officer. Drafted in alongside Nance was 23-year-old First Lieutenant Clyde Tidrick from Beloit, Kansas. When war came, Clyde enlisted in early 1942 and was very quickly selected for officer training where he excelled in leadership and was always popular with any unit he served with and then he was posted to Company A – probably because he had such courage in command and was certainly cut out for promotion. One of the boys from New York was First Lieutenant Alfred Anderson. Working as a driver with his father when war broke out, Alfred was another for whom war created an opportunity to excel in so many new ways and, having made sergeant, he was also selected for officer training, no doubt the great pride of his father who was also a driver in Queens, and promoted to first lieutenant before being posted to Company A, 116th Infantry. Right up until the very last few days, the battalion reinforced their leading companies with extra officers and men – almost as if they were aware of some new information.

Within the other ranks there were men who had joined the company as early as 1942 when the roll stood at only ninety-four. They had been with Captain Fellers and his fellow National Guardsmen from Bedford through the journey of *Queen Mary*, Tidworth and Ivybridge. Private First Class Dominic Surro, whose parents were from Ariano, Italy, was from Worcester Massachusetts. Private First Class James Elam was from Scott County, Virginia where his parents owned a small farm. Tall and rangy, he was a handsome and confident soldier as was New Jersey born Private First Class John Cerone who had worked in a laundry in 1940 before being drafted very early and allocated with Company A along with John Barnes. Private First Class Thompson Dicks was from Williston

South Carolina and all the way from Delaware came Private First Class Water Brinton. Brinton's father was a machinist in a shipyard in Wilmington – not where the *Empire Javelin* was being built, but in Wilmington Delaware. Another soldier from West Virginia was Private Arnold Baker. One of the oldest men in the Company, Arnold had been born in 1909 in Monroe County. Again, his family owned a small farm and he was almost as much a boy from Bedford as the rest. Assigned to Company A because of his physical fitness and strength, Private Baker caught up with the unit in Ivybridge in 1943 along with Private Lester Laing who had run a pool room in Faquier County before the draft and was now also based at Uphill Camp, Ivybridge.

Arriving in 1943 to catch up with Company A in Ivybridge had been Private First Class Joseph Humbert from Indiana and 30-year-old Private First Class Melvin Ellinger from Augusta County, Virginia who worked in a manganese mine before the draft caught up with him and posted him to Company A. All these men had survived and completed the massive training programme that Company A had been through and they were as ready as any Bedford Boy to land in Normandy. Numerous sons of Polish families also served in the 29th Division one of which was Private Michael Dziuma who was also drafted in early 1943 and sent as a replacement to Company A of the 116th in Ivybridge where he would have met Sergeant Harry Pope Hamilton who had joined Company A in 1941.[52]

Sergeant Orville McNew was born on 6 September 1921 in Middlesborough, Kentucky. His father Hugh was a coal miner and Orville was drafted in August 1942 and, after basic training, was posted to Company A of the 116th. Showing good leadership skills and strong character, Orville was one of the platoon sergeants on D-Day. Living in Lehigh County, Pennsylvania, but originally from Randolph County in West Virginia, was Staff Sergeant Samuel Baker. Samuel was drafted in August 1941 and joined Company A in Tidworth and remained with the company as a key personality of the unit. Aged 29, he was only a few weeks younger that Captain Fellers and was one of the dynamic leaders of the Company and was always first out of the boats in any training exercise. Another of the Company A Staff sergeants on whom Captain Fellers depended was Edward Andrew Vargo. Born in Prince George's County Virginia, he was the fifth of eleven children – his parents were emigrants from Slovakia and were farmers. Edward decided to enlist, which he did at Richmond VA on 3 May 1941 and was immediately assigned to Company A of the 116th and trained with the unit from then on both in the USA prior to embarking on the *Queen Mary* and serving at Tidworth and Ivybridge. Staff Sergeant Vargo suffered from bronchitis and tonsilitis and struggled with the training on Dartmoor but was so well respected that he stayed on in the Company right up to and including D-Day and was a member of boat team number 6.

Working alongside the four companies of the 1st Battalion were the support teams which included the Medical Detachment that saw to all the illnesses and training accidents of Companies A, B, C and D. Leading that detachment was an officer who became well known to Captain Fellers and that was Captain Robert Barnes Ware. Born on 30 December, 1914 in Amherst County Virginia, Robert Ware married Martha Wood on 30 July 1938 and they had a son Robert Barnes Ware Jr. Graduating from medical school in 1940, at the outbreak of war Robert Sr. was working at the General Hospital in Lynchburg before volunteering for service where he was posted to lead the medical detachment of the 116th Infantry. It was Captain Ware that tried to help Captain Fellers deal with his acute sinusitis and keep him going up to and through D-Day. Captain Ware declared that he was determined to be landing in the first waves even though his role did not require him to do so.

All these men were now trained, they were resolved to see this mission through and they were part of a very close-knit family of warriors. All they needed now was good weather, for the Air Force to do its job and good luck.

The third of those three requirements was already struggling to be on parade. The next day, on 27 April, the second day of the practice landings where a much larger scale landing was due to unfold, poor communications between the supporting naval ships of 'Force U' for UTAH and the LSTs carrying men of the US 4th Division dogged the movement plans of the larger formations of ships. A slower convoy time across Lyme Bay meant that a change in H-Hour was needed and an extra hour of H+1 added to the landing time – crucially, the new time of landing did not get communicated to the landing ships. The result was that the first waves landed successfully from the large LSTs – down ramps from the sides of boats beached on the sand but they noticed there was no live covering fire bombardment – but the second wave an hour later and now landing at the original H-Hour, was heavily shelled by their own ships, who were firing from ten miles out to sea and at the new time for H-Hour, and as many as 450 infantrymen may have died struggling to get off the beach. Many bodies were never found as they had simply been blasted to nothing and the shell holes that were meant to cover their way in now became the only places to survive on the beach from their own friendly fire. Had it been the day before, then there would have been no Company A to remember and many if not all of them would have been anonymous and covered up losses in the preparations D-Day – which is what happened to the men on 27 April.[53]

The epic failures in communications should have been the main lessons from Exercise Tiger but on the second day, 28 April an even worse episode occurred when Convoy T-4 moved across Lyme Bay in the early morning where they were ambushed by the unexpected arrival of nine German E Boats of the 5th E-Boat Flotilla. At 01.30 all hell broke loose as four pairs of E Boats attacked at right-angles to the long line-ahead formation of the convoy. Two hours later, after fighting in the pitch-dark night sky punctured by flares, flames and explosions, four of the heavily laden transport ships had been sunk. There was only one instead of two Royal Navy destroyers to protect them as HMS *Scimitar* had been sent back to Plymouth having collided with one of the LSTs and her replacement arrived after what was called the Battle of Lyme Bay. Poor communications were again partly to blame as the LSTs and British naval headquarters operated on different frequencies so could not communicate with each other.

By morning, two LSTs had been sunk – LST-531 sank within six minutes of being torpedoed and with a loss of 424 US Army and Naval personnel. Another LST had been hit by friendly fire and one limped back to port. In all, 749 men of the US 4th Division were killed that night. Trawlers and mine sweepers were sent out to save what survivors they could, but the water was so cold that many died of hypothermia and fell under the water asleep before they could be saved. Bodies in full packs with lifejackets – many unopened – were washed up on the beaches of the south coast for months after the disaster and, for the sake of public morale – Eisenhower ordered that the whole tragedy be covered up and the losses merged into the post D-Day casualty lists.

The results of this tragic event were far reaching, not least on the morale of the senior officers of the 29th Division. If the Naval bombardment was again to fall at the wrong time and short of the cliffs and bluffs of OMAHA, then D-Day would be a slaughter for their men. The Navy had to get the time and the distance right. If the communications were so poor that landing ships could not talk to supporting escorts, then what would happen off OMAHA and UTAH when not dozens, but thousands of ships were present?

Eisenhower's conclusions were rapid and far reaching and included the provision of small rescue ships with the landing craft to collect survivors, standardised radio frequencies across all the landing forces and lifejacket training was ordered throughout the commands. Eisenhower also had to worry about leaks of the invasion preparations to the Germans. Not only were the E Boats able to report back to Paris and then Berlin that allied invasion preparations were well advanced, but ten American officers were amongst the missing – all of whom had the vital BIGOT level of security clearance. The 1994 study of D-Day by Stephen Ambrose suggests that Hitler noticed the similarity between Slapton Sands and the beaches of the Cotentin Peninsula which resulted in more reinforcements arriving on the Normandy coast in May 1944.[54]

Another less considered result was the attitude of both the British and American Navies. Dropping hundreds of high explosive shells onto a narrow beach was an intricate task at the best of times and now that nearly 500 men had been killed, there must have been a real determination that this should not be repeated on D-Day. There is no evidence to support the notion but it would certainly make logical sense for captains of ships to ask their gunnery officers to make sure that whatever else they did, the shells must not fall short. When Company A eventually landed on DOG GREEN, there was not one shell hole from the vital naval bombardment – every round had overshot the target and fallen inland – even over the German defences and this was to be a critical failure in the attack plan. Were naval gunners so acutely sensitive to what had happened at Slapton that they did not wish to risk shelling their own men again? Were the ranges of the naval guns increased to avoid another case of friendly fire – but so much that they missed the beach altogether? These were small but vital decisions that could have a pivotal impact on the progress of the initial landings by the 116th infantry.

For the rest of the Division the orders were clear – the disasters of the Exercise Tiger operations were to be forgotten and not discussed at any time. The survivors of the 4th Division units were sworn to secrecy pending courts martial and it was viewed as critical that the civilian population did not become aware of what had happened. As things turned out, it was impossible to keep such an event secret – even today, rumours swirl about temporary graves being dug in their hundreds in the ploughed fields of Devon, bodies being loaded onto special night time trains and corpses washing up on beaches along the English Channel. Debates continue about both the causes and the effects of this event, but one thing is certain, the news of these large-scale training exercises onto large open beaches still did not cause enough alarm in Berlin to alter the German strategic position – if it had then the history of the war and the world could have been very different.

Within Company A, Captain Fellers and his officers knew what had happened – briefings tumbled down the various command levels and a gag order was put in place. This of course did not stop new fears and concerns striking the stomachs of the officers. Captain Fellers had been feeling increasingly gloomy and depressed about the coming operation and the euphoria of being chosen to be the first Americans to land on D-Day had been replaced by the reality that they may not live to see the beach being taken or to climb the cliffs where the Germans were waiting for them. Slapton Sands just made things worse and seemed like a bad omen. Long after the war, Lieutenant Nance, one of the few officers who survived from Company A, recalled how:

'He (Fellers) was all excited when he told me about the disaster. It upset him a whole lot. He said it could have been us guys. We had done exactly what they had done, only two days before them. [Operation Tiger] made us even more aware of our responsibilities. We had these young men's lives in our hands. It deeply affected us.'[55]

Captain Fellers shared the news of the recent events with the other lieutenants in Company A – Ray Nance was one, John Clements was another. Between them they agreed not to discuss any aspect of what had happened with the men – even though they too – as is the nature of gossip – had heard the news on the wind – they then also decided not to discuss the matter with their officers. While a certain sober glumness descended over the unit as the men took in how lucky they had been and how dangerous the situation they now faced, huge Marshalling Areas (MAs) had been set up across southern England. Each MA was commanded by a Brigadier from the British Army and, together with a Brigade level staff, every aspect of feeding, arming, fuelling, preparing, entertaining and medical cover was put in place before the troops received their movement orders. It was simply a mammoth effort and the backdrop to OVERLORD which is so often overlooked. Within each MA the sausage shaped camps were erected to hold a specific number of men and vehicles and each was given a code letter and number. For the 116th Infantry the MA was D and the sub area D6 which could take the 3,600 men and 510 vehicles of the entire Regiment.

The Sausages are Stuffed.......

'Brave men rejoice in adversity, just as brave soldiers triumph in war.'
Lucius Annaeus Seneca

The final move for Company A, now composed of fit, emotionally ready and focussed men from across the United States came on 18 May as they were loaded with all their equipment onto trucks to take them to the forward containment area – or D6 – in preparation for D-Day. As the *Empire Javelin*, now anchored off Portland Bill along with hundreds of other ships of all shapes and sizes, waited for their return, Company A and its fellow companies of the 116th Infantry plus all the Headquarters units moved into their vast tented sausage.

The fields of tents were reminiscent of a Roman legionary camp that stretched for miles in the distance – except that these tents were green to camouflage them from any remaining German reconnaissance aircraft willing to take a chance by flying over the south coast. Erected over the previous three weeks, the men of the entire 1st, 4th and 29th United States Infantry Divisions could be found in tented communities together with the 82nd and, together with the 101st United States Airborne Division, comprised the assault troops of the largest amphibious invasion force ever assembled in human history.

Totalling some half million men, the sausages within the MAs were a marvel of military precision. Containing sleeping areas, messing, medical and equipment storage areas, they could be found in farmer's fields – the cows having been removed elsewhere – in woodland, parallel to the sides of roads, rivers and great stately homes. The 116th Infantry found themselves on the garden boundary of Dewlish House just northeast of Puddletown in Dorset and now only fourteen miles from the *Empire Javelin*. The elliptical shapes of the tented towns lent themselves to the nickname 'sausages' and had been in the planning phase since COSSAC had begun its work back in 1943. The faceless and nameless planners were still weaving their web around the Bedford Boys whose destiny was no longer in their own hands and the men could feel it.

Two further layers of design ensured that all was now ready. A ring of steel with fences and sentries surrounded each sausage and there was very little movement in or out. Local village communities had been forcibly removed from the surrounding area to reduce the potential for spying and even shops and pubs remained open – inside the security area – allowing locals to make money but not be allowed out until the invasion had begun. How they managed to get any fresh fish inside remains a mystery. Secondly every unit area from Division Headquarters down to Company level had a BIGOT tent. Inside every BIGOT was a different landscape model that directly resembled their area of beach and their mission targets. This was the first time anyone was now able to take in where they were going and what their mission was – an awe-inspiring sight after all the months of training and no mean feat of production by the war games departments of the War Office. Inside each tent was the final summation of years of the brave sacrifices of thousands of French resistance agents, many of whom languished in German prison cells or concentration camps. Aerial photographs accompanied each model of the beach on boards around the tent and the size and shape of the defences, as far as they could tell, were discussed in detail with what type of charge was needed to destroy them.

Captain Taylor Fellers and his young officers now stood in their green, high security intelligence tent and finally got some long, detailed looks at the target they had been trained to take. As Fellers discussed the landings, it was clear that it was vital to get off the landing craft as fast as possible. They were going to have to get out in single files because of the design of the LCCs they were using – these were not Higgins boats as people had assumed where a single ramp dropped and men three or even four abreast could exist at the same time, but the LCA (2) that was discussed in earlier chapters and this meant the centre file followed by the left and then the right. While they were in the boat they were a sitting target for any machine gun and fanning out right and left would at least help – but they had to get out – and hopefully straight onto shingle or sand and not into water.

Fellers must have felt numb in his own stomach trying to pump up the confidence of his young Lieutenants Nance, Anderson and Tidrick. They were so very young and had never been under live fire, they were National Guardsmen, their time would come and with that would be the awareness that battlefield casualties fall all around and for all sorts of different reasons. They had never experienced mortars landing amongst them or shells aimed towards them – they had always gone way overhead. They had never seen men screaming, real fear and faced death right there in front of them – how would they react? Would they go? Fellers looked to his cohort of strong and experienced staff sergeants, men like Vargo, Baker, Hamilton, Earl Parker and McNew. These were men he had worked with, laughed with, barked orders at, praised and condemned for eighteen months at least and now they were very close to that time when their roles – to be first out the boats with their officers – faced the final test. Of course, there was always Master Sergeant Wilkes – there as an anchor and stick to keep them all moving forward, ever forward.

In that tent and looking at that model on the board, none had any idea of the names of their enemy or what they were doing at that particular time. They had been told it was going to be something of a cake walk. The 716th German division was an 'ear, nose and throat division' static, unable to fight in a mobile way and would already have collapsed by the time of the landings due to the massive bombardments in advance. They didn't know the 716th Division had been recently reinforced and replaced.

They did know that Rommel had been helping to prepare the welcome they would receive on DOG GREEN beach but they did not know of Lieutenant General Dietrich Kraiss, whose division had so recently moved in to man those positions they now assessed in detail. Nor had they any idea that Lieutenant Colonel Fritz Zeigalmann was ensuring that each and every 'nest' was replete with as much ammunition as they could store or that Oberleutnant Hahn was the young Wehrmacht officer in charge of the Wilderstandnests they saw on their models of the beach. Lastly, they might never know that manning one key resistance point – WN72 – was a young private soldier Henrik Naube who at that very moment was testing firing the most powerful machine gun in the world – his MG42. As they stood in that tent there was so much that they did not know but what they did know was that it was the Verville Draw – D1 – that all their training had been preparing for – take the draw in the centre of their section of beach and they begin the start of the bridgehead that would begin the end of the war.

The Bedford Boys had come all the way from Virginia and trained for nearly three years for a mission that they only now understood. There it was. On a model board it did not look too much of a challenge but so much was not in their hands. Captain Fellers related to Lieutenant Nance more than once and more increasingly as D-Day drew near, that he felt he was not going to make it and that they could all be killed. Fellers had been unusually outspoken at a briefing by Colonel Canham pointing out that one man with a machine gun could control that entire beach. COSSAC had done everything it could think of to neutralise the defences with heavy bombing by the air forces, heavy shelling by the Navy and tanks on the beach to give them shelter – 'everything would be blasted to smithereens – a pushover' according to Lieutenant Ray Nance but even so, Fellers revealed that he was sure they would all be killed no matter how fit or equipped or well-trained they were as a Company.

As men wandered around, their heads full of instructions, orders and images of their own piece of the infinite jigsaw that was OMAHA beach, every company found itself on a 'street' – their own place to find via large blackboard maps around every sausage and, miraculously, the exact equipment for each unit was also stored on that same street. There was a sense that the Army had done its job well and was now 'fattening them up for Christmas'. Over a year previously, Chief of the Army, General Marshall, had made the planners look ahead to this very moment. In his mind's eye he wanted every man to be as well fed as they could manage. Again, the planners had reacted well and chicken, ham and steak formed the main meals whilst coffee and doughnuts were available 24 hours a day – especially necessary for the paratroopers all of whose exercises were at night. Movies were run in tents in every sausage to try to dull the boredom and therefore the fear and some units ran their own little shows and theatres to keep the men's minds occupied and generate laughter amongst the millions of butterflies in hundreds of thousands of stomachs across southern England.

Perhaps seeing the wooden box walls full of explosive charges and brand-new equipment in camp, together with now being able to mix with all their friends from the other companies inside the wire, gave the Bedford Boys a feeling of growing confidence that they were going to complete this mission and survive. Certainly, their letters home suggested an upbeat message hidden within the fear that they suppressed. In his interviews with surviving wives and sisters, Alex Kershaw relates how many of the men wrote home at this time and, despite Captain Fellers' strict instructions to his officers to be very tough with censorship as they read what would soon be the final letters to be posted, the sentiments arrive with us so many decades on with the same feelings that they were written in May 1944. In those green tents within the sausages of the Marshalling Areas, the Bedford Boys were able to sit and think calmly about the very long journey that they had been a part of and which was now very nearly over.

For Sergeant John Schenk, training and membership of Company A had always been positive and he had been committed since the earliest days back in Bedford. The offer of a commission had come his way and this would have seen John promoted to Second Lieutenant but it would also have meant leaving the unit and not landing with them on D-Day. According to Alex Kershaw, Lieutenant Ray Nance tried to persuade him to take it but Ivylyn Schenk recalled that her new husband, with his slight frame, sparkling blue eyes and great smile, felt that such a thing was the equivalent of desertion and he turned it down. Since marching out of Bedford on 18 February 1941, John Schenk had stuck to his agreement with Ivylyn to think about her every day at 8pm and she at 5pm Eastern Standard Time. This was a ritual for them both. For over three years war had kept them apart and their young, married lives were blighted by separation, but every day for that whole period each kept their vigil and this continued right up until 6 June 1944 when, on that day and forever afterwards, he would not be able to continue the same commitment.

Raymond Hoback wrote to his parents about his severe nosebleeds and how he had been offered a medical discharge which of course he had refused as he wanted to be part of the assault with the men who had been his childhood and adult friends all his life.

Earl Parker always asked after his daughter Danny, the child conceived before he left Bedford but whom he had never seen. Mrs George Parker did everything she could back in Bedford to help the war effort and wrote to her son Earl as if he were in the next room, bringing him up to date with all the little events that composed her world and from which he was so far away.

Sergeant Grant Yopp enjoyed his twenty-first birthday on 27 May. Still so very young and yet so experienced in warfare and a key part of the Bedford Boys as anyone. Captain Taylor Fellers was a young man, in years at least, and looked forward to his thirtieth birthday on 10 June – less than a month away now.

Nick Gillaspie had more time than ever now that final training was over to write even more letters and one can imagine him sitting on his low camp bed composing his thoughts perhaps more clearly than he had ever done before. His flow of letters would continue to arrive long after he lay dead in the water and sand of Normandy.

With each day that passed in May, the tension throughout all the camps increased. Each man has a breaking point and some showed this with short-tempers, others by playing baseball for hours on end and, no matter what they did to while away the hours, no one knew when the call might come to get their kit and move out. On one occasion Sergeant Allen Huddleston, as recalled to Alex Kershaw, was playing unarmed combat exercises with another Bedford boy, Sergeant Robert Goode. Huddlestone broke his ankle and, despite all his training, he was out of the invasion. One more disaster befell the regiment when sixteen men of Captain Zappacosta's Company B were killed or wounded by an explosion. Men were transferred from the other companies to cover the losses – one of whom was Hal Baumgarten.

As May turned into June, Colonel Canham asked that a letter be read out to all the men in his regiment. Trying to inspire determination and common sense into men now riddled with a lack of confidence and uncertainty could not be done with words alone – he was going to have to do it on the beach. But he did say one thing that the men would remember as they crossed the channel: 'To each one of you Happy Landing and come off those craft fighting like hell.' A further sign that D-Day was coming any day was the issue of life insurance policies each worth $10,000 and each man made out his will assigning the policy and any other items to those he loved back home.

More new arrivals.......

With all the attention on the final paperwork, it was down to Captain Fellers to welcome the last new arrival to Company A in the form of First Lieutenant Kearfott. Aged 25, Benjamin Rives Kearfott had been born in Henry County, Virginia in November 1919. His father was Dr Clarence Kearfott, a druggist in Martinsville. Like Taylor Fellers, Benjamin had volunteered for the Virginia National Guard and served in the enlisted ranks until he was commissioned on 3 February 1941. Just prior to leaving for England, the then Second Lieutenant Kearfott was married to his sweetheart Mary Thebo Jennings at Lynchburg – on Valentine's Day, 1942. Another young officer marked out for promotion in the 29th Division, Kearfott proved himself to be a talented and popular officer, driven to command and with that sense of duty and determination that characterised the men of Virginia. There are two possible reasons to account for this. One of the platoon leaders could have dropped out – unlikely at this later stage but still a possibility. Another more plausible reason is that, given we know Captain Fellers was still suffering from his serious sinus infection, it was possible that Lieutenant Colonel Metcalfe wanted a replacement company commander alongside Fellers in case he just could not function before or on D-Day and Kearfott was selected for that role – in other words he was sent as an insurance policy alongside Captain Fellers. This would account for Kearfott being a member of LCA 1015 – the landing craft led by Captain Fellers on D-Day itself. A further even more likely reason is that the regiment expected heavy casualties in the first wave and over populated the leading companies with men. In fact, Company A would be well over strength in both officers and enlisted men by the time of D-Day.[56]

But Kearfott was only one of a number of new arrivals. A letter written to Cornelius Ryan dated 24 June 1958 tells us a little more. Ryan had advertised throughout America for information on survivors for the first waves on D-Day – naturally there were not many but the VFW – Veterans of Foreign Wars Association based in Pittsburgh, PA did know of one. T-5 Woodrow Welsch was one of the very few men from Company A who would survive D-Day. They mentioned that Woodrow landed in boat No. 7 but also that 'The company was overstrength – expecting heavy casualties. Which it did.'

The letter continued that there were 226 men on the Company roll for the invasion – hence the need for seven LCAs and not the standard six for a company formation. Lieutenant Kearfott was clearly there as an additional officer – someone who could stand in when the others fell and everyone knew this.

One other new officer also arrived at some point before D-Day and that was a young Second Lieutenant Edward Marcellus Gearing. Like those before him, Gearing would have been brought into Company A because of his leadership skills, his suitability for the role and his courage. He joined perhaps the best team of officers in the regiment.

Edward Gearing was born on 16 January 1924 and grew up in Woodstock, Virginia. The son of a local and respected doctor, who was also the physician for the Massanutten Military Academy, Edward and his two brothers all attended the military academy for their education – so a military way of life, self-reliance and discipline were well established in his character. A career in medicine seemed to beckon Edward, but he was tempted into joining the officer school in Fort Benning, Georgia where his qualities were recognised and encouraged. We know that Lieutenant Edward Gearing (the middle name Marcellus taken from his paternal grandfather) was based in Devon in 1943 – perhaps with Company A at Uphill Camp but more likely with another company in the 116th. His regular service marked him out as a valuable junior officer for this Virginian regiment and, prior to D-Day, Gearing became part of Company A.

Final Orders are received......

On 2 June, Company A received their final movement orders: they were to pack immediately and be ready to move the next day to Portland just a few miles south of their camp, ready to embark for France. As this moment arrived, Captain Fellers had been admitted into a local medical unit in Dewlish House on the edge of the camp. Suffering from sinusitis is awful at the best of times, suffering from the complaint just as you are needed to go into battle and cross the English Channel was a whole new level of discomfort. The choice was stark – stay where he was and be treated or drag himself out of bed, take what pain killers he could, sweat through the nausea and discharge himself – he chose the latter and within an hour stood, looking very sick, in the Company A mess where two boys from Bedford – James Crouch and Cedric Broughman – were checking all the feeding supplies were in order.

After some hours of sleep, Fellers was dressed and packed with the rest of his men. According to Alex Kershaw his words on that final parade were:

'I've trained you, I'll die with you too if it comes to that.'

Chapter Fourteen

The Final Departure for Portland
and the *Empire Javelin*

'It doesn't take a hero to order men into battle. It takes a hero to be one of those men who goes into battle.'

General Norman Swarzkopf

'Early in June the Javein arrived at Portland and took on board from Weymouth Harbour the 1st Battalion of the 116th Infantry Regiment, 29th Division along with other support units. They were a friendly but buy shy bunch of fresh-faced country lads who must have felt at home in Ivybridge – a small town in Devonshire, where they had trained for the invasion.'

Sub-Lieutenant George 'Jimmy' Green[57]

In the last few days of a very hot May heatwave, Weymouth, Portland and all the ports of the south coast of England were a seething mass of ships, men and stores waiting to be loaded. The men and equipment of nearly forty divisions that had been parked and camped were now on the move towards their embarkation points. During the previous four weeks, much of the heavy equipment had already been loaded – there was just nowhere near enough wharf capacity for all the ships to dock and load at the same time. The big supply and logistics ships had been already loaded weeks before and these were followed by artillery, tanks, field hospitals and command elements – the infantry were loaded last of all and this began in earnest on Sunday 4 June. As each ship was loaded, a barrage balloon appeared in the sky above it, manned by a Black crew of five. These men appeared on every ship – not a problem on the British ships, but certainly had to be catered for on the US ships. The loading went on 24 hours a day and the roads around the small villages and towns slowly started to clear until one day, they had all disappeared.

By 4 June the SS *Empire Javelin* had been cleaned, fully fuelled, the sick bay was primed and ready, guns were manned, she was armed and ammunitioned and, on that Sunday afternoon, Captain McMahon and her crew awaited the arrival of the 1st Battalion, 116th Infantry and expected to see them marching along the quaysides towards their ship at any moment. Numerous contemporary images exist capturing the atmosphere of vast numbers of men and ships collected in tiny British ports, yellow life jackets pepper every image of men marching in columns to their destination and destiny. That destiny had been scheduled to begin in Normandy on Monday 5 June and the ship needed to leave the previous afternoon if she was to be off the coast of Normandy at 02.00 the next morning.

The patchy sun had almost disappeared and peeped through increasing cloud on the south coast during 4 June occasionally lighting up the zig zag camouflage and glinting off the grey steel hulls of hundreds of ships – troop transports, rocket ships, Landing Ship Tanks, Landing Ship Infantry, Destroyers, Frigates, Minesweepers and everywhere one looked there were landing craft. Either hanging on the sides of ships from davits out at sea on the larger ships like *Empire Javelin* or stored in the decks of troop transports ready for thousands of men to scramble down the nets. The air was full of noise as if a stick from the heavens had roused a wasps' nest of green, yellow and grey. Swarms of infantrymen marched in step and in different directions along the harbour side – some led by their officers and others by guides in Royal Navy blue and white but all of them wearing combat uniforms, some with scrim nets over their helmets, some with chin straps undone. It was easy to recognise men from the 29th Infantry division as 'Uncle Charlie' General Gerhardt had specifically stipulated that his men would have their chin straps done up – much to the annoyance of his 15,000 officers and soldiers.

The tight-knit family of men from Bedford Virginia were there too – at last – and mixed in with them were the old comrades of 1941 and 1942, officers and men, together with guys who arrived only the day before – they were now all in this together. Arriving and halting by platoon, then company and battalion sized chunks, men were able to exchange glances at each other, noticing small details and perhaps remembering something that they had been told not to forget, their minds checking and rechecking that all was where it was meant to be. The Blue & Gray '*monad*' shoulder patch shone out from the drab light brown combat jackets of the Americans and it could be seen everywhere on this particular section of Weymouth Harbour. Glances became shouts, shouts became insults and nervous jokes; runs to the 'heads' for that last minute pee were a constant giveaway that all was really not normal anymore. Brave young men, unaware of what was ahead, cocky and innocent, guilty and demure, they were all the same now and all embarked on the same journey.

Officers greeted each other, relaxed saluting of those only just senior to them, crisp parade ground salutes to colonels, brigadier generals and above. Shaking of hands with those of equivalent rank while NCOs cajoled and encouraged rather than barked as they organised the men into tight formations ready for boarding. PFCs whistled to the Red Cross and ATS girls serving tea and delivering messages from the innumerable headquarters units across the harbour.

As they looked up at the hull of the SS *Empire Javelin* it would have been a familiar sight, they knew her smell, green colour and noise, they knew the noises her engines made and they recognised the white pale faces of the 'limey' naval crews manning the anti-aircraft guns high above them. Looking up they would also have noticed the new layers of grey clouds flooding up from the west coast – the weather was indeed changing rapidly. The drab dull green paint of the hull was in good order as the *Javelin* was still not much more than a year old. Hand-painted on by hundreds of dockyard workers back in Wilmington just for this event and here for this moment where courageous infantryman and dedicated ship, finally came together, she looked fit and ready for duty – her landing craft fuelled and checked ready to go. Both stood in the grey clouds and partial sun of a blustery Monday afternoon. Boarding time for the 116th was scheduled ahead of all the other units on OMAHA as they, together with the very slow LCTs with their tanks on board, needed to be ahead of the rest of Force 'O' on the morning of 5 June 1944.

Carrying Bangalore torpedoes, radios, satchel charges, rifles, packs, ammunition, first aid kits, maps, binoculars, machine guns, mortar tubes and mortar plates, ammunition boxes and all the equipment needed to break through Rommel's Atlantic Wall. At last, after hours of waiting, Master Sergeant John Wilkes got the nod to start his men boarding. Wilkes himself was not immune to the need to constantly suppress the emotional pulls of memory – those days of being at a basketball game or on a picnic with Betty up on Smith Mountain overlooking Bedford must have seemed like a different life in a different world as his friends as well as soldiers filed past, some with a comment or a quip, others in silence as they started up the gangway onto the *Empire Javelin*.

Long after the war was over, Ann Ferguson Cooper in the United States was given a bundle of papers. On behalf of Francis Henderson, who was on board the *Empire Javelin* later that year on 28 December 1944, and her father Chauncey Dwight Fergusson Jr who was also on board, Ann Henderson passed these documents to Maritime Quest – an international website dedicated to collecting material on ships. In amongst these was a long letter entitled Schoichet's account of the sinking of the *Empire Javelin*. We are not concerned with the sinking at this point of our story but part of this account described what it was like trying to get on board the Javelin from the point of view of a soldier in full kit:

There have been varying estimates on how long we waited before we were permitted to board HMS Empire Javelin *which was laying at anchor when we arrived. It must have been well over four hours. The end of this period found us sitting, lying down, in short, sprawled all over the docks and grumbling at the apparent unnecessary delay. At long last the line started to move jerkily and we struggled back under our gear to board.*

The ship was long and sleek and rode easily beside the pier. Most of us, as we mounted the gangway, were mentally comparing the Empire Javelin to the Aquitania, on which we had made the Atlantic crossing.

The decks were very narrow in many places. She had not been built as a troop carrier. In spots it was impossible for a man to squeeze by with full pack and duffel bag. So, frequently, we had to turn sideways, dragging the bags after us or pushing them before us. There was a good deal of bad humoured muttering at this.

Our arrival only added to the confusion and shouting. The line crawled around corners and along walls. We descended what seemed to be innumerable stairways. Then the line stopped completely. We fidgeted and griped until word filtered back up to us that there was no more room below."

From Schoichet's Account[58]

This short but telling extract tells us just how awful the conditions were – unable to move forwards or backwards, laden with equipment in corridors designed for one man at a time. One can imagine how the crammed passageways on board the *Javelin* for Company A and the other four companies of men added to the signs of pre-battle tension – which were everywhere. With grenades and ammunition, it was not just explosive from the point of view of loaded weapons. Both Master Sergeant Wilkes and Captain Fellers felt the tension more acutely than the rest of the company as they knew full well that tempers were already running high and any little spark could ignite into a fight amongst trained killers. Their clothes reeked of waterproofing oil that they had soaked into their clothes, together with the sweat of anxious waiting, their weapons also carried that sharp unmistakable smell of gun oil with barrels cleaner than a scientist's microscope ready for them to start pumping through the masses of ammunition hanging from their limbs. Smells enliven the senses more than anything else and each individual smell triggered a subconscious thought but a combination of these fragrances created a heady, drug-like mix of anticipation of battle and put then men on edge. Those who had once been chirpy, cheeky and could always see a joke somewhere were suddenly stilled as they put their boots onto the decks of the *Javelin* and all the Navy could do was watch and compare the men with their new nickname – 'the suicide wave'.

In fact it was not just Company A and those coming in shortly after them that felt like the suicide wave – someone had to get them to the beach and that meant that Sub-Lieutenant Jimmy Green was also part of this elite group. He and his naval ratings had their vital part to play and they had some pretty good notions of what the run into the beach was going to be like from their training in Scotland and at Slapton Sands and past acquaintances were now renewed as he and Taylor Fellers saluted each other and moved through the ship as Company B now started to make their way up the gangway. On the quayside stood Companies C and D and mingling with the men was Lieutenant Colonel Metcalfe, putting a smile on for the display of confidence his men needed to see and leading his officers up onto the *Javelin* looking every inch a graduate of one of the best military academies in the world – West Point. His regular army service stood him in good stead as he moved in between his National Guard platoons and welcomed his young, battle inexperienced officers to what General Bradley had already called 'ringside seats for the greatest show on earth.' Alongside Lieutenant Colonel Metcalfe was Major Thomas Spencer Dallas as Battalion XO – Executive Officer – together with the signallers and men of the Headquarters Company of the 1st Battalion, 116th Infantry.

The burdens of command

As Captain Taylor Fellers walked around the green tents of his men in their sausages on 3 June, under a sunny sky with a whiff of change in the air and battled with his own personal demons, fears of imminent death and burdens of command, so did a fellow officer, second only in seniority to the commander of the entire American Army General George Marshall.

Amongst the many documents and papers of the Eisenhower Presidential Library in Abilene in Kansas, sits an inconspicuous typed letter which is in fact a memorandum dictated or written from notes by General Eisenhower as a record of his thoughts on 3 June 1944. No doubt composed for posterity, these paragraphs display the thinking of the Supreme Commander of the Allied Expeditionary Forces in Europe as he sat at his desk in Southwick House.

Eisenhower reveals his thoughts on a number of subjects and through the prism of a man that cares for his troops. All generals care, but some are more caring than others. After revealing his frustrations with General de Gaule – who seemed as interested in securing his control over post war France as he was in defeating the Germans – and the consequent difficulties of communicating with essentially political groups within the tangled web of the French Resistance and their role in only two days' time, Eisenhower reflects on the most important unknown, the weather. It was not just a question of getting the men over the Channel without sinking – it was being able to assess how they would fare in a landing with unfavourable weather. It was not Kansas where Eisenhower could set his watch by the seasons and he starts the section off by saying:

'*The weather in this country* [the UK] *is practically unpredictable. For some days our experts have been meeting almost hourly and I have been holding Commander-in-Chief meetings once or twice a day to consider the reports and tentative predictions. While at this moment, the morning of June 3rd, it appears that the weather will not be so bad as to preclude the landings and will possibly even permit reasonably effective gunfire support from the Navy, the picture from the air viewpoint is not so good.*'

Memorandum, 3rd June, 1944[59]

Finding suitable weather that suited all parts of the military colossus that he commanded was going to be impossible and waiting for another month for the tides to be correct did not guarantee anything. What worked for the Airborne troops was high on his agenda – the infantry could manage, but high winds and terrible visibility would be disastrous for the Navy and the Paratroops.

'*My tentative thought is that the desirability for getting started on the nest favorable tide (5th June) is so great and the uncertainty of the weather is such that we could never anticipate really perfect weather coincident with proper tidal conditions, that we must go unless there is a real and very serious deterioration in the weather.*'[60]

What we can deduce from Eisenhower's thinking is this: there is no point in my checking reports from Stagg to see if there is going to be an improvement in the weather for the next few days, that's just not going to happen. What I need to make sure of is that it's not going to get any worse. In other words, Eisenhower was fixed on going from 3 June onwards, it was just making sure things did not deteriorate further.

There were other things on Eisenhower's mind. He was by profession a staff officer, and a brilliant one at that, although he had held many different commands including commanding officer of an Infantry regiment, the Fifteenth, and he knew the challenges the infantry would face. His concern over the beach obstacles was very real, and uppermost in his mind was getting the tides right so that his combat engineer units could work on blowing paths through the obstacles to allow the ongoing masses of reinforcements and materials needed to defend a bridgehead. Eisenhower knew that the losses amongst the engineers could be heavy but the entire plan rested on packing materials and men onto the beaches to overwhelm the enemy and thus it was a sacrifice worth making.

There was no port in the OVERLORD plan, the Mulberries would come into play later, but the beaches had to be cleared to allow tanks and vehicles onto the beaches and inland within 24 hours.

'It is because of their [the beach obstacles] *existence that we must land earlier on the tide than we had originally intended. This gives us a chance to go after them while they are still on dry land because if their bases were under water they would be practically impossible to handle.'*[61]

And then came the pivotal and crucial remark:

'If our gun support of the operation and the DD tanks during this period are both highly effective, we should be all right.'[62]

That same afternoon of 3 June, Eisenhower and his large team of planners, advisors, senior generals, admirals and air marshals attended endless meetings mostly centred around the weather forecasts. Now relocated to the combat Headquarters of Southwick House, just five miles north of Portsmouth, Group Captain Stagg increasingly took centre stage as the most important individual in the entire invasion forces as he and his meteorologists pored over every possible indication of coming weather. His burden was to inform Eisenhower, to whom he reported directly, what the chances were of decent enough weather for the invasion to proceed. The next day was earmarked as D-Day but the weather was changing fast – if they could not go on Monday 5, or by Tuesday 6 or Wednesday 7 June at the latest, then it would be another month of waiting and the entire invasion plan would have to be put on hold.

Out of the windows looking south towards the Channel, the Sunday afternoon clouds had gathered over Plymouth, Portsmouth, Dover and all the rest, the wind was up and sea was changing. The Bedford Boys and the 116th Infantry were already aboard the *Empire Javelin* and ready to go – if they were to arrive as the first wave at H-Hour then every second counted and the clock had been running now for over a month. As other units arrived from their sausages, the sun began to fall and the grey shadows lengthen – their landing times were long after the 116th would have landed – wave after wave was scheduled almost every twenty minutes for the whole of the next day but *Empire Javelin*, if she was going to make it on time with the rest of Force O, was heading towards her own deadline after eighteen months of waiting. The burden of command was heavy on Captain McClean – to him fell the task of delivering his prime cargo of determined, talented and courageous young Americans to the exact spot at the exact time that the OVERLORD planners had determined.

With 1,400 men on board, the *Empire Javelin* was packed and tense. All her holds were full of resting, joking and smoking young men, some up on deck, officers grouped together for yet one more final briefing or just trying to keep active. The smell of men, oil and sweat reminded some of the *Queen Mary* only this time they were not going to England, they were going to Normandy and the next morning. Climbing on board with their compatriot division, the First Infantry Division, combat cameraman Robert Capa quickly made new friends with some of the infantrymen of Colonel Taylor's 16th Infantry Regiment – Capa would land just up the beach from Company A of the 116th about an hour after the first wave and find himself pinned down on the beach – which is where 'The Magnificent Eleven' images were captured on film and for eternity.

As he had his equipment tightened by the infantrymen, Capa wondered what the hell he was doing there but as he looked right and left or forwards or backwards, he knew he was now part of something very special, very important and was recording history in the making. Whether he would survive to tell the tale was another matter.

The 551st

What Sub-Lieutenant Jimmy Green RN regarded as shyness was probably mistaken for unadulterated fear and foreboding as the Bedford Boys finally boarded the *Empire Javelin*. They had been away from home now for over eighteen months and boarding the wooden ramps up to the entry deck of the *Empire Javelin* must have felt similar to what a man felt climbing the scaffold to his untimely death. Was there a desperate desire to turn around and run, of course there was in some, but this was overridden by comradeship and the fellowship of arms that soldiers feel before a battle.

In his memoirs, Jimmy Green spoke proudly of his Royal Navy boat crews – the men of the 551st Landing Craft Assault Flotilla, RNVR. Like Jimmy, these men had been reservists before the war. Some of their colleagues would have been drafted into front line ships and already seen action in the North Atlantic, Mediterranean or on the Baltic Convoy routes, but they had been sent by Combined Operations Command to crew the LCIs of Operation OVERLORD. Allocated to their landing craft just like any other able seaman was posted to his combat ready ship, the ratings under Jimmy Green's command had practised so often all the aspects of getting their cargo of heavily armed men to shore, that they just wanted to get it over with. They knew that their LCAs were shallow in draught to enable them to get as close to the beach as possible, but this also meant that their stability was fragile and any sort of heave above half a metre would make them difficult to control. With an experienced RNVR officer in control of each landing craft, the attack plan stipulated that they must be in the water and ready to go by 04.00 – Force O having arrived off OMAHA, through its swept channel, by 02.00. Between 04.00 and the signal to proceed towards the beach, the LCAs of the 551st had to organise themselves – in partial dark and what were to be choppy seas – into their respective waves ready for their run in to hit the beach at H-Hour which was set for 06.30hrs on 5 June.

The Plan for the assault of DOG GREEN Beach

We might recall that the COSSAC planners had envisioned a preliminary saturation bombing of the beaches on OMAHA during the early morning to both destroy, disable and disorientate the Germans on the cliffs and bluffs. Then, ten minutes before H-Hour, or H-10, and over the heads of the ranks of advancing landing craft all along OMAHA beach, the US and British Navies would fire a crushing barrage onto the beaches to create the shell holes so vital for cover to get across the beach in case any German positions were still active.

The idea in the minds of the planners was for Company A, in their six LCAs, to sail slightly behind the tanks, by five minutes, on their five plus kilometre final run into the beach. We must bear in mind that the timing had been fixed for H-Hour to correlate with a turning tide and so each minute that the battle continued, the tide would be coming in further and covering the beach obstacles.

The Sherman tanks would land first five minutes before H-Hour at H-5 or 06.25 and on DOG GREEN this meant 16 Duplex Drive Sherman Tanks of Company B, 741st Tank Battalion. The tanks would provide further fire on any German positions and offer cover for the first wave of infantry to land five minutes later. To the right of the tanks on another beach this time codenamed CHARLIE, seventy men of the 2/Rangers would land just after the tanks at H-Hour itself, or 06.30, to secure the right flank of the main landing. Then the main landing would begin at H+1 with Company A, 116th Infantry in six LCAs with thirty Bedford Boys amongst their ranks, who would hit the beach at exactly 06.31 and OVERLORD would begin in earnest. The six LCAs from the SS *Empire Javelin* would fan out in a line across DOG GREEN beach with Sub-Lieutenant Jimmy Green and his crew in the lead boat with Captain Fellers and his company headquarters staff. The rest of the day was then to be wave after wave of carefully choreographed landings based on the clear expectation that within thirty minutes, Company A would already be engaged in clearing the resistance nests of lacklustre and second rate German infantry and on their way into and up to their objective which was the Verville Draw – D1 and thus off the beach. The Engineers could be kept busy starting to clear the beach obstacles which, with the rising tide, would become a real problem if they were not blown apart quickly.

Quickly getting his six (it would actually end up only being five) boats reversed off the beach, Jimmy Green would then see, following in close behind him, three LCAs of Engineers and another two LCAs of Rangers who were set to land at H+3 – only two minutes behind Company A. This was extremely tight as, even in the best practice runs, Fellers could not get his men off the boats in much under three minutes. The idea of a constant saturation of the beach in large numbers is clearly exemplified by the tight timetable. As Jimmy Green headed back towards SS *Empire Javelin* he would then expect to see the third wave coming in at H+30 or 07.00 and this would be the seven LCAs of Company B under Captain Ettore Zappacosta, who should have been circling waiting for their order to go. The third company of the battalion, Company D under Captain Walter Schilling would then land in their six LCAs at H+ 40 or 07.10. Landing with them, Company D would also have another batch of Engineers from the 121st Engineer Battalion and 149th Beach Clearance Company.[63] Finally, the last elements of the 116th Infantry Battalion would land. At H+50 three LCAs carrying Battalion Headquarters and Lieutenant Colonel Metcalfe would arrive along with a further six LACs of Company C under Captain Berthier Botts Hawks III with the intention of hopefully landing closer to the cliffs on the rising tide.

For the officers and men of Company A of the 116th Infantry, D-Day could now not come soon enough. They were briefed and ready. They did not know that events in France were already in motion – an event that could now not be stopped, only postponed.

The final hours in Normandy

'The troops were very receptive, very motivated, and discipline was good. I am not exaggerating when I say that the general spirit of the bunker was first class.'
Leutnant of Artillery, L. T.J. Wergens, Merville Battery, Normandy

What first hand participant accounts exist from the German side of the Normandy landings, and there are quite a number, suggest that, apart from continuing to build more tank obstacles and 'Belgian Gates' amongst the sand dunes of Normandy, all was pretty much as ready as it could be. It was now June and the weather forecast for the first week was dismal and felt the same as in Portland – winds were up, grey clouds had gathered and rain was on the way. Rommel felt so confident that nothing would happen that he briefed his subordinates in Paris and took his staff car home for a quick visit to his wife for her birthday. The waiting game had been going on for well over a year and the German troops of the 352nd were well ensconced into the defensive routines of life in Normandy. For them, the alcoholic Churchill and the risk averse Montgomery could ponder for as long as they liked about what to do and when to come – the tides came and went, French chickens were producing eggs and the milk and butter stocks were good – plus ammunition boxes were packed in every corner. With grey windy weather coming it did not seem likely that anything was happening this week. Mind you, it was not all quite as normal and one by one visible signs were there for those with the vision to see them and formed the basis of evening conversation inside the sleeping quarters of the resistance nests.

It was all about the Pigeons.

Inland bombing raids on transportation infrastructure had been increasing in recent weeks. A long way from the beaches maybe, but nevertheless there seemed to be a pattern to what was happening and in the various divisional and Army headquarters there was a sense of increased tension as reports came in of increased activity by the French resistance. Blowing up telegraph lines was not just something that happened at the last minute on Cornelius Ryan's *The Longest Day*, it had been steadily causing concern for some weeks – little did they know how much the resistance would do on the night of the invasion itself with disruption and murders in numerous locations.

In the monumental Heiber and Glanz edition of the stenographic records of Hitlers conferences there is a very small section on page 432. Under the heading Evening Situation Report, 18 May 1944 at the Berghof it comments as follows:

Present	*The Fuhrer*	*Rear Ad. V. Puttkamer*
	Colonel General Jodl	*Lt. Col. Borgmann*
	Maj. General Scherff	*Lt Col. Waizenegger*

Beginning 11pm

The West
Today there were two reconnaissance missions – rather, we can't call them missions. They were attempts to locate obstacles off the coast and to photograph them. A patrol of the 18th Luftwaffe Field division on the left wing eastward of Calais noticed some movement. An exchange of fire occurred. First, we thought they were our own forces, clashing with each other. But flashbulbs, spades and American flashlights were found – one man was wounded – so we have to assume that Americans had tried to photograph the obstacles. Likewise, two British officers were captured at the mouth of the Somme [River]. They had gone in with a rubber dinghy, and, according to interrogation completed so far, had been dropped by a British motor torpedo boat.'[64]

This rather plain and unspectacular section, of what was a far longer report, is attractive for our purposes for a number of reasons. Firstly, it shows that allied command was still sending in night-time reconnaissance efforts right up until almost D-Day itself – scheduled for only two weeks at that moment in time. Secondly, Hitler made no comments whatsoever in response, the verbal report simply went straight on to the next item. This suggests that Hitler had already made his mind up that the invasion was coming in the Calais area and such reconnaissance efforts merely confirmed this – exactly what Operation FORTITUDE had intended and the Special Operations Executive (SOE) spies had been working towards – there was no need for such missions anywhere near Calais other than to keep drip feeding misinformation even if it did result in the capture or death of the men sent on them. Interestingly the Germans noted that they were carrying American equipment and immediately, and incorrectly, inferred that it was an American raid because the Americans were the ones landing in Calais. Perhaps the brevity of this minute in the meeting also suggests that Hitler had many other problems to deal with in Russia, the Balkans and Italy tending to take up his time until something concrete happened in France.

One of the two officers captured at 'the mouth of the Somme' was Lieutenant Roy Wooldridge who was in fact taken to Rommel, after an initially painful interview with the Gestapo, where the Field Marshal asked to interview him personally. Unlike Hitler, Rommel was able to focus on just one area of the strategic battles being fought against the allies. Rommel also knew that the successful opening of a third front (after Russia and Italy) would be the end of Germany. Rommel's ears were already burning with the constant whispers amongst his closest officers of an assassination attempt on Hitler but maybe he saw stopping the allied landing as a way of also stopping the threats to Hitler's life too.

Wooldridge was a Royal Engineer and he had been sent on a real mission to check for mines along the SWORD beach area. His story is unique in meeting Rommel but also in as far as Rommel did not press him for information – he was just interested to see who was being sent to look at his beaches. Rather than being handed over to the Gestapo – where he would have been tortured and shot – Wooldridge ended up in a prisoner of war camp. Very lucky indeed given that he was not in uniform or carrying any papers when he was captured. We will never know what Rommel made of this but it is just possible that recent research that points to Rommel's complicity in the July Plot to assassinate Hitler may have influenced his decision to do nothing more than make sure Wooldridge was safe – rather than further reinforce his front.

Attacks on bridges, railway junctions and German staff officers had also increased with new orders to restrict movement between positions at night. While

Captain Fellers and his men emptied their tents and looked for their trucks to take them down to Portland Harbour, German higher echelon headquarters in Paris and Berlin, became so concerned that the invasion was coming that on the weekend of 3–4 June, the entire front was put on high alert:

> 'I remember that on the weekend just before [D-Day], there was a big alert, and the Divisional command put the alert code to the highest level. I don't know how they decided the levels, maybe due to intelligence or reconnaissance of shipping. So we actually expected an attack over the weekend. It was a warm weekend, and it seemed to go on forever, I remember that. But then on Monday 5th, the weather broke, and it rained, and the alert was reduced aswell, and we thought, "Well we're ok again".'
>
> Gunner Paul Breslau, Sturmgeschutz III self-propelled gun, 200 Assault Gun Battalion, 21st Panzer Division based south of Sword Beach.[65]

There was however, another, more subtle but vital sign that the invasion was imminent. Writing down his post-war memoirs in the United States, Lieutenant Colonel Zeigalmann recalled that the men of the 352nd stationed on the coastline had agreed – there were a lot more carrier pigeons trying to get to England from the OMAHA area than in the past. They had been shooting down far more than usual – and no doubt eating them. This increase in activity by the French Resistance may not have been substantial enough to make it onto the evening briefings at the Berghof but they were a clear signal that traffic to and from the French Resistance was at a peak. As the 116th Infantry had trained, moved and trained again so too had SOE dropped agents into France – both male and female – to help the resistance coordinate their actions in the run up to D-Day. The overall mission was to cause as much disruption and panic in the rear of the German lines as they could, to break their channels of communication, to sow disorder in military communications and confuse the enemy about what was happening.

As long ago as 1941, while the *Empire Javelin* was still just part of a paper file on a desk in Washington and St James's Park in London, and as A Company guarded the east coast of America from German submarines, the unknown and forgotten planners of COSSAC had been communicating with resistance groups across France.

From another London residence taken over for the war effort, not far from a hotel where the Headquarters of the Polish Army now resided and around the corner from where the Norwegian Resistance operated, the French had their own Etat-major des Forces Francaises de L'Interior (EMFFI). In theory, this group of rooms co-ordinated resistance activities throughout the whole of

France and represented the myriad of political and military opposition groups. Working with specialists from SOE, four plans had been developed, disseminated and resourced. As D-Day approached these plans became effective and were all part of yet another arm of the OVERLORD plan – so many arms that it is a miracle they all came together in the way that they did. Captain Taylor Fellers, his young officers, the men he had been comrades with now for over ten years and the entire 1st Battalion of the 116th were in a sort of wrap around cocoon of efforts to ensure that their mission was a success.

As 5 June approached, Plan VERT was activated which was a fifteen-day operation to sabotage the rail system surrounding Normandy to cut off supplies to German forces;

Plan BLEU began which was a mission to blow up all electrical facilities;

Plan TORTUE was a nationwide effort to disrupt reinforcements being sent to Normandy after D-Day (notable in history as the movement of the *Das Reich* Division from the south of France northwards); and finally

Plan VIOLET which was the cutting of underground cables.

All of this in the hands of thousands of heroic resistance fighters of both sexes and all ages from age six to 100 years old was now under way just as Taylor Fellers dragged himself out of bed and onto the SS *Empire Javelin* to play his part in one of the greatest dramas ever mounted in human history.

It was not all about trains though. Readings from literature were transmitted by radio from the BBC in London to France that carried hidden codes – activation codes in fact – for the many groups of the Maquis waiting for the invasion. Through German intercepts and the barbaric activities of the Gestapo, it was known that certain key phrases indicated that the invasion would come within 24 hours.

Sleeping outside in his tent, Gunner Paul Breslau on SWORD Beach was not to know that it was exactly one of these signals that had put the entire 15th Army on alert. Again, famous lines from Ryan's *The Longest Day* echo in our minds. The Special Operations Executive or SOE, had already been communicating with their resistance groups since the fall of France in 1940 – if not before – and it was to be the transmission of verses from the poem '*Chanson d'automme*' by Paul Verlaine that would reveal when the invasion was coming. It would be down to Eisenhower to make the final decision and then, cascading out of Southwick House via every available telephone and telegraph line, orders would flow like Niagra Falls to over half a million men and thousands of ships and aircraft to get moving.

On Saturday 1 June 1944 and as Captain Taylor Fellers languished in his hospital bed struck down with his agonising and debilitating sinus infection, he was not to know that SOE was already transmitting from London the first of the two most vital phrases of the war to France.

> *Les sanglots longs,*   'The long sobs
> *Des violins*   Of violins
> *De l'autome'*   Of autumn'

This set all the resistance groups throughout France into a subtle agitation as these three lines revealed that the invasion would come within two weeks. An increase in resistance activity was noted by the German High Command in Paris and Rommel, now away from the front, was informed but the weather just seemed so unlikely to clear that any thought of invasion now, at this moment, was put aside. As Company A of the 116th rested below decks or stood smoking above decks on the *Empire Javelin,* thousands of Frenchmen, women and children were already active and under arms waiting for them to arrive and for the second part of the poem – that invasion could be expected within 48 hours. The German weather forecasters, seemingly nowhere near as well advanced as the allied meteorologists, could not see what Group Captain Stagg and his team could see – that a small break in the weather was possible – not on 4 but on 5 June making 6 June, 1944 the only possible day for the invasion.

84 Avenue Foch

Once a beautiful Parisian family home, but now a place of torture and terror, numbers 82 ,84 and 86 Avenue Foch stood, and still stand, in the 16th arrondissement near the Arc de Triomphe. Commandeered by the Germans in 1940 all three became home to different component parts of the Sicherheitsdienst or SD – the feared counter-intelligence branch of the SS. It was in these buildings that Standartenfuhrer Helmet Knochen oversaw the torture and murder of thousands of prisoners and controlled the deportation of French Jews from Paris and the north of France. Although it probably never occurred to the men of A, B, C and D Company aboard the *Empire Javelin*, it is a certainty that the casualties resulting from the preparations for Operation OVERLORD already ran into hundreds when one adds up all the military accidents, training catastrophes, aircrew losses over Normandy, torture and execution of resistance workers and deaths of SOE agents working to prepare the way for the allied invasion of Europe.

It was also in the same building, on the second floor of No. 84, that Dr Josef Goetz led the offices of Section IV which listened in on captured SOE radio sets to allied traffic and had already worked out what the two key messages of invasion alert meant for the resistance and immediately picked up the 1 June broadcast which is what triggered the alert across Normandy that weekend. With no invasion in sight, the Fifteenth Army stood down again.

In his expansive book *D-Day, The Battle for Normandy*, Anthony Beevor dwells momentarily on the events at Southwick House where the immense pressure of making the decision about if and when to implement the ground attack elements of OVERLORD were weighing heavily on Eisenhower. Group Captain Stagg had an unenviable task – to read the weather reports, to make estimations and give his best advice. It was not only the ships that could struggle, there were thousands of parachutists and glider-borne troops to consider. On Saturday 3 June, as tens of thousands of men tried to rest as calmly as they could on board their respective ships, knowing that this could be their last night on earth, writing yet more last letters, smoking endless cigarettes and trying to remember unfunny jokes that they had all heard before, a provisional postponement of D-Day was agreed – the weather crossing for the 5th looked pessimistic. On the 4th, as the *Empire Javelin* was ready to depart that late afternoon, the provisional aspect was confirmed and D-Day for 5 June was off.

All through Sunday it seemed as if the whole world was full of the same questions. From privates to generals it was the same problem, how could we keep all these men on board for much longer, what about ships already taking up positions – the minesweepers had already left just in case it had been the 5th after all – and how long before the Germans stumbled across the direction of the landings? On the evening of Sunday 4 June, Group Captain Stagg held a screening and displayed their maps showing that the large-scale depression about to arrive over Normandy and the Channel coast was slowing down. It was already raining outside now and the winds were throwing the rain at the glass panels as if warning of impending doom. At 21.30 hirs in the Library at Southwick, Stagg spoke:

'*Gentlemen, Since I presented the forecast last evening some rapid and unexpected developments have occurred over the north Atlantic....*'

Stagg continued and the general tone and line of his summary was that there was a small window of opportunity that the full depression would take 24 hours longer to arrive and hit on 7 June. The weather would still be far from ideal but the landings would not be going ahead in a storm. The warmth of the room added to the colour of the various uniforms and no amount of tea and discussion could hide the fact that it was now down to Eisenhower. Montgomery had already announced they should 'Go' and Admiral Ramsey had also announced to the assembled might of the allied high command that if they were landing on 6 June, he needed to give the command to his various 'Forces' within the next thirty minutes – but if there was a second recall it would be impossible to sort things out in time for another go on Wednesday 7. It was agreed that Ramsay should get his front-line ships moving – the minesweepers – and that they would have a final conference in the early morning.

As dawn broke on Monday 5 June, the weather was still drizzling all along the south coast but Stagg was able to re-confirm what he had said the previous night. It was done. As the waterfalls of paper and signatures on orders began, so did frantic telephone calls to ships, divisional headquarters, airfields, Bomber Command, Headquarters of the Royal Navy in Plymouth, encrypted telegrams went in code to Washington and finally a signal arrived on board the *Empire Javelin* – the mission she had been built for was under way.

Never had the four silver stars on Eisenhower's green uniform been under such pressure. During that morning in SOE and at Bletchley Park a second batch of messages began to buzz their way through to all parts of France. One was the second three lines of Verlain's poem:

'Bercent mon Coeur	*'Wound my heart*
D'une langueur	*With a langour*
Monotone'	*Monotonous'*

The invasion was beginning but, in a quiet moment of reflection, Eisenhower picked up an HB pencil and notebook and sat and scribbled out a short message to be typed and used in the event of a disaster the next day.

Orders filtered down through the various commands like a virus. Orders reached the 116th Infantry on board the *Empire Javelin* and the officers and men took in the reality of the signal that the mission was on. At that moment another officer of the 29th reacted sombrely.

Moored not far from the *Empire Javelin* was the USS *Charles Carroll* – a coast guard vessel now given over to the 29th Division and Brigadier General Norman Cota with his 'bastard brigade' staff.[66] Cota received the news that OVERLORD was now proceeding calmly. No rush of adrenalin filled excitement that at last the division was going into battle, instead a reflective and trepidatious reaction and relief that what he had foreseen many months earlier was now coming to pass.

Cota, as the assistant divisional commander to Major General Gerhardt, was in effect the advance guard of the main divisional headquarters. On board the *Carroll* Cota called a final briefing meeting for his staff – he was scheduled to watch the landings of the 115th and 116th infantry on their respective beaches and then land himself later that day when they had taken the beaches, secured the bluffs and were well on their way through Verville-sur-Mer.

Lieutenant Jack Shea, an aide to Cota, writing to Cornelius Ryan in the 1950s, described the scene:

'The last meeting of this staff was held in the officers' aft wardroom of the Carroll on the fifth June, 1944 at 14.00 hours. Every member of the staff realised that this was the final review of the plans. The hushed problems of several months were covered for the last time. Questions were asked. Finally General Cota addressed the little group with some remarks that he had been saving for just this moment. He had withheld them until that time in order to emphasise their critical nature. True they had been pointed out singerly in other discussions of their plans and in the Slapton exercises. But these were the factors in essence, factors that had to be remembered, they were quite vital.

"This is different from any of the exercises that you have had so far," said Cota as he began a final address to the staff. "The little discrepancies that we tried to correct on Slapton Sands are going to be magnified and are going to give way to instances that you might at first view as chaotic. The air and naval bombardment and the artillery support are reassuring but you're going to find confusion. The landing craft aren't going in on schedule and people aren't going.... are going to be landed in the wrong places. Some won't be landed at all. The enemy will try and will have some success in preventing our gaining a lodgement. But we must improvise, carry on, and not lose our heads, nor must we add to the confusion. You all must try to elevate the confusion, but in doing so be careful not to create more. Ours is not the job of actually commanding but of assisting. If possible, always work through the commander of a group. This is necessary to avoid conflicts, duplications of both orders and efforts. You are my staff, my staff and my tools. Keep informed at all times of the situation that confronts you. Particularly in your respective departments. Keep those in a position to need this information informed; don't merely keep it to yourself.... yourselves. This vital information loses all importance unless it is a real tool in the hands of the men who must use it. Keep recommending your ideas to me. In that way I will understand that which must be accepted, that which must be employed to insure its highest degree of usefulness."

They went off to their bunks to try to sleep, to try to rest, to try to prepare themselves for the task which was but half a day from them.'[67]

Part V

The Destruction, But Not the Death, of a Regiment

'And ye shall hear of wars and rumours of wars: see that ye be not troubled: for all these things must come to pass, but the end is not yet.'

Matthew 24: V6

Probably the first signs of panic were when the SS *Empire Javelin* started her engines. There could only be one reason why Captain McClean had ordered his men to their stations and, when the ship started to tremble with noise of her screws turning deep in her hull and she cast off, all was confirmed. She was not alone of course. On that grey Monday afternoon everyone woke up to the reality of the situation – in less than 24 hours where would they be?

By mid-afternoon most of the men of the four companies of infantry plus the Headquarters company and a unit of engineers were all on deck. Apart from the fresh, salty wind blowing in their faces, there was nothing to calm their emotions. Specks of white horses flecked the seas all around the horizon – they were sailing in the calmer waters before the storm that Stagg had predicted, again they did not know it, but rough weather would arrive before the *Empire Javelin* reached Normandy.

Looking up at the single great funnel it was possible now to see the large black and white identification sign on the side of the bridge and 'S 551' marked out the *Javelin* and what she was carrying. On the rear of the two large metal masts, one fore and one aft, Captain McClean had raised the identification flags of the ship – two blue Saltires, flags of Scotland, with a yellow and red lined central flag and a plain yellow to finish indicated her call sign of MYMQ. At the back of the ship, proudly blowing hard in a strong wind was the large 'Red Duster' of the British Merchant Navy. Over the public address system, the captain or one of his officers gave out orders to the crew across the decks of the *Javelin* and occasionally her loud bells would ring in the hods and on deck for the men to report to their respective boat stations to practise drills – as if the *Empire Javelin* were talking to them and taking them through the drills over and over again.

To left and right ships began to gently break away from each other and spread out into their lanes as they steamed on the exact course that would take them to where they needed to end up across the Channel. This was the longest route to France – something that Hitler had always doubted Eisenhower would ever risk – and certainly not in bad weather. With a speed of only 5–6 knots in order to stay in formation it was going to feel like a very long journey. At this speed in this weather the *Javelin* should arrive off Normandy at around 02.00 and drop anchor 10 km from OMAHA beach.

The crossing saw many vignettes of men facing an imminent death. Alex Kershaw tells of Sergeant Earl Parker chatting with Roy and Ray Stevens and showing them a photograph of his sixteen-month-old daughter, Danny. It had been a lot more than sixteen months since he had been home and he had yet to hold her in his arms or kiss her. The longing, in the face of such uncertainty, must have been torture. 'If I could just see her once', he muttered, 'I wouldn't mind dying.'

The anxiety and agony of the crossing was partially relieved by having to face the weather. By mid-channel around 20.00, the weather began to change and the ship started to heave in the growing swell. Surgeon Lieutenant Naunton would have handed out sickness pills across the ship and it was difficult to walk outside with the salty spray on the steel decks.

There was a complete blackout amongst the fleet and no-one wanted a repeat of Operation TIGER in mid Channel or to attract the attention of a wandering U-boat or reconnaissance aircraft. This made life on deck hard and most men retreated back inside for a while then wandered back out again wondering how long it would be before they saw the coast of Normandy. It was quiet everywhere. Deep in one of the humid holds, sweaty, warm, very noisy and reeking of oil and vomit, the regimental chaplains held a final mass for those wishing to attend. There were Jews, Catholics, Protestants, Baptists and all manner of heathens aboard and the services were well attended in the hope that God might react kindly to a conversion or hear a plea to look after their loved ones – or simply let them see lunchtime tomorrow.

For Captain Fellers and his young officers there was the operations room on the main deck where they could chat to the Master of the Ship and to the Royal Navy officers. Men including Lieutenant H.C.A. Middleton RN, DSO who was the Senior Naval Officer Transport and there to liaise with the American commanders like Lieutenant Colonel Metcalfe and Major Dallas. There was also the Flotilla Officer, Lieutenant F.B. Grant RNVR and where the officers had cabins and double bunks. Here he could lay on his bed and try to lose his fear for a few minutes pretending he had seen some new feature of the beach on a map or worked out a better line of attack. There were desks and tables to sit and ruminate or discuss with his younger officers, drink coffee and check and re-check everything over and over again.

Fellers tried to envisage what the ramp going down would reveal and how the beach would look through all the smoke and disruption of the preliminary bombardments. It should be a moon-like landscape of shell holes with occasional sporadic fire here and there allowing the men to use all those 400 metre runs in full kit that they had done so many times back on the sands at Slapton. He was fit, he was the school athlete, he could imagine dodging from hole to hole working his way up the beach until he was able to get his men into position to take on the remaining defences and edge up to the pill boxes and use the explosive charges just like they had practised.

The tough discipline meted out on Dartmoor by Captain Walter Schilling now seemed a world away to his solders as he wandered around them all with a fatherly gesture and words of encouragement to his sergeants but, privately, Schilling was very worried. He confided to a fellow officer that night that he didn't believe he would make it. Later that night, perhaps as the men were lining up for their boats, Schilling made the following prophetic speech to his men on the deck of the *Empire Javelin*:

'This is the real McCoy. The dry runs are over, the amphibious assault training is concluded. I am proud to lead this company into battle…Cross the beach fast, gain the high ground and get into perimeter defence…When I call the roll call tonight in Isigny, I want everyone to say "Here!" Good luck!'[68]

With the battalion Headquarters also on board the *Empire Javelin*, it was normal for men wandering the decks or sitting in huddles to bump into and chat to senior officers such as Major Dallas, the battalion executive officer. In a letter to Cornelius Ryan, Dallas recalled that:

'Personnel were tense, the fear of being afraid seemed the be the basis for tension. Conversations were, in large measure, further discussions of the specific details of landing. Everyone generally, seemed genuinely concerned about carrying out his specific part of the task ahead. Off colour stories were told occasionally and seemed to have a beneficial effect on the overall tension. One abandon ship drill was held. Religious services were held aboard ship; additionally, the Catholic Chaplain did a land office business in confessions and absolutions.'[69]

Also making his way around the SS *Empire Javelin* would have been Captain Robert Ware. As part of the Medical Detachment of the 116th, Captain Ware already knew many of the men of the 1st Battalion and he was there, in advance of where he needed to be, as he knew there were going to be a lot of casualties – Ware had decided that he was going in with B Company in the first wave. Again. Just coming up to 30 years old, Robert Barnes Ware was the youngest of eleven children and from Amherst County in Virginia. Married with one son, Robert Barnes Ware Jr, he was working at Lynchburg General Hospital in 1940 and volunteered for service. Popular and a stable, steady personality, his conversations no doubt calmed many nerves on that crossing – after all, this was a National Guard division and the vast majority of men had never seen combat or been under enemy fire. There were a lot of nerves permeating through the adrenalin rush of youthful exuberance and the 'Heads' on board the *Empire Javelin* were being well used.

Joining Captain Ware were many medics attached to each platoon. The two A Company medics were Privates Cecil Breeden from Iowa and Thomas Mullins from Worcester. They were kept busy handing out what pills they had remaining on the crossing, but as the seas lifted even more there was no stopping the vomiting below or on decks – facing the Germans felt like nothing compared to the awful yawing of the heavy steamship, the smell of the oil throughout the ship and trying to hold a conversation without blasting the empty contents of one's stomach over a friend. The men sweated that night, in cramped, dark conditions and would be exhausted even before they got into their boats. Others played poker with the two-hundred French francs they had been given, anything to pass the time away.

The Navy also had their own medical men on board and the SS *Empire Javelin* benefitted from a well-run surgical team led by Surgeon Lieutenant W. J. Nauton RNVR. Sitting on deck was also a small unit of Combat Engineers. Easily identifiable by the white half-moon lines on their helmets, they carried packs of explosive charges and sat near the black rubber dinghies also packed with high explosives. These brave men were part of the operation to clear the beach obstacles, under fire, to allow landing craft to get closer to the beach as the deep tides came in and, eventually, for vehicles to land. They were scheduled to go in with the first wave – as were sixteen similar units all along Omaha beach.

On the cliffs of OMAHA, young Oberleutnant (First Lieutenant) Hahn had woken long ago, drunk some coffee and, for some hours now, sheltered from the rain and drizzle of the early morning. By 02.00 there was a lot more activity than usual overhead and rumbling gunfire from anti-aircraft batteries to his left along the Cherbourg Peninsula and to his right from the direction of Caen. Sentries had reported seeing tiny lines of ships on the horizon some 20 kilometres off shore – they just did not know for sure where they were going. Perhaps a channel convoy on its way out or returning.

On board the *Javelin* and the seas began to calm a little, it was possible to see the most amazing sight of the silhouettes of hundreds of ships in convoy all heading in the same direction – the invasion was in full flow. As the *Empire Javelin* rolled motionless in the swell, so, at around 02.00 the drone of hundreds of aircraft crossed over their heads heading for the Cotentin Peninsula – it was the Airborne divisions of the American 82nd and 101st. Ahead of the aircraft and off to their right, the men of the 116th could see red and yellow flashes and hear the rumble of gunfire in Brittany as the 88mm anti-aircraft shells were pumped into the skies. On the ground, the French resistance were now carrying out Plan TORTUE and already considerable confusion and failed communications were disabling German reactions to events. Then, without warning, the engines of the *Empire Javelin* suddenly began to grind as she went into reverse, there were no brakes and she shuddered as she slipped forward steadily and then more slowly and came to a stop. There was a brief silence and then the grating and hellish noise of the chains linked to her anchors ran across the steel decks hitting the cold, black water with a crash. All around to the left and right, hundreds of ships were doing the same thing as the huge fleet came to a slow stop and there, peering through the dark haze of a cold grey morning, was the coastline of Normandy.

T-5 Woodrow J. Welsch was also a member of Company A and recalled his journey over that night on the *Empire Javelin* in a letter to Cornelius Ryan in 1958:

> *'The water was really rough. We had made a lot of dry runs in the channel but I think this was the worst. Some of the boys wrote letters others played cards, read books and a few talked about home wondering if the folks back there knew what we were about to do. There were also a few that thought this was another dry run. In fact, I did a little bit myself until I saw a boat section get a direct hit.'*[70]

For those on board who still harboured a belief, or more likely a hope, that this was another practice exercise the announcement by the captain of the *Empire Javelin* that they had received a message from General Eisenhower to be read out to all the men in the invasion forces, must have disappointed rather than enthused them.

Chapter Fifteen

The Landing

'No matter how far or how fast you run, the world is not big enough to hide you from me.'

The words on an MG42 bullet, Anonymous

Getting off the *Empire Javelin* now seemed a luxury. 'No one that has never seen the latrines of a troopship that has been in heavy weather can describe the disgusting and dreadful mess left behind once the infantry have gone.' This comment can be seen all the more acutely as these National Guard soldiers now took on what even the very best in the United States Army would have found challenging.

The men of all five companies of the 116th now had time at last to stand and stare, but there was no rush, just time to gather their thoughts and chat and wait. The boat had stopped moving and men could at last feel their stomachs return to some sort of normality – even though there was more to come in the landing craft.

At around 02.00, Sub-Lieutenant Jimmy Green was tucked away in a dark corner of a small bunk half asleep and his imagination halfway to the beaches – rehearsing over and over again exactly what it was that he had to do to get the first wave on the beach. As Sub-Lieutenant John Swift, who was the Assistant to the senior Naval Officer Transport, later wrote in his After-Action Report:

'The beach is very flat, having a gradient of one in a hundred, and sandbanks and shoals lie dotted around, between two hundred and four hundred yards from the shore. The tide rises and falls extremely quickly, at a rate of one foot every ten minutes, and with westerly winds the sea becomes very choppy and an easterly wind brings heavy surf upon the beach...the outstanding feature of Vierville was its church spire which could be distinctly seen two or three miles off shore. This acted as guiding line for the run onto the beach....

H–Hour was at 06.30. This meant that the craft would beach on a rising tide, which would make it impossible for the LCAs to remain high and dry on the difficult beaches. The First wave was designed to proceed to the Rendezvous Area, then to the Line of Departure with Sub-Lieutenant Green in command ...

Sub-Lieutenant Drew with half of the First wave, was to beach on the western side of the valley, and Sub-Lieutenant Green on the eastern side...

The beach obstacles consisted of a staggered line of element 'C'. Element 'C' is similar to a five-barred gate, about ten feet high and seven feet wide. Astern of these were steel ramps, the tetrahedra, pillar like constructions of four stakes. Following these were single stakes then hedgehogs. The majority of these obstacles were heavily mined.....'

[With thanks to Kevan Elsby.]

A hurried knock on an open door summoned Jimmy Green to the flotilla commander who told him that, because of the sea conditions, they estimated that it would take longer to reach the beach and that the time of departure had been brought forward. As Jimmy Green grabbed a cup of tea from the wardroom and a sandwich, the men of the Merchant Navy began their work and up on the chilly and grey-lit decks the chains and cables of the davits were connected to the first six landing craft. At just after 03.00, and as over three hundred Liberator bombers were warming up their engines back on air bases across the south coast of the UK to make the bombing run over Normandy, the first boats were hanging over the side, forty feet above the waves which were now hammering into the sides of the *Empire Javelin* with increasing force. Instructions now reverberated across the ship from the Tannoy loudspeakers and bells rang to get the men to their boat stations and stomachs churned from a toxic mixture of panic and sea sickness.

As the tension in the atmosphere built, the master sergeants of all the companies started barking out to their men to get into the boat parties and stand by their boats. At the same time Jimmy Green ordered his Royal Navy crews, in their blue sweaters and flat topped British helmets, to get aboard first and they showed the way over the gently rocking 'rails' and took up their positions in each boat. Command now moved over to Sub-Lieutenant Green as he was now the commander of the invasion force of the first wave of LACs. Once these seven were in the water and A company was ready to go, the next six boats would start loading straight away – just as they had practised endlessly in Holy Loch off the Clyde near Glasgow and again on Slapton Sands. A seventh LCA of Company A would follow in the second wave, with Company B, with Lieutenant Nance in command bringing the Company HQ radios, ammunition and support weapons.

The landing schedule for D-Day from the SS *Empire Javelin* was described by Sub-Lieutenant Swift:

03.45   Hands to Operation Stations
       Gripes and tackles were cleared so that the craft were free and ready to be lowered.

03.50   Troops embarked in the landing craft

04.10   First Flight lower away (Actually part of the Second Flight was also lowered, and was joined a few minutes later by the remainder of their craft).

04.50   Six craft of the SS *Princess Maud*, a troop carrier standing off at sea, near the *Empire Javelin*, were hoisted: embarked troops to complete the Third Wave.

05.15   The Third Wave was lowered away.

As Company A were to be first into the water, the guys now said their final goodbyes to friends and brothers. Bedford and Ray Hoback found each other on their way to their station and promised each other they would meet on the beach, Roy and Ray Stevens were in different boats but grabbed each other as they passed for what was to be the last time, and all-around men of Company A and especially the boys from Bedford shook hands and wished each other good luck, saying 'see you on the beach then by the sea wall'. Lieutenant Clyde Tidrick ordered his men to stand by boat position No. 2 and he and Private First Class Leo Nash were at the front of their men ready to walk over the 'rails' – two wooden planks into their hanging and swinging landing craft. The RNVR officers were in the boats to greet them:

Sub-Lieutenant A.L.C. Drew RNVR who was the Assistant Leader of the First Wave
Sub-Lieutenant D. Doodson RNVR was the Leader of the Second Wave
Sub-Lieutenant T.E. Arlidge RNVR Assistant Leader of the Second Wave
Lieutenant D.W.L. Barnett RNVR Leader of the Third Wave
Sub-Lieutenant L. Q. Le Couteur RNVR Assistant Boat Group Commander

A sombre and serious Captain Taylor Fellers and Lieutenant Benjamin Kearfott got their thirty men ready to board LCA 910 where Sub-Lieutenant Jimmy Green RNVR, Leader of the First Wave, was waiting. Next to their boat, Second Lieutenant Edward Marcellus Gearing, along with his Sergeant Roy Stevens, had his men lined up alongside LCA 911. John Barnes recalled that:

'Gearing was just a kid with a buzz saw cut but you never realised it. He had been to a military academy in Virginia and was the kind who just took charge, was sympathetic to all the men, a very good officer.'[71]

Roy Stevens also remembered Lieutenant Gearing:

'He didn't stand back and tell you what to do, he did it. He was a leader.'[72]

In every boat the men were directed to their positions either tucked under the port or starboard wing of the LCA or right in the middle on the wooden bench along the centre – just as they had done so many times in training. Shouting across to pals in the other boats while hanging forty-feet above the water, the men were trying to make the best effort they could to say a few last words to their buddies but it was not easy. If we recall, these LCAs had been designed by the British specifically to land Royal Marines, probably covertly and not under fire hence little thought had gone into the width of the doors which now looked really small with all the equipment each man had to carry. Marines land light and fight heavy. The men of the 116th carried packs weighing sixty pounds and it was obvious from just trying to get them sat down in the landing craft that getting them off again, most likely under some sort of fire, was going to be tough. Jimmy Green noticed their struggles with seating in a rocking boat:

'They had far too much weight. I don't know why the first wave did not go in light. We had worked before with British commandos, and they would not have gone in so heavily weighed down.'

> Jimmy Green, Interview
> with Alex Kershaw

As Company A departed the *Empire Javelin* for the last time Captain Ettore Zappacosta's B Company were lowered away. Behind Zappacosta was Private First Class Robert Sales:

'When we left the Empire Javelin and boarded the landing craft, Captain Zappacosta was the first man at the front. I was behind him being his radio operator. He was very quiet going in. He was not a talkative man anyways but he was very, very quiet on the way in.'[73]

As the landing craft full of the men of A Company tossed around, the waves began to build and it was clear that the weather was again changing ahead of morning. A dim light now hung over the French coast. Although they did not know it, the invasion had been underway for some hours now and inland Normandy and the Cotentin Peninsula was already a mass of small conflicts. To the extreme left of the *Javelin*, while the men of Company A were boarding, British gliders had dropped a company of British troops who had captured

Pegasus Bridge – they now had to hold the bridge until the landings and relieving forces arrived. To their right, the flashes and fireworks of anti-aircraft guns indicated that their Airborne brothers of the 82nd and 101st were already fighting all over the dykes, villages and roads of central Brittany and, with more aircraft overhead, the invasion was clearly under way. A few miles along the coast to their left, a German military policeman was guarding two tank officers having a meal in a small hotel just two miles from the British beaches.

Had Hitler decided to release the 21st Panzer Division within the next few hours, then D-Day might well have failed. Positioned as the armoured reserve near Caen, they were well within range of all the beaches and such a powerful and experienced formation could have thrown the allies back into the sea. As it was, Feldgendarme Lange was not thinking about strategic issues but looking up at the same aircraft as the men of the *Empire Javelin*. One of the officers, a Hauptmann or Captain emerged from the pretty stone house and chatted with him – just then a pretty French waitress came out and offered some real French coffee and rolls. Both German soldiers could feel that there was something tremendous happening above them but they had no idea what was anchored offshore just a few miles to their front. The officer went off to a bedroom 'for some rest before the morning'. Although Lange disapproved, it was not his job to interfere. Mind you, after over an hour had passed, he went to locate the Hauptmann. Pushing open the door Lange found the Captain of Panzertruppen upstairs laying on the bed. He had been shot through the side of the head and his brains and blood were all over the pillows. A one-shot Browning assassination pistol, often used by the resistance, was on the floor, and all the hotel staff had disappeared.

As the LCAs came down the side of the *Javelin*, immediately some of them started swinging into the side of the the ship in the increasing wind and swell and Sub-Lieutenant Green – or 'Jimmy the One' being the Executive Officer, felt a large bump as his LCA910 was hit in the stern by LCA911. Green pushed through the tightly packed infantrymen in the wet and dark to check the damage and Signalman Webb agreed with him that if he kept pumping on the way in they could probably make it.

Salty spray now covered the men as they arrived on the water. Jimmy Green ordered the engines to start and clouds of diesel fumes enveloped each boat as they slowly started to pull away into the dawn light. Now it was possible to see the menacing Normandy coastline far more clearly on the horizon as well as hundreds of ships off to their left including the USS *Charles Caroll* – eastwards along the Normandy coastline. The LCAs started out away from the *Empire Javelin* and into a circular holding pattern waiting for B Company to form up in the same way and within forty or so minutes both A, B and D Company under Captain Schilling were circling ready to go along with the interspersed waves of Engineers and Rangers. It is interesting to note that the *Empire Javelin* carried more troops than she had boats to embark them and they had to hoist further LCAs from the *Princess Maude*, fill them and then lower them down in order to complete the Third Wave which was Company C and Captain Hawks.

Keeping a regular eye on his watch, Jimmy Green was forever recalculating how long he had to deliver the men of the 116th – between that moment and H-Hour he had around an hour and half to get his boats onto the beach exactly as planned at 06.31 and H-Hour. Over to his right he could already see that the LCA rocket firing ships were sailing ahead into the grey early morning mist to take up position to the west of them and add to the firepower dropping on the Germans. Given the order to proceed, Green signalled his six boats to move forward as they had practised so often through the waves and towards Normandy – still just a faint line on the horizon – his LCA910 leading two other boats and alongside was Sub-Lieutenant Tony Drew in command of the next three boats. Similar scenes were repeated all along the coast to his left as the landing craft of the 1st Division were also on their way. Sub-Lieutenant Jimmy Green also had under his command a further two LCAs from HMS *Prince Charles* which carried two platoons of C Company 2nd US Rangers whose mission was to scale the cliffs at Pointe du Hoc.

Moving ahead in two columns of three, Jimmy Green noted that the men were now starting to feel very sick and throwing up on the floor of the landing craft. There were no jokes now, everyone was wet, cold, frightened and staring dead ahead to this coastline where they knew the enemy was waiting to fire at them and kill them. The swell was growing and Jimmy Green had to target his boats at a slight angle to the right, or west towards Pint du Hoc, so that his struggling engines could make headway against the strong tide. Thankfully another new invention was on hand to assist them and they were following in a guide boat kitted out with a new radar set which, even through the thick sea-spray, could direct them on target and stop them drifting onto a different beach or crashing into some other flotilla on the way in.

Everywhere he looked there were landing craft. At eight miles from shore and after forty minutes of bucking, swirling and heaving progress, just ahead on the right the men of Company A could see the reassuring sight of the landing craft of the 2nd Rangers who were set to land five minutes ahead of them exactly at H-Hour, 06.30.

Green kept a close eye on his flotilla and all were still where they needed to be. Way back behind them, Green saw rows and rows of black shapes of ships of all shapes and sizes and imagined the thousands of pairs of eyes watching their progress in towards the beach – he could see the grey ominous shape of the

Empire Javelin disappearing behind him but as they reached the five mile mark his attention was grabbed by the sight of a group of LCTs struggling towards the beach. These were the Landing Craft Tanks of the 743rd Tank Battalion. Green and the men of Company A were not to know that over to their left, the duplex drive tanks of the 741st had been launched in advance of the 1st Infantry Division and were 'swimming' in to the beach individually only to be swamped by the swell – their waterproof canvass covers and bilge pumps, just as predicted, were not high or powerful enough for the wave conditions and twenty-seven of the thirty-two tanks simply sank like stones with heavy losses of men. Seeing the tanks sinking one by one, the commander of the 743rd decided not to launch his tanks and instead land them directly from the LCTs onto DOG GREEN – but this meant that they would not land ahead of the infantry and the first part of a series of failures in the plan unfolded – just as Von Moltke had also predicted. Shouting at a very wet, cold and grey faced Captain Fellers, Jimmy Green asked what he wanted to do – in his interview with Alex Kershaw Jimmy Green recalled the conversation went:

> *'What are they doing here?' asked Green.*
> *'They're supposed to go in ahead of us,' replied Captain Fellers.*
> *'But they won't get there in time for six-thirty,' said Jimmy Green. 'I think we might have to go in ahead of them. Is that all right?'*
> *'Yes, we must get there on time', responded Fellers and they continued past the large LCAs towards the beach.*

As a Captain of infantry, Fellers would have known that not having the tanks already on the beach would deprive his men not only of vital cover as they moved up the beach but also firepower on what defences remained. But his hopes would have rested on the knowledge that the air bombardment was about to arrive and that and the naval gunfire should have damaged the German positions so effectively – and provided huge shell holes all over the beach – that it would still be okay for a frontal assault. Fellers knew that they had no option but to push on and his Virginian sense of honour and duty would have held his emotions together even though this was to be his first combat mission. We can only wonder what went through his mind as he thought about the challenges in front of him and the men that depended on him who sat shivering behind him.

At just before 06.00 and twenty minutes before the tanks had been due to land, high above the advancing forces of the 1st and 29th Divisions, 329 American Liberator bombers approached the beach through thick low cloud. Planners had been wary of them flying parallel with the beach for fear of bombs falling on the advancing troops and so the angle of attack was frontal. With the noise of the engines, dealing with sea sickness, fear-gripped stomachs and mental prayers, the men of Company A saw and heard nothing as the formations flew over and dropped their bombs as planned. What had not been planned was that they would miss their target completely and the second catastrophic failure of the OVERLORD plan unfolded. Worried about dropping short, the bombers added one thousand yards too much to their bomb sights and dropped their entire loads inland – some as far as three miles inland – killing many French civilians, destroying buildings and killing cows but they did not do their vital job of disorientating and destroying German defences.

From the German positions on OMAHA, Grenadiers such as Henrik Naube had been witnessing the great saga unfurl in front of them. Awake from 02.00 and with a formal invasion alarm at 04.00, the Germans were already in their positions ready to repel an attack and had been watching developments through the steadily improving light. Reinforcements had joined them in their positions and they had been told to expect a landing on the beaches in front of them at any time.

'At this point, a very large formation of enemy bombers came over us. These were the big four engine bombers; I think they were the Lancaster type [they were in fact Liberators]. *We saw them streaming towards us over the ships on the sea, and a nearby 20mm Flak gun fired on them, but they were too high in altitude. They bombed us, and we threw ourselves under the steel covers, fearing the worst. These bombs came down at an angle from the sky, and the explosions made the whole cliff shake and sway under us. But we realised that they were missing us, if we were the target, and the bombs hit the inland areas behind us. This was a great relief, and we laughed in a nervous, apprehensive manner as the sound of the planes moved away inland too. We climbed up and prepared ourselves, with the massive fleet of ships on the sea getting closer by the second.'*

Henrik Naube
325th Infantry Division[74]

In the tank turret occupied by Gefreiter Gustav Winter of the 716th Static Division, the effect of the naval bombardment and the aircraft saturation bombing was felt much harder as his position was inland of the beaches. With both the naval guns and the aircraft overshooting the beach, the positions around him received the full force of the explosions and they seemed to just merge into each other:

'The intensity of the bombardment was more than anything that I had experienced on the Eastern Front. When one of those naval shells exploded near us, the shock

*wave came through the ground and travelled through the panzer, which felt
like a punch in the stomach. The blows came again and again, every time a
kick in the belly, and making my ears ring terribly.*

*The Czechoslovakian lad who was my loader got down on the floor of the
panzer and began sobbing, the poor idiot. He was not very bright as I told you.
I told him to shut up, but he was only seventeen, and had not been in action
before. What a way to start! After that I think we were bombed by aircraft,
but I'm not sure.'*[75]

Gustav Winter
716th Static Infantry Division

The various waves to hit the beach one after the other were now forming up
around the larger landing ships and preparing to move off. Just behind Jimmy
Green were the LCAs of the combat engineers and Rangers scheduled to land
just two minutes after he had dropped his troops and then came Company B
with Captain Zappacosta in the lead boat with Lieutenant Nance and the rest
of A Company and then Company D under Captain Schilling.

Back on the *Empire Javelin*, it was the turn of HQ Company and Major
Dallas who was already under fire from an unexpected direction:

*'…after rail-loading my control group into a British landing craft, while lowering
away the davits became jammed leaving our craft suspended about half way
between the rail and the water level. Repairing the davits took approximately
20 minutes. Our craft was hanging about 4 feet directly below the outlet of the
forward port head [toilet]. The head was in constant use during this 20-minute
period and we received the entire discharge from the head. It seems funny now,
but I must confess that at the time it seemed otherwise.'*[76]

At three miles from the beach, it was now possible for the men in LCA 910 to
see the grey cliffs and bluffs of DOG GREEN beach and, with their binoculars
in hand, both Jimmy Green and Captain Fellers could start to pick out some
ominous dark grey pillboxes at either end of their part of the beach. Situated
well back and under the cliffs, Jimmy Green confessed to himself that if they
were still fully functional then the boys in his boat were going to have a very
tough time getting up that beach. It was at that moment, with maybe fifteen
minutes left to hit the beach, that all sorts of things occurred simultaneously.
As is the way in war and in battle, the best laid and prepared plans begin to fail
the minute you engage with the enemy.

First the rocket firing ships began sending up their first salvoes and the men
of all the boats looked away to their right and saw masses of red and yellow

flames followed by huge palls of smoke. Looking to where they were landing, it was clear that they were falling short and into the water – a fact that was confirmed by Sub-Lieutenant Swift in his After-Action Report. Disappointing and concerning though that was, no doubt adding to the trepidations of Fellers, there was no time to dwell, as Sub-Lieutenant Jimmy Green signalled for the engines to roar into full power and, as the bow doors of the landing craft lifted higher it was no longer possible to see the beach – they just knew that they were on the final approach. The order to release safety catches was given and that meant that now it was only a matter of minutes before they hit the sand. The unmistakable sound of M1 Garand rifles being cocked and Thompson sub machine guns at the ready, the men could feel this was nearly it.

As the noise of the aircraft had faded away over the cliffs and into northern France, it was now the turn of the Navy and a sudden and terrifying series of booms rang out across the whole of the fleet as the twelve 12″ guns of the USS *Arkansas* and the ten 14″ guns of the USS *Texas* opened fire on OMAHA beach. The thunderous noise made everyone duck as the huge shells screamed overhead towards Normandy and a pall of thick acrid smoke now started to envelop the landing craft as if in a race with them to the beach. It was a version of hell that few could have imagined with vomiting so hard, some men were already exhausted, the smell of the gunfire, the noise of the engines right underneath them and the pitching waves. All many could think of was getting off the boat and if they were killed then let it be quick. It would be.

Debate over the effectiveness of the naval bombardment continues to this day. We know that Cota, and others, had argued for a far longer bombardment for example as the Americans had done in the Pacific where Japanese held islands were shelled for days on end before American troops were landed. Of course, this did not guarantee minimising casualties but it was a strong argument. On the other side one could argue that such a long period of bombardment would convince the German High Command of where the invasion was coming and enable them to move reinforcements to meet them – a short bombardment did not necessarily betray the allied plans. In reality it seems that the bombardment was effective in disrupting a small number of German positions but it failed to provide the shell hole cover that the infantry were so sincerely relying on – and had been promised. From the German perspective, we can again look at the experience of Grenadier Henrik Naube:

'...*the intensity* [of the bombardment] *was astonishing. It was heavier and was far more accurate than the bomber planes that had just hit us, I had been under artillery fire on the Eastern Front, of course, where I learned to brace myself against it, both physically and mentally....The power of the explosions made the concrete of the trench ripple and fracture, and if I glanced up, I could only see enormous spouts of earth and sand hanging over the dunes and the beach. The shockwaves punched all the air out of our lungs, and made our eyes bleed…..One man, near me, could not take the stress, and he tried to run by ducking outside of the trench zone which was covered overhard by steel screens. I saw him try to run. He was caught by an absolute stream of shrapnel, and his torso was ripped across and broken open. Absolutely ripped open, from front to back. He fell in the open part of the trench, and countless other bits of debris fell on him, mutilating him further. His body produced a lot of steam in the cool air, which filled the trench for a while.*[77]

Over on his LCA things were not going well for Lieutenant Ray Nance. Coming in alongside Company B and with less than three thousand yards to go, Nance was busy trying to help his radio man John Clifton repair the radio antennae. They shouted at each other asking how it had become broken but it was too late to do anything now and instead of leaving it, Clifton strapped it on his back, saying that they could repair it somewhere later once they had landed. They would need it for Company A to be able to communicate with Battalion HQ – now in the water behind them and trying to wash away the smell.

Lieutenant Gearing and his Sergeant Roy Stevens were also having problems on their LCA 911 which was now taking on water fast – her collision with Sub-Lieutenant Green's boat had clearly damaged her too and she was sinking fast. On board with him were Private First Class John Barnes and their radio operator Private James Padley. Jimmy Green could hear cries for help behind him and just as he turned around, he saw the nose of the LCA 911 dive under and the thirty men of that boat went with it. Heads bobbed up here and there, in the intensity men scrambled over each other to stay afloat. Those with their wits about them, grabbed their bayonets and cut off their heavy packs allowing them to come back up to the surface. Gulping sea water, most of the men were excellent swimmers – either thanks to their summer picnics in the Blue Mountains of Bedford or to their training off Torquay where Colonel Canham made them practice over and over again. Only one man was lost at that point – Private James Padley was dragged under by not only his own kit but the weight of his forty-pound radio. The first Company A casualty, the first of many. The rest of the men were bobbing, swimming and helping others to drop ammunition and anything they did not need to stay alive.

Green was under orders not to stop if boats were lost but he shouted over that he would come back and pick them up.[78] Green now ordered the remaining five boats up into line abreast and within less than a minute they were going straight at the beach just as they started to receive the first German fire. Mortar rounds started dropping around them sending up large plumes of white water as well as the sound of artillery shells screaming past the boats. Obviously being fired at a low angle, some of these were from the 88mm guns low down on the cliff faces while others were hidden relics of the 1940 campaign and French artillery pieces which were identified after the battle.[79]

On the LCA to his left, handsome 26-year-old Technical Sergeant Frank Draper Jr. from Bedford was huddled in the centre row of his boat team ready to go. He would not live long enough to see the beach he had come all this way to take. The Germans were firing anti-tank rounds to try to sink the landing craft and a shot had pierced the port side and gone straight through the boat but took off Draper's upper arm on its way through. Shrieking with pain, he was bleeding profusely when, despite the boat heaving up and down, his friends tried to get him to lie down in it. 'But he wouldn't do it, he kept trying to stand', Draper's sister Verona told Alex Kershaw after the war. Eventually he fell onto the floor of the boat, mixed in with the seawater and sickness and lost consciousness. He would end up in the water as this LCA sank taking in water and would still be alive for a while longer before eventually passing away back on board the *Empire Javelin*.

Back on the cliffs, the Germans were quickly recovering from the naval bombardment which ended after fifteen minutes:

'The cessation of the noise and blast waves came as a great relief, as you can appreciate. My ears were ringing, and I had blood on my face from my eyes. We knew that a halt in the shelling meant that the landing must be imminent, and so we washed our eyes in water from our canteens, and slid away the metal covers, and we slowly emerged from the bottom of the trenches....In the time that we had been under cover, the ships and boats of the attackers had come very close to the shore, and now we could see vessels which I would have called 'invasion barges' but later I learned were 'landing craft.' I did not yet know the nationality these troops were. There were very many of these landing craft approaching the beach; there were at least ten facing me....'[80]

Henrik Naube recalled the 88mm guns now opening up on the landing craft:

'These were 88mm PAK guns sited in concrete positions further along the cliffs. These 88mm gunners were very accurate, and shot into the landing craft straight through the tall vertical bow. They fired high explosive, and the shells pierced the bow and exploded inside. I saw one of the landing craft opposite my location being hit in this way. The 88mm shell detonated beyond the bow, and the bow door, which I then realised was a ramp, was throw into the air.

Inside the craft, I could see a large number of troops who had been injured in the explosion, surrounded by men who were still able bodied....I saw from the shape of their helmets that these were Americans.[81]

That early hit on the landing craft was not the only one the German 88mm and French guns made that morning. Some forty minutes later, as the landing craft of D Company arrived at the beach at H+40, Captain Walter Schilling, in the lead boat of the 3rd wave was overheard shouting 'I told you this would be easy' when a shell ploughed through the bow of his landing craft and sent one of the steel doors right into his head killing him instantly on the deck of the sinking boat. It will never be known what gun fired that round but the effect was equally devastating and Captain Schilling would have known very little about the impact and his prophecy on board the *Empire Javelin* had come true.

At 06.32 Green had the five boats in line abreast and all was quiet except for the noise of the engines and shells fizzing overhead from the German positions. The naval bombardment had stopped and they were maybe two hundred yards from the beach as Captain Fellers stood up and took a look at what was in front of him. We will never know what went through his mind as he took in the fact that there was nothing, absolutely nothing by way of cover for his men. Jimmy Green recalled long after that the beach 'was as flat as a pancake.' The rockets had fallen short, the bombs of the aircraft had fallen long and the effects of the naval gunfire were uncertain until the ramps went down. Scanning quickly left and right there were still two very threatening large bunkers and, up on the cliffs, he could clearly see lots of Germans running left and right across the tops of the cliffs and then disappearing.

Riding in on the churning white surf beneath the boats and at H+6 the five landing craft landed one after another in water just below the start of the beach obstacles. Maybe two seconds before the ramp was dropped, Captain Taylor Fellers thanked Jimmy Green for getting his men to the beach on time at which point, through a cold, grey drizzle and with no time to think, Sub-Lieutenant Green ordered the bow doors to open onto the steel ramp which was now dropped into the water.

Chapter Sixteen

The Beach

'Good luck' were the last words Jimmy Green was able to shout to Captain Taylor Fellers but he doubted that he heard him, as he was possibly the first man on D-Day to land in Operation OVERLORD. The men filed out quickly to the right and left into the waist high water as they had been trained, this was it, this was their turn. The tide was turning on OMAHA, and in the war at large.

The 1st Bn, 116th Infantry

It took a while for the men to clamber out of the boat and they did it quicker than they had ever done at Slapton Sands but then they had not been under fire – not like their compatriots would be when they landed. As the last men exited, Jimmy wasted no time in ordering hard astern and the roaring engines grabbed at the hull of the boat like lions to pull back from the sand with its doors still open and the ramp in the water. As he looked right and left all the other boats were doing the same thing. There was still no machine gun fire, just mortar shells and explosions all around and further out maybe they had been neutralised after all. Sub-Lieutenant Green recalled after the war that:

> 'Taylor Fellers was gone as soon as the ramp was lowered before I could wish
> him luck, followed by the middle file, then the port file and the starboard file
> as practised and in good order. They all made the beach safely and formed a
> firing line at a slight rise. At this time there was a lull in the German firing.'[82]

As he turned the boat away to port and engaged the engines at full power, it was then he heard a crackle of gunfire but the noise was lost in the melee of engines, the smashing of the sea and the explosions still popping all around him. In less than a minute he was passing the three LCAs of the Engineer combat team and the two of the 5th Rangers scheduled to land only two minutes after Company A. Although Jimmy did not know it at that moment, over half of Company A were already dead or dying.

The men slowly stumbled into the water of varying depths and started moving forward; their packs were heavy, their guns were heavy and the water was heavy, everything felt heavy. In places the water was at least at waist height and in places deeper as the men searched for their footing. All was quiet and they were briefly able to scan the view in front of them as they moved and the water got slowly lower around their bodies. A perfectly flat slowly sloping sandy beach was ahead, with about four hundred metres to the shingle at the top and the small sea wall. In between were hundreds of beach obstacles of various types. Beyond that were the cliffs rising up like the backdrop of a theatre stage and right and left two large concrete bunkers with black slits but no noise other than the surf and the roar of engines behind them. Between where they were and that wall were dozens of wooden obstacles sticking up out of the sand like a forest of poles with mines on top and, some 100 yards further up the beach dotted in lines beyond them were the black and brown rusting shapes of the welded metal tank traps which were instantly recognisable. Perversely, these obstacles placed here by the Germans formed the only cover on DOG GREEN beach.

In fact, it was probably the eery silence of wading through the water that struck the 150 or so men of Company A that had made it to the beach – before the bullets did. Jumping into the water and then pushing through the waves may have felt like a cleansing experience – they had been bouncing around now for nearly two hours after nearly twenty-four hours on *Empire Javelin* and just for a few, a very few, seconds, they could feel their feet on dry land and to their right and left their friends and brothers were doing the same thing. Those few surreal moments in time were the last that most of them would ever sense.

'I continued to look through the slit of the parapet, and in that way, I could see that, despite the losses, these men inside were starting to emerge and enter the water down the ramps. It was orderly, very orderly. The craft were stopping at a point where the water was about chest or neck hight, and the men were running down the ramps and stepping into the water, holding their guns, plunging down and then bobbing up again with the sea up to their shoulders or chests. In most cases, the men tried to advance in the water one behind the other, with each man holding or reaching for the pack of the man in front. It was as if they were conducting a drill or exercise.'[83]

Of course, that is exactly what the men of A Company were doing. They had been trained to move this way through water so many times in Devon that it was second nature to them. Later waves would not have this experience as the carnage that was unfolding all around them was not in silence but on a beach that looked like hell. But for the boys from Bedford and elsewhere in the United States, the beach was all quiet so they did as they had practised so many times before.

> '...they began to advance in this way into shallower water, and the waves came to their chests and then to their waists. That is when we opened fire on them, as our orders stated....These troops were about four hundred metres from us. I did not sight on them individually at first, but I began firing and I swept the gun [MG42] from left to right along the beach. This knocked down the first few men in each line of men; you must remember that the MG42 was so powerful that the bullets would often pass through the human body and hit whatever was behind. So it was that many of these men were hit by a bullet which had already passed through a man in front, or even two men in front. After that, I aimed more selectively, to make the ammunition last as long as possible. I fired short bursts at small groups of men and hit them that way.'[84]

In his book, *The Bedford Boys*, Alex Kershaw describes how the men were actually lying in the sand 250 yards from the Vierville Draw before they began to move off and then started taking fire.[85] The after-action reports, however, suggest that they were in fact a lot further out and Jimmy Green states that he landed the men at the water-line just before the beach obstacles which would make the distance a good 400 yards. In one sense it does not matter where they were when they were killed, but if they had managed to get to the sand then at least one set of German machine gunners had ignored their orders to catch the first wave in the torso in the water. The result was the same. The last Jimmy Green saw of Captain Taylor Fellers was his kneeling with his men issuing orders before they charged up the beach.

Fellers and many others would feel nothing of his death nor did his entire boat team of 29 other men as every single one was mowed down by machine gun fire – and probably from both sides as well as in front. There really was no escape. Only those that were wounded would see the carnage around them. The MG42 ensured that multiple rounds would hit – at 25 rounds per second it may have only taken less than five seconds for that group of men to be hit. Five seconds after four years of waiting. Hit by multiple machine gun bullets with Fellers, after only seconds on the beach at Normandy, were men like Lieutenant Benjamin Kearfott who had only know Captain Fellers five days and some of the Bedford Boys – Clifton Lee, Dickie Abbot, raised by his grandmother who back in Bedford said a prayer for him every day, the budding writer Nick Gillaspie and the pool hall king, Wallace Carter.

To the left and right of Fellers and his men, it was a similar story. When Lieutenant Alfred Anderson's LCA dropped its ramp, he was the first off the boat into the water which was over waist height and he was followed by his thirty infantrymen including George Roach, Thomas Valance, Gil Murdock and two Bedford Boys – Dickie Overstreet and Master Sergeant John Wilkes. Heavily laden and shouting to get onto the beach, some of them actually made it to the sand before they too were targeted and cut down. The Germans now aimed directly into the boats as they landed. According to Alex Kershaw's interview with some of the very few Company A survivors:

'Wilkes and Roach spotted Lt Anderson, thirty yards in front of them. He waved for them to follow him across the beach. Then Roach was knocked down. The next thing he knew, the sea was licking at his heels. There was no sign of Anderson or Wilkes. According to some eye-witnesses, Anderson was cut in two by a machine gun. It is thought that Master Sergeant John Wilkes was shot and killed as he fired his rifle at the defensive installations at the base of the D-1 draw.'[86]

Such accounts were repeated within a few seconds of each other and the whole drama of the loss of A Company was over within minutes. Dickie Overstreet was one of the few Beford Boys to survive those first few minutes – shot in the stomach and leg, he made it to the sea wall and miraculously survived until 04.30 on 7 June when he was able to be taken back off the beach. It would take nearly 24 hours to secure OMAHA and wait for the tides to change to get some boats in to take off the wounded. During the morning, the incoming tide claimed many bodies of Company A infantrymen who were never found. The rolling tide came in quickly and as so many men were shot in the water; their bodies were just removed out to sea by the tide.

In his oral history recorded and stored in *The Peter S. Kalikow Oral History Archive*, Sergeant Thomas Valance of A Company recalled how many men just sheltered in the water, lying flat and hoping not to be hit by a stray set of bullets from the MG42s that were raking the beach. The bunkers were alive with firepower and had not been touched by any of the preliminary bombing and Valance saw the sea and gulleys in the sand run red with blood – some of his own as he was shot through the hand. Private Henry Witt was screaming at Valance: 'Sergeant, they're leaving us here to die like rats.' Somehow Valance managed to get up as far as the sea wall; wounded in numerous places, he patched himself up and lay there for the rest of the day with a handful of other survivors from A Company.[87]

Within fifteen minutes there were hundreds of bodies rolling in the water as the tide inexorably rolled in and lifted up their bodies as if Mother Nature wished to clear the beach of the slaughter; all their training, all their commitment, their long journey and their lives had ended within minutes on OMAHA beach. To stay in the water meant drowning as the tide rushed in over the flat sand, to move forward risked being hit. Clusters of men sheltered behind the beach obstacles and often that is how they died – in a cluster targeted by a German machine gunner with a good eye. There was no need for rifle fire yet from the rest of the German infantry as very few American troops had got anywhere up the beach but they began to pick off the survivors with rifle fire as stragglers started to make it to the sea wall.

In the After-Action Report for A Company, seven survivors of Company A reported what they had seen. One of the other boats in Captain Fellers group of five had landed off to the right but short of the beach and on a sandbank. The After-Action report stated:

'They [soldiers] *crumpled as they sprang from the ship forward into the water. Then order was lost. It seemed to the men then that the only way to get ashore with a chance of safety was to dive head first into the water.'*

Pte Howard Grosser[88]

'Some of them were hit in the water and wounded. Some drowned then. Others, wounded, dragged themselves ashore and upon finding the sands lay quiet and gave themselves shots [of morphine], *only to be caught and drowned within a few minutes by the on-racing tide. But some men moved safely through the bullet-fire to the sands, then found that they could not hold there; they went back into the water and used it as cover of underwater obstacles. Many were shot while so doing. Those who survived kept moving shoreward with the tide and in this way finally made their landing. They were still in this tide-borne movement when B* [Company] *came in behind them.'*

PFC Gilbert Murdock[89]

Able bodied men lying in the water were trying to pull their wounded comrades forward onto the sand to prevent them from drowning, often only to see their bodies pop up in the water as more machine gun bullets finished them off. 'The able bodied who pulled them in stripped them of their equipment so that they could move more freely in the water, then cut away the assault jackets and the equipment of the wounded and dropped them in the water.' Many wounded had to lie in the water and drowned as the sea washed over them. There was nothing that could be done, all order was lost and it was a matter now of personal survival. Even a boat team of medics was machine gunned and all were killed trying to stumble from their boat.

The After-Action Report for A Company continued. 'One hour and forty after the landing, six men from 'A' from the boat which had landed on the far-right flank had worked up to the edge of the cliff. They saw no others who had advanced as far.' That was boat team six and Staff Sergeant Edward Vargo from Prince George's County, Virginia, was killed trying to exit the boat along with twenty more men from that boat who were hit by an MG42 face on and most died in the boat. Other NCOs who did not make it on to the beach were Staff Sergeant Samuel Baker from Randolph County in West Virginia and Sergeant Orville McNew from Kentucky. One of the six men from Company A who survived the massacre and reached the cliff face was Private Arnold Lester Baker from Monroe County in West Virginia. He was killed in action only eight days later moving inland into Normandy.

Of the remaining boys from Bedford, Sergeant John Schenk was hit by a sniper near the waterline. He had done as he had always done. The day before on the *Empire Javelin* at 08.00 EST or 13.00 as he was waiting for the ship to leave Weymouth, he had spent his usual few minutes thinking about his new wife Ivylyn. She would be thinking about him again later that day at 5pm in the States, but John was somewhere on the beach at Omaha waiting for his body to be collected and identified. The handsome and charismatic Corporal Weldon Rosazza was killed by machine gun fire straight into his boat before he could get off the ramp, as was Sergeant Grant Yopp – who had lived with Roy and Ray Stevens after his father had left home. Raymond Hoback's body was never found and was probably one of those taken by the sea – although his bible was miraculously found by another soldier who mailed it home to his family. His brother Bedford was killed instantly leaving a landing craft – the family never recovered from the loss of both boys. For Earl Parker, all his fears were grounded and he never would get to meet his new daughter Danny; his new wife Viola, who once told him that she doubted he could never shoot anyone, was proven right as he was one of those killed leaving his landing craft. Private First Class Gordon White had been killed almost as soon as the ramp in his boat had dropped. After the war, Gordon White's family received some personal possessions that he had on him when he died. They were soaking wet even after so many months, leading them to believe that Gordon never reached the beach and he died in the deep water thirty yards from the beach.

Then it was the turn of Company B. They landed on time but into a chaotic scene covered in smoke and noise of battle. The intention of the planners all along had been that B Company would land to support and reinforce A Company. In fact, A Company was all but wiped out and only one of the officers remained unwounded. B Company were in reality landing on their own. On the way onto the beach Captain Ettore Zappacosta was ready to go, but with the bows up on the LCA as it headed for the beach at full speed:

'About a thousand yards or so off the beach, the only words he [Zappacosta] spoke were 'Sales. Step up there and see what's going on the beach, if you can see anything.' I looked over. I could not tell anything. I said "A Company. I can't see 'em. It looks likes bodies lying on the beach, but I cannot tell." And I sat back down. It wasn't but a brief while after that and the only words from the coxswain were "I cannot go any further. I'm going to drop the ramp." This was the last time I heard the coxswain speak, and I do not know to this day whether he got out alive or not, but when that ramp went down mortar shells were hitting on both sides of us. Machine guns were all over the top of us, just like you were in a bees' nest.

The captain was the first man to get off the boat and he was hit on the ramp and fell into the water. Sergeant Wright was next off, followed by a first-aid man. I was fourth off the boat. The sea was rough, the ramp banged up and down, and I caught my heel and went over the side into the water. When I got up, Captain Zappacosta was up and calling to me, "I'm hit!" He went down and I did not see him come up. His body was washed up on the beach later.'[90]

The ramp had been dropped 75 yards from the beach partly because the in-rushing tide was now starting to cover many of the beach obstacles, but also because the boat had grounded on a hidden sandbank. As the men jumped, they found themselves in nine feet of water and started to drown. At the same time the Germans, no longer waiting for the first wave to make its way onto the beach, were already pouring machine gun fire into the boats. Technician 5th Grade, or T/5 Kenser jumped towards Captain Zappacosta to try to save him but was also shot and killed in the air and slumped into the water. When Sales bobbed up from under the water himself, men from his boat team were simply falling like flies into the bottom of the landing craft and the coxswain, sheltering behind his steel panel screen was already pulling the boat back off the sand. It would take Sales two hours to survive in the water and gingerly find footing in the sand holes and even reach the beach – a distance of only twenty yards, moving with the steadily moving tide and he found himself by the obstacles and a part of a log that had been blown up by the engineers and that's where he sheltered. He was the only one from Captain Zappacosta's thirty men to have got onto the beach.

Lieutenant Elisha Nance landed with B Company as planned and was able to quickly see the chaos ahead of him. He fell forward into the water which probably saved his life as the waves took him down and then spat him out onto the sand with sea water choking his lungs. As Nance crawled ashore, he watched as young Lieutenant Clyde Tidrick was then hit in the throat as he jumped from the ramp into the water. According to the After-Action Report for A Company, Lieutenant Tidrick struggled on to the sands and then:

> '.... *flopped down 150 feet from PFC Leo J. Nash. He raised up to give Nash an order. Nash saw him bleeding from the throat and heard his words "Advance with the wire cutters!" It was futile. Nash had no wire cutters, and in giving the order, Tidrick had made himself a target for just an instant, and Nash saw MG bullets cleave him from head to pelvis.'*[91]

Lieutenant Ray Nance managed to crawl a little way up the beach and away from the inrushing tide that had claimed so many wounded and dead men. MG42 bullets peppered the sand and zinged over his head, thumping into men still trying to get out of the landing craft which was already pulling away and around him he could see bodies everywhere – the remains of A Company. Nance recalled to Alex Kershaw that he recognised two dead Company A officers laying face up in the water, rolling back and forth in the surf. The German machine gunners were voracious in their appetite to deal out death and any movement on the sand caught their eye and like hawks they quickly fired making sure wounded men died. Suddenly Nance was joined by his radio operator John Clifton with his massive 40 lb radio on his back. Clifton cried out that he had been hit and as Nance turned around for a second time he had gone – either blown up by mortar rounds which were dropping nearby or the tide sucked him back into the water.

More mortar rounds peppered the beach all around him killing three men outright who were huddled together and still tracer fire fizzed off stones and caught metal on the bodies of the wet and dead. Off to his right, Lieutenant Nance recalled that he saw Private John Reynolds from Bedford, the man whose mother had begged him not to go, decide he was not going to wait to be killed on the beach. Reynolds hauled himself up with his wet 60lb pack on his back and ran forward trying to zig zag but was caught by a burst of fire and just slumped forward dead like a heavy sack. Soon after, Nance felt a piercing pain in his right ankle – part of his heel and boot had been ripped apart by a stray MG bullet and he was bleeding badly. Using some slight tidal pool depressions, Nance edged himself forward, trying not to catch the eye of the gunners and slid down into some warm water and this way he slowly edged up the beach.

Bob Sales continued in his interview with Alex Kershaw to describe the chaotic scenes:

'I'd seen a wall, maybe 150 feet away. I thought: "If I can get to that wall, I got a little protection. And maybe I can get another gun or something." Had fifty yards to go – a long way, especially when you're expecting a man to kill you. So, I started using dead bodies. I would crawl to one, and then real easy, I'd move to another one. That was the only protection.'[92]

The sad reality was that, with new boats landing every few minutes, the German machine gunners saw a better return for their ammunition by focussing on the bow doors of an incoming landing craft than they did trying to hit one wounded man – thus giving individuals like Sales, Gearing and Nance the opportunity to crawl their way gingerly up the beach. It was only through sacrifice of boat loads of infantrymen that any individual made it to the low, sloping sea wall or the base of the cliffs. Somehow Lieutenant John B. Clements Jr, who was one of those additional officers posted to Company A in anticipation of heavy losses, nearly made it up to the right-hand bunker that protected the Vierville Draw. Back in the United States his new wife would have had no idea of his bravery that morning as his obituary on the 29th Division Roll of Honour states that he was attempting to destroy the bunker when he was caught by machine gun fire and killed.

After what must have seemed like an eternity, Nance too finally reached the base of the cliff and sheltered there as stragglers arrived with him. About an hour later he was joined face down in the sand by the last of the Company A officers, 19-year-old Lieutenant Edward Gearing who had somehow survived getting up the beach. Within seven to ten minutes, both A and B companies of the 1st Battalion, 116th Infantry had ceased to exist as combat formations and all the officers but two had been killed.

At H+40 or 06.46 it was the turn of Company D to head in and try to land in the confusion of DOG GREEN beach. With Captain Schilling already dead, their boats were now landing into continuing MG42 gunfire – along with two more boats of engineers and a beach party. The After-Action Report for Company D tells the story of how, with the wind picking up, the six landing craft were constantly hitting waves and being swamped with men needing to bale with their helmets to keep their craft afloat.[93] Schilling's boat had sunk, putting thirty men into the water, many of whom would drown trying to get to the beach some four hundred yards, or thirty minutes of swimming, away, although the incoming tide would help. Sub-Lieutenant Swift from on board the SS *Empire Javelin* noted that with each landing wave, the time of approach had slipped further so that the Third Wave was actually 'some twenty minutes late'. This merely added to the scene of confusion out at sea as each wave backed up upon the other waiting for its turn to proceed into the growing carnage on the beach.

Another LCA, that of Lieutenant William Gardner, the D Company Executive Officer and therefore now the Company D commander, hit a sandbank 150 yards out and the men poured into the water under continuing machinegun and mortar fire from the cliffs above – it was just before 07.00 and it would take over an hour and a half for these men to get ashore crawling and crouching through the water which tells of just how murderous the machine gun fire was at that stage. Other LCAs churned the waters around them trying to get on and off the beach as they lay sheltering from the gunfire and trying to stay alive by washing in with the tide. Losses were heavy and only fourteen of the thirty-two men made it onto the beach. Lieutenant Gardner, a popular 28-year-old regular officer, was born in Beverly Massachusetts, a suburb of Boston and was another highly thought of young officer transferred into the 116th in preparation for the first wave. Nicknamed 'Porky' at West Point, Bill Gardner was one of the many killed in the water by the MG42s raking the D Company boats as they tried to land.[94]

A third LCA of Company D was also sinking and, 400 yards from the beach, the British coxswain shouted he could go no further and started to lower the ramp when Sergeant Willard R. Norfleet blocked the mechanism and insisted the boat go further in. The LCA carried on through the noise, raking gunfire and mortar explosions, but at 200 yards the bottom of the boat was ruptured by a German beach obstacle and sank immediately in five feet of water and the men then emerged into the gunfire and again took very heavy losses as they staggered onto the beach. By 07.30, Company D of the 1st Battalion was also now an ineffective combat unit.

By the time he reached the cliff base, Second Lieutenant Edward Gearing's pocket book notes would later state that there were only fourteen men left alive from the entire A Company roll of 232 men. Gearing had only survived thus far because his LCA had been hit by an 88mm shell at 06.30 on the way in and about 300 yards from the beach allowing him time to survive while the most intense period of the battle was under way – only by nearly drowning, Gearing, and what was left of his platoon, managed to get through that first ten-minute massacre by the German machine gunners. Crawling through the surf about an hour later, Gearing's note book pages confirm that he came across the wounded Lieutenant Nance and, under the smoke, noise of machine guns, explosions, screams and boats still landing near them he shouted at Nance 'What's happened to A Co.' and Nance shouted back 'As far as I know the officers are dead and everyone else is too.'[95] All the officers bar Gearing and the wounded Nance were dead as were all the NCOs. The company had ceased to exist.

Gearing noted that he picked up some nearby weapons and left Nance at the foot of the cliffs and made his way through the gunfire off to the side of the beach towards the Vierville Draw where, later in the morning he would bump into Lieutenant Colonel Metcalfe and some of the 1st Battalion headquarters company and then go on to earn the Distinguished Service Cross.[96] In a 1958 letter to Cornelius Ryan, Edward Gearing wrote:

'I have read all of the material that has been brought to my attention concerning the D-Day landings and feel that little justice has been done on the early portion of the invasion, particularly during the 24-hour period that Mr Ryan intends to cover. I imagine that this is due to scarcity of the people available to give eyewitness accounts.

It would also be very interesting to read the activities of other individuals on that day. When you are in combat and especially when there was as much confusion as on that day, a man is only aware of what is happening to him and his immediate vicinity.

Although there were many heroic deeds performed on that day, many of which were not recognised, I was among that group of fortunate to receive the Distinguished Service Cross for my days' work.'[97]

During this time, the rest of the men in Gearing's boat had been paddling water. Gearing had swum the 1,000 yards onto the beach and made his way up, where he found Lieutenant Nance but John Barnes and Roy Stevens were trying to stay afloat. Others around them were helping each other avoid going under; they had cut their kit away, inflated their Mae Wests and lost their helmets and weapons, but their boots were heavy.

2nd Rangers

Some twenty minutes earlier, Sub-Lieutenant Jimmy Green had reversed his boat off the beach and promised to go and pick these men up. However, while they were trying to survive in the deep water about one mile off shore and, as Jimmy Green, explained:

'....I was itching to return to the survivors of LCA911 hopefully still afloat about a mile offshore. I looked to my left and saw Tony Drew up to his neck in water around the stern of his LCA and obviously in some sort of trouble. He told me much later that he had reversed off the beach into a tank.... I was intending to see if I could help Tony Drew when my coxswain told me that there were some of our lads on the beach. I thought it was unlikely but he was right. The two craft with the Rangers on board had landed just behind us and to our right. The crew of one of these craft were waving frantically at us and wanted us to take them off. I thought twice about it, with Tony Drew and the

survivors from LAC911 in mind, but I couldn't leave them on the beach so 910 went into the beach again, grounded and picked up the crew. One of them was wounded and had to be supported by his shipmates. They told me they had been hit by four mortars on landing which destroyed their LCA and killed a number of the Rangers.'[98]

Shortly after, Green remembered that he was supposed to send a signal reporting the landing. He did this, or rather Signalman Webb did and sent 'Landed against light opposition' and then went on to pick up the survivors from LCA911.

The men in the water could hardly believe it when through the din came a British voice shouting over and the quiet engines of an LCA drew up beside them – as he had promised, Jimmy Green had indeed returned and found them. Clyde Powers was hauled out of the water and then helped grab Ray Stevens, Russell Picket and John Barnes. They expected to be run back into the beach but Jimmy Green told them their fight as over for now and he headed back to the *Empire Javelin* and safety. One other who was hauled on board and still alive was Sergeant Frank Draper. Despite his gaping shoulder and chest wound and blood loss, he was still breathing, and Alex Kershaw writes that men could see his heart still beating through the open wound with only an hour left to live. Green had no idea what had happened to the rest of A company, just telling these half-drowned survivors that he had landed them safely – they expected them to be up on the cliffs by now.

By 08.30, Sub-Lieutenant Swift noted that the first LCAs had arrived back at the *Javelin* and with the waves now reaching twelve feet high, it was quite a task hoisting them back on board. Taking them back alongside the *Empire Javelin*, through the masses of boats still heading towards OMAHA, Jimmy Green found it hard to hook the boat onto the davits – the swell was heaving and the storm gathering strength – but eventually his LCA was lifted up back in place as were eleven others – six of the *Empire Javelin*'s original complement of eighteen boats had been sunk, damaged or destroyed. Swift wrote:

'After many failures, which nearly ended in disaster for some of the craft, twelve LCAs were hoisted, six craft having failed to return. The other LCP (L) had also returned and Lt Grant held a meeting of the coxswains to try and discover the fate of the craft and crews. It was then learnt that all but one boat's crews could be accounted for. Incidentally nearly fourteen days elapsed before we were informed that this crew was safe, with the exception of the coxswain who had been killed after the loss of his boat. Thus, out of 118 men in the Flotilla, only one man was killed, although six boats were lost.'

[With thanks to Kevan Elsby.]

The 149th Engineers

The fate of the combat engineers that landed with the 116th has been overlooked, but they were suffering every bit as badly – except that they could not even try to get off the beach. Their job required them to stay in the ever-deepening water and try to lay charges to destroy the beach obstacles so that larger boats could land closer to the beach later that day. They had travelled on the *Empire Javelin* that morning, trained hard for their role and they died just the same as their comrades in the infantry.

There were sixteen 'gapping teams' allocated along the length of OMAHA and, as the name suggests, their job was to create gaps or lanes through which tanks or landing craft could move right up onto the beach at high tide. Their landing craft towed black rubber dinghies behind them full of various types of explosive charges. The impact of the German artillery was devastating – not only were the 88mm gunners accurate in hitting the landing craft, they were effective at aiming for the dinghies too and more than one blew up with massive, thunderous explosions, killing all the engineers hovering around them.

One of the problems faced by the engineers who managed to get off their LCAs was that what was left of the infantry – both Company A and Company B – in that first hour, refused to get up and move from the obstacles which were providing the only shelter on the beach and it took officers to order them to move up the beach – as soon as they showed themselves, most were cut down as they feared. After the war, many of the surviving combat engineers criticised the OVERLORD plan for cramming too many waves of men so close together. All that did was encourage the German gunners to rake the beach as more landing craft arrived and just added to the confusion. The engineers also observed how many wounded men drowned in the incoming tide, unable to move due to the weight of their equipment and their wounds. The strong tide pushed on by the winds of the rising storm also pushed some of the landing craft eastwards and even men of the later companies of the 116th ended up confused on the neighbouring beaches of Dog White or Dog Red having drifted down the coast by 1,000 yards in the smoke and the power of the tides. Jimmy Green had aimed his boat at Point du Hoc, far to the right, to ensure that his boats drifted onto Dog Green with the tide.

Private Shotwell was a member of the 149th Amphibious Combat Engineers who landed with Company D:

'*The noise was deafening. Big guns fired, engines roared, men shouted and geysers of water erupted around our craft. It seemed like mass confusion. I felt excited, probably because I had no combat experience at all. Like those kids, I had this feeling of invincibility and I thought nothing could happen to me.*'[99]

That euphoria did not last once the ramp came down and men were dropping straight into the water. The engineers struggled off their boats and made it to shore huddling together behind some rocks with a depression behind it:

'To lift your head up was almost certain death from a sniper or machine gun. But we couldn't stay behind the shingle, because the tide was coming in. Bits and pieces pop into focus…a hand. An arm with nobody around it. A foot. A helmet with a head still in it. I wondered if the next shell would be mine.'[100]

By the end of the 'memorable and terrible' first day, between 45 and 55 per cent of the combat engineers had been killed or wounded. (Corps of Engineers: *War Against Germany*.)

By 10.00 the smaller destroyers were able to get closer to the beach and start firing their 5″ guns at the cliffs to destroy the artillery positions – zeroing in on their gun flashes. But this created further problems as large chucks of cliff face fell down on the able bodies and wounded men sheltering at the base of the cliff. The Catholic chaplain for the 1st Battalion of the 116th had somehow made it to the cliff base and was administering the last rites where he could and assisting with medical aid when these huge explosions blew the cliffs out over them raining rocks and sand down on the men. Sergeant Ernest Ward Haynie was there with them and he recalled how the chaplain made a red cross sign using the blood of one of the dead soldiers onto a white service cloth and held it up in the hope that someone on board one of the destroyers would see it through their binoculars and the smoke and haze.[101]

While inroads had been made further along the coast on the British and Canadian beaches and UTAH to the west was falling quickly into American hands, General Gerhardt and his deputy Norman Cota gazed in anguish at what was happening to two of their three fine infantry regiments. The Germans still held the dominant positions overlooking both Dog Green and Dog Red. Small groups of men were firing back with small arms fire but the main problem now for the Germans was that they were starting to run low on ammunition. In addition, the barrels of the MG42 were notorious for heating up fast due to the tremendous rate of fire – and then the German gunners picked up their rifles. There was no mercy. The aim was to kill everyone that they could and, by 10.00 the incessant OVERLORD schedule meant that larger LCAs were now arriving with trucks and jeeps – totally out of step with the reality going on around them on the beach as Henrik Naube of the 352nd relates when the tide was almost fully in:

'I remember that one of the landing craft came close to the shallows, and whoever was in charge of it seemed to hesitate. The craft slowed and steered carefully between other craft and the obstacles, as if selecting a place to land.....as this craft turned away, it presented its flank to the 88mm guns and it was shot immediately, below the waterline. The explosions tore off large pieces of its side, and the craft began to capsize rapidly as the water flooded in. I could see the troops inside as the hull rose up, the whole interior of the vessel was exposed to us. There were various vehicles in that craft, Jeeps and trucks, as well as troops. These vehicles were falling on to the troops...other men were jumping from the sides into the sea.

The 88mm fired again into the middle of the interior, and this exploded the vehicles as they lay crushed together. I saw the whole landing craft go up in flames within seconds....'[102]

One of the few survivors of A Company sheltering under the cliff face was T-5 Woodrow J. Welsch – whom we might recall, while coming over on the *Empire Javelin* that morning, thought that this might just all be another dry run. When asked if he recalled anything in particular about that morning, he said he did:

'I recall something sad as I lay on the cliffs and watched our medics trying to get some of our wounded on the LCVPs. The Germans would machine gun them. They didn't have a chance for that Big Red Cross they wore meant nothing to the enemy.

They trained us hard to run 300 yards on a sandy beach in England for that was about the distance between the water's edge and the cliffs on Omaha beach.'[103]

Those additional men that Company A had been given had just disappeared with all the rest.

Headquarters Company

'The dead were piled up like brown firewood in stacks at the base of the cliff, brought in by the tide...'

Having cleaned away the smell and faeces off the deck of the boat that had poured in while they were stuck under the Heads of the *Empire Javelin*, by H+50 or 07.20 it was time for the 1st Battalion Command Group and Headquarters company with Lieutenant Colonel John Metcalfe and Major Dallas to land. The storm had really developed and the seas were rough leading to one of the three boats sinking on the way in and the other two stopped to pick up survivors.

According to the After-Action Report prepared by Major Dallas, with the tide now well up the beach, they were able to navigate their way in and land in only two feet of water. The German gunners still had control over the watery beach and bodies and equipment floated everywhere and would do all day and that night – hence many were never recovered when the tide retreated taking its tithe of men with it.

After a few yards they too came under heavy machine gun fire from the cliffs. Only one-third of the men reached the foot of the slope alive:

'And they made it because the men ahead caught the bullet which might have felled them and so saved them from the fire.'[104]

Unable to move up towards the objective of the D-1 Draw, Dallas and Metcalfe quickly realised just how few men were still alive out of the first four companies that had landed. Only small pockets of men could be seen sheltering from the gunfire as more and more boats tried to land disgorging men into the shallow water. On the radio system Dallas could only get a response from Metcalfe some 100 yards away and to move meant almost certain death. To his right it was possible to see a cluster of men from his battalion so Dallas ordered Lieutenant Wayland Hooks, who was killed in action later, to get what weapons he could, get the men together and scale the cliffs and knock out the MGs that were doing so much damage. Staff Sergeant James B. Smallwood went with Hooks and kept the infantrymen supplied by sending back down the cliffs to take ammunition and grenades from the many dead bodies now washed up like piles of firewood at the base of the cliffs. Around sixty men went up to the right through the sloping dunes and engaged in fire fights with the German defenders. The fight up on this section of beach was hand to hand, brutal and visceral as Henrik Naube of the 325th Infantry could now see right beside him near Vierville:

'I could see hand-to-hand fighting on the cliffs directly across the ravine from me, with Americans and our troops so close that I could not fire into them because they were mixed up together. The ferocity of that fighting astonished me. Men were lunging at each other with fixed bayonets, and even with their rifle stocks, and even with entrenching tools or shovels. The Americans were charging upon our German gunners in the barbed wire entanglements up there. Some men were in flames, and other men were shooting or stabbing them as they staggered on fire. I could no longer see which men were from which army, as the smoke and flames made them all a similar outline as they fought.'[105]

This type of close quarters combat was to go on for most of the afternoon and spread out into the hinterland and into Vierville through fortified houses and numerous German entrenchments with Polish conscripts of the 716th still in position. It was not until 5pm that pockets of Rangers and 116th infantry were able to move further along the top of the cliffs without being caught by machine gun fire. This contrasts completely with the many fictions of the Steven Spielberg film where the 2/Rangers were able to get off the beach and up the cliffs within minutes. Sadly, we have very little information on the actions of Lieutenant Colonel Metcalfe at this time other than he was up there leading and arrived in Vierville in the early evening – John Alfred Metcalfe Jr was wounded in action on 29 June and died of his wounds, despite being evacuated to England, on 15 July 1944.

Throughout the mid to late morning, all around beached and damaged ships collided with new landing craft coming in on the new approaching high tide mark right up through the now underwater beach obstacles. Company L of the 3rd battalion landed in the wrong place, as did numerous other waves on the stormy waves and high tides. Private Valentine de Pace recalled to Cornelius Ryan how:

'One soldier came in from the ocean unaware that a smoke grenade had gone off in his behind pocket. With yellow smoke streaming behind him, everyone was trying to get his attention so that he may rid himself of it because he was a living target! As he was running up the beach, someone finally got his attention. When he turned and saw what had happened, he stopped running abruptly and turned and ran back to the ocean where he stayed down in the water and flushed out the smoke grenade. All during this everybody wondered why he wasn't hit because tracer bullets were striking near him. After he got rid of the grenade he got up and ran back up the beach safely and everybody cheered when he made it!'[106]

Back with Major Dallas, another British destroyer had closed up to the beach to help and was firing 5-inch rounds directly into the cliffs. Keeping the fire up almost all day, numerous men were killed or wounded as they tried to fight the Germans and duck the shellfire which only stopped at 17.00 hours when Dallas managed to get a radio message through. Dallas commented later that he lost more men that afternoon to the destroyer than he did to the enemy.

Lieutenant Colonel Metcalfe was pinned down most of the morning and early afternoon. He could hear and see pockets of men trying to get up the cliffs but they were all well short of D-1 and could see that the 1st Battalion no longer existed. Headquarters had already lost many officers getting off the boats.

Recalling that morning, Private Sales recounted to Alex Kershaw how he had seen Captain Robert Ware fall along with other officers as the HQ Company boats dropped their ramps. The MG 42 gunners had the exact range and knew what was coming and with each boat they repeated their harvest of death, hitting Captain Robert Ware between the eyes – he who had chatted to so many men on the way over in the *Empire Javelin*:

> 'He [Ware] had brought himself in on an early wave rather than later in the day because he knew there was going to be a lot of wounded. When that ramp went down, they opened up and they got him. Just cut the boat to pieces. He'd got me a three-day pass to London. Treated my knee after a river crossing in England, came from my home in Lynchburg.'[107]

The After-Action report goes on to add other officers who fell dead or wounded as they exited the command boats. Apart from Captain Ware, Colonel McQaid of the 158th FA Battalion was hit as he stepped off the LCA and died in the water. Lieutenant James Limber, the Battalion S2 was shot in both legs – he crawled and pulled himself onto the beach only to be hit square in the face by a mortar shell fragment. The battalion was not only leaderless at company level but almost at Battalion level too. As the MG42s maintained the slaughter on the beach, Captain Thomas Callahan was shot in the leg and Lieutenant Mortwest was shot in the buttocks while trying to pull a wounded Ranger from the water.

Private Donald A. McCarthy was a member of Headquarters Company of the 1st Battalion of the 116th. After the war, Donald remembered how he was yet another infantryman to find that his LCA had been unable to cope with the waves. His LCA, along with five others, was also blown eastwards along the shoreline by the heavy winds that had bothered Eisenhower so much. As the morning continued, increasing numbers of landing craft had found it impossible to motor at an angle to hit their beach and were drifting down, eastwards, onto DOG WHITE or even DOG RED and mixing in with the US 1st Division – depriving DOG GREEN of badly needed reinforcements. This made for a colossal log jam of damaged, sunk and burning boats in between beach obstacles, men in the water and German gunfire.

In places along OMAHA it really was chaotic later that morning until resistance up on the bluffs had been snuffed out by individual and courageous groups of men. Indeed, it has often been said that OMAHA was eventually won, not because of the plan but because of the bravery of small teams of men desperate to get off the beach – some had been under gunfire nearly all day. McCarthy, a veteran draftee from July 1943 who had been with the battalion in Ivybridge as well as Slapton Sands and had been with the five companies on board the *Empire Javelin* later recalled how:

'Again, I was fortunate to have survived the landings of the third wave… Although the flotilla was originally scheduled for DOG GREEN sector of the beach, the British coxswain and the entire flotilla of LCAs from the SS Empire Javelin were carried in an easterly direction by the tide toward the DOG RED sector and the Moulin Draw.

My LCA had taken on water, was swamped and sank about two-hundred yards from the low watermark and beach obstacles. Several of us swam in behind bodies and attempted to hide behind the obstacles from machine gun and artillery fire. Although the MG fire was intense, the Germans on the bluff were unable to see us because of smoke from burning grass and buildings blowing east from the Vierville (Vierville-sur-Mer) area. The smoke screen provided an opportunity to run from the water's edge, and the fear of getting run down from incoming landing craft, and find protection from the high-water shingle.'[108]

Memories of Lieutenant Colonel William C. Purnell

The Headquarters of the 29th Division including Major General Gerhardt had crossed the channel that morning from Plymouth and their LCI positioned itself behind the main waves of the Division and their 115th and 116th infantry regiments.

They had watched from their LCI all day and tried to piece together the fragments of information as they came in either from radio signals – although there were few of them given the disasters on the beach itself – or from observers with other units and from the Navy with their large binoculars on the various bridges of ships. Their views were obscured by the smoke of battle mixing with the grey dimly lit daylight, but around mid-day it became impossible to see how the fighting was going on because the brush and dry grass of the cliffs had caught fire – created by accident as the 2nd battalion of the 116th Infantry managed to penetrate the defences over to the left of DOG GREEN later that morning.

'There had been great controversy at Supreme Headquarters about whether or not a smokescreen should be laid.'[109]

Clearly a decision had been made not to lay a smoke screen – posterity can only muse on what sort of a difference that would have made to the first waves of men onto OMAHA beach.

As Assistant Chief of Staff of the 29th Division, Lieutenant Colonel Purnell headed for OMAHA beach at around 16.00 and landed an hour later. During the preceding hours, his LCA had come in close and then retreated again due to the fire from the cliffs – this had receded by later afternoon as pockets of men from the 116th had managed by then to get up there and fight through the opposition and were heading inland. One comment Purnell did make in his note to Cornelius Ryan was:

'That night on OMAHA beach rows of wounded lay against the sea wall, stranded by the high tide and a very heavy wind. Unavoidably, they were there until morning, when the Navy might get in. Sometime during the night, the medial supplies ran out. It was pretty awful.'[110]

The regimental Headquarters Company, with Colonel Charles Canham of the 116th was also due to land as part of the third wave onto DOG GREEN – reinforcing and pushing on up with what was supposed to be the rest of the 1st Battalion RCT (Regimental Combat Team) except it largely did not exist any longer as both A and B Company had been decimated, while C and D Company had both lost over half their strength. In the event, the strong winds and tides blew the LCAs from the *Empire Javelin* further along the beach and they in fact landed on DOG WHITE.

Brigadier General 'Duch' Cota came ashore as planned, with the divisional staff of the 29th, also onto DOG WHITE. Linking up with Colonel Charles Canham, both men could quickly see that the landings were in trouble. As their respective LCAs delivered them about 800 yards to the left of DOG GREEN beach, they could see over on their right that the 1st Battalion had had a very hard time of things and in front of them on DOG WHITE the 2nd battalion was struggling too. Emerging under small arms fire and thankfully not the heavy machine guns, they ran over the beach far more easily than their own heavily laden troops who had struggled earlier in the deep water and wet sand. The tide brought them in quite high up the beach now – although their LCA had had to wriggle in between the mines on the beach obstacles now only just above the water. Major John Sours, the 116th's S4 intelligence staff officer, was shot in the chest and fell dead as they ran in – it could so easily have been any one of them and they took cover by weaving from one destroyed tank to another. It was clear that the tank landing on that beach had failed – just as it had further along the beach on DOG GREEN. The specialist gunners of the 88mm guns had enjoyed easy pickings with Sherman tanks emerging so slowly from the water and struggling in the sand and shingle – had nothing been learnt from

Dieppe in 1942? Clearly the infantry had had to do the job alone, naval gunfire, aircraft bombing and tanks, all had failed.

Colonel Charles Canham and Cota went on to distinguish themselves by showing their faces to the men, exhorting them to gather weapons and to regroup and press on. It was through their drive and courage that the 116th got off the beach on DOG WHITE and saved OMAHA from becoming a total and unmitigated disaster – it could so easily have been the beach that the allies failed to take that day. Canham was wounded in the hand 'about ten minutes after landing' as he took fire from the cliffs above him but carried on with a handkerchief around his wounded hand and, with his pistol in the other, inspiring the men who had once hated him, to now follow him – and they did. Canham was awarded the Distinguished Service Cross for his actions on D-Day. His reputation as a hard and strict disciplinarian was well known – that is why he was given command of the 116th for two years in the first place. At the end of the day, Canham took into this battle the only National Guard unit on D-Day – and he took them into OMAHA beach.

The challenge was immense. In a letter to Cornelius Ryan dated 21 May, 1958, from Colonel Canham's son, Captain Charles D.W. Canham II, the reputation and reticence of his father was well recognised – by then Major General Canham had answered Cornellius Ryans' request for information from survivors of OMAHA with the crispness and conciseness of a man not used to wasting words. Captain Canham on the other hand was keen that his father's reputation not suffocate his service on the beach that day and said the following:

> 'I felt called on to write to you this because I know he wouldn't. Among his most treasured possessions is a stack of letters from members of the regiment which all run in substance as the one I will quote. 'I used to think you were a hard bastard for the way you drove us in training in England, but now I know that the training you gave us and your personal leadership were responsible for saving my life…'[111]

But Colonel Canham and Lieutenant Gearing were not the only men who distinguished themselves that day. As is so often the case in close combat fighting, many men deserved the highest awards for gallantry but either were not seen or those that had seen their bravery died before anyone could report what had happened. Another hero noted by Ray Nance was the Company A medic from Iowa Cecil Breeden who, in the eyes of fellow Company A infantryman Hal Baumgarten, 'was probably the single greatest hero of D-Day.' The later report cited in Kershaw's book from the United States Army Medical Department stated:

[because of the] '*actions and example of men like the medic Breeden,* [Company A] *survivors found the will to rescue many of the wounded from the advancing tide and move off the beach to a sheltered position where the remnants of the company rallied. Were it not for Breeden all of them might well have died on the beach.*'[112]

Chapter Seventeen

Reactions, Repatriations & Remembrance

Reactions

Back on the *Empire Javelin*, news had been filtering through all day of the fighting on OMAHA beach. One by one as the landing craft returned and were winched back on board, the damage from bullet holes and the empty davits told their own story of the severe fight that had taken place earlier that morning. There was a gloomy and depressed air amongst the crew of the ship and more news came when Sub-Lieutenant Jimmy Green brought back the first survivors from the sunken LCA911.

Rescued from almost certain death by Jimmy Green the men sat on the decks of the ship where, only a few hours before, so many of their friends had been sitting and playing cards on the journey over – after so many years and experiences together, they now lay dead, rolling around in the surf of that Normandy beach. Destined to spend another two nights on the *Javelin* before she weighed anchor and headed back towards Plymouth, the survivors on board the *Empire Javelin* from Bedford included Lieutenant Elisha (Ray) Nance, Charles Fizer, Harold Wilkes and Sergeant Roy Stevens but there was also Private First Class John Barnes – still alive but not sure how he had managed it. Also from Bedford was Tony Marsico. From a bed on board the *Empire Javelin*, Nance remembered how, while still on the beach, unable to move and bleeding out from his ankle wound:

'Then, all of a sudden, a navy medic wearing green overalls was leaning over him. Nance was soaked and covered in oil and grease. The medic looked immaculate, dry as a bone. He knelt at Nance's side and started to examine him. He had been in combat before. That was clear from the way he handled himself under fire.

"This is worse than Salerno", he told Nance.

The medic gave him a shot of morphine, opened up his hobnailed boot and dressed his heel wound. At some point, Nance had also been shot in the hand and again in his foot.'[113]

Meanwhile beach parties had tried to clear the beach of bodies from 7 June onwards, even with the occasional shells still dropping on the coastline during early June. Given the unexpected scale of the losses, it took some time for the command structures to assimilate what had happened and how many good men had been lost. But decisions had to be made quickly and the 607th Quartermaster Graves Registration Company established a temporary cemetery on the bluffs overlooking OMAHA and began the task of collecting the hundreds of bodies from the beach from the day before. Many were still rolling back and forth in the surf while others had disappeared altogether.

Up on the shingle beach around the right-hand bunker that had done so much damage and probably wiped out Captain Fellers and his men as they assembled before moving up the beach, the piles of bodies still seemed like bundles of driftwood from a distance. Contorted bodies but somehow resplendently peaceful in death. Men from Bedford lay there intermingled with their lifelong friends and with men from New York – tangled in distorted and contented shapes having made the ultimate sacrifice the day before.

On 6 June, nineteen men from tiny Bedford Virginia had been killed on OMAHA beach but they were not alone – almost the entire company had been lost around them. The few that survived went on to fight in a reconstructed Company, but nineteen of their comrades were dead on the beaches of Normandy. In total twenty-two men from Bedford were killed in the Normandy campaign – men who would now become known as the Bedford Boys. From Company A and killed on OMAHA beach were:

Leslie Abbott	Joseph Parker
John Clifton	Jack Powers
John Dean	John Reynolds
Frank Draper Jr	Weldon Rosazza
Taylor Fellers	John Schenk
Charles Fizer	
Nicholas Gillaspie	Ray Stevens
Bedford Hoback	Gordon White
Raymond Hoback	John Wilkes
Clifton Lee	Elmer Wright
Earl Parker	Grant Yopp

But let us not forget the dozens of other men from that company that were also killed. Apart from the Bedford Boys, a further 180 men of Company A were killed that day and now lay in the cemeteries of Normandy or back to their homes in the United States. Long after the war, in 1987, Thomas Valance – a survivor from the LCA in which Master Sergeant John Wilkes was on board – wrote:

> 'I've wondered over the years about one thing, and that is why we, in Company A of the 1st Battalion of the 116th Infantry, 29th Division, were chosen to be the American equivalent of stormtroopers. Was it because we had such potential? We had no combat [experience], and the other troops that were around and with us in the invasion, such as the 1st Division, were highly trained. Or was it simply because we were considered expendable?'[114]

Back in Bedford

First news reports that the allies had landed in France reached the United States airwaves in the early hours of the morning of 6 June. With the time lag, it was around 08.30 in Normandy but 03.32 in the small town of Bedford. Across America, the same statement was read out in every state at the same time: 'Under the command of General Eisenhower, Allied naval forces, supported by strong air forces, began landing Allied armies this morning on the northern coast of France.' President Roosevelt had been woken at 03.00 with the news that the landings had begun and he immediately rose and remained on the telephone to various of his commanders until 09.00 that morning.

As morning broke, doors had opened to the sound of church bells ringing and, in every town, city and state, worried mothers ran to friends and family for consolation. Fathers went silent and brothers clamoured for more information. The mail from England had recently stopped arriving in Bedford and expected letters home seemed to be held up but no one had known why – now it became clearer that their husbands, sons, brothers and fathers had been unable to write as they had been preparing to land in France.

America reacted in many different ways and specially scheduled services were held in churches in every state to pray for victory and the lives of their loved ones. Kieth Huxen, Director of Research at the National World War Two Museum wrote:

> 'The reaction of many Americans, whenever they found out what was happening that day, was to attend religious services. Churches and synagogues were reportedly packed across the country.'[115]

Roosevelt used his evening address to the nation to emphasise the need for ongoing prayer – he knew only too well that this was just the start and nobody knew how the German reaction and response would play out, or whether the toe-hold the allied forces had in Normandy could be maintained. In Times Square, passers-by paused to look up at news flashes posted on the Times Building and the Mayor of New York, Fiorello La Guardia, led New York in a mass meeting at Maddison Square Gardens, praying for the 'liberation of the world from tyranny'.

In Bedford Virginia, Alex Kershaw paints a picture of calm forbearance, a sense of shock about a day that they had always known would come coupled with a determination that life had to go on.

> 'In her parlour in Bedford, Ivylyn Schenk sat with her mother close to an old radio. "Mama brought me what she thought I would enjoy eating, and she sat there with me most of the day as we listened to all the reports" recalled Ivylyn. "I knew that John would be involved in the invasion. He had not told me anything directly but in a round-about way I knew."'
>
> 'Bettie Wilkes switched on the radio while eating breakfast. At 7 a.m., she had to be at the Belding Hemmingway plant, where she made material used for parachutes – the same parachutes used by the 101st Airborne on D-Day. "I caught the early news. I thought John might be involved but I hoped he was not. We were just hoping to get through the war, begin our lives together...In his most recent letter, John had said: 'I probably won't be able to write for a while, but I will as soon as I can.'"[116]

In ports all along the south coast of England, ships started returning from Normandy. When they had left only a few days previously, there was an air of great patriotism and pride in the fleets with their colours flying from the hundreds of masts as the great armada set sail. But the return was far more sombre. From a distance it was possible for the hundreds of nurses and ambulances to see men laying on the decks of the ships. As they edged closer to the quays and wharfs, flecks of white bandages speckled with red came into focus and when the ships were finally docked, the scale of the losses was visible for all to see.

After almost eighty years since D-Day we are now very close to exact figures of deaths and casualties and those returning ships brought back just under 10,000 wounded men from all the beaches combined – many of these would subsequently die, adding to the actual death toll number which today stands at 4,414 allied deaths on D-Day itself. Of these, 2,501 were Americans composed of soldiers, sailors, coastguardsmen and airmen killed on the first day of the Normandy campaign. On OMAHA alone, within the 116th Infantry regiment the losses were high. Of the 3,100 men of the regiment that went into combat on 6 June, 1,007 became casualties – basically one in every three men was either wounded or killed with Company A annihilated and many of the others down to under half strength. For the exceptionally tough 43-year-old Colonel Charles Canham, the losses were no doubt hard to accept, as indeed they were for many as word started to seep out.

Amongst the survivors of Company A from Bedford were Charles Fizer, Harold Wilkes, Clyde Powers and Sergeant Roy Stevens. Climbing down the ramp of the *Empire Javelin*, they were soon re armed and equipped and, together with batches of other men who had similarly been brought back recused from the sea, they were sent to Southampton and, from there, back to France on the next transport to rejoin their units. Forbidden to discuss anything with anyone, Roy Stevens was amazed when they were landed back on DOG GREEN beach only this time there was no gunfire and it was as if the whole American army had set up camp there. The bunkers were silent, the German defenders either dead, wounded or prisoners of war and, before they went off to find their unit, they wanted to find where the casualties from that day were buried.

At Coleville-sur-Mer the men, carrying their new rifles and equipment, came across a temporary graveyard covered with crosses from which dog tags hung. By the time they had wandered past only a few the names of their friends from Bedford began to appear and then one by one they realised that almost the whole contingent from Bedford was laid there, dead all around them – including Ray Stevens, Roy's brother and Jack Powers – Clyde's brother. The total number of men from Bedford who had landed with A Company from the *Empire Javelin* was thirty-four and now nineteen of them were lying here in the field around them. How many others were still out there – explosions may have seen some bodies disintegrate never to be found again and others washed out to sea? As the black servicemen of the burial details continued their work of collecting bodies and laying the remains in white sacks, they realised that the field was covered in dozens of bodies waiting to be buried. In under a month Charles Fizer would be killed by a strafing Luftwaffe aircraft as he slept outside and he himself would be sown into one of those white bags, another casualty from tiny Bedford.

Repatriations

Long before anything official was posted out to families, the wounded started to communicate in advance of the official news. For the rest of June, families across America wondered and waited for news – had their sons been involved in the landings or were they now going in? Were they in France now fighting in Normandy or had they been wounded in the first days of the invasion? Many of the wives in Bedford occupied their evenings by rolling bandages for the war effort. Viola Parker recalled 'We knew the casualties were high, but we always hoped it wasn't ours. As time went on, we had no letters. We were lucky not to have had any televisions then because we would've seen what happened.' Other families in Bedford had already lost men in the war and the 'Gold Star Mother' patriotic symbol of sacrifice already hung in numerous windows across America and indeed in Bedford – but would there be more? It was impossible to find out information and the agony continued day after day, night after night – it was the not knowing that was the worst anguish of all. Then, slowly at first, in late June letters began arriving in the town from men serving in the 29th – they commented on how noble the sacrifice of the division had been and the immortality of the men who had given their lives on D-Day.

According to Alex Kershaw, Earl Parker's mother was one of the first to receive notification that her son was listed as missing in action. Her daughter in law Viola refused to take the information in and focussed on Danny, the daughter Earl had not yet met. Even a month later, on 6 July, there was still no official news but that day the Bedford Bulletin did carry a story about D-Day. Apparently, Company A had indeed landed in the first waves on D-Day and had been commended for their role and commented on the 'uneasiness' about the fate of the men that now permeated the town. A few days later Bettie Wilkes, walking down towards Green's the drugstore that everyone knew, bumped into a friend who told her she had received a letter saying that John had been killed. On that same day, 10 July, the younger sister of Taylor Fellers, Bertie, was in the sunny garden with her parents when a letter arrived from the United Kingdom. It was from Mrs Lunscomb – whose dinner invitations to Taylor and other officers had lightened their training and routine in Ivybridge. Mrs Lunscomb wrote of her great sadness that Taylor had been killed – she had been told by letter from a fellow officer in Company B who had kept in touch with her. Bertie apparently knew there was something deeply wrong when her birthday card to her brother for his thirtieth birthday on 10 June had been 'returned to sender'.

Then the avalanche of pain truly began as, in the early morning of 11 June, Elizabeth Teass turned on her teletype machine which was part of the Western Union national telegraph system:

'Teass's heart sank as she read the first line of copy: "The Secretary of War desires me to express his deep regret". Teass had seen these words before……Line after line of copy clicked out of the printer. Within a few minutes, as Teass watched in a "trance like state," it was clear that something terrible had happened to Company A. "I just sat and watched them and wondered how many more it was going to be."[117]

The sadness in so many families in Bedford was crippling. That first flurry of telegrams accounted for nine men but there would be more, at least another ten within a few days and the inconsolable families cried long into the days and nights. Eventually all nineteen men who lost their lives on D-Day would be named to be followed by another three in the fighting in Normandy and the town was changed forever, as it is today, marked by such a tremendous loss in such a short space of time. A generation was very nearly wiped out on a far-flung beach that few had even heard of, in a country they would never see and were buried in a graveyard without their family beside them.

Just after news reached the parents of Taylor Fellers that Mrs Lunscomb had heard of their son's death, a poem appeared in the Bedford Bulletin on 15 July. Written by Naomi Newman, Captain Taylor Fellers' wife it read:

> *I mourn for you in silence*
> *No eyes can see me weep*
> *But many a silent tear is shed*
> *While others are asleep.*
> *Never did I know that the gift I sent*
> *Would mean so little on your birthday, June tenth,*
> *It will always break my heart and will cause many a tear*
> *Just to know your burial day would have been your thirtieth year.*

Part VI

The Death of a Ship

'…. the day I first experienced war – a day I'll never forget – a day the end of which I (and now, you) will never cease being thankful for – a disaster and a miracle.'

Major Joseph C. Hazen Jr.[118]

The *Empire Javelin* docked at Plymouth and needed to take on a fresh crew and make repairs to the remaining landing craft – all as quickly as possible as there were many more runs across the English Channel to come over the next few months. Sub-Lieutenant Jimmy Green continued to work with the 551st Flotilla and completed a number of trips across to Normandy and his LCAs continued to be dropped from the davits and take men to and from the quaysides – the same craft that had done such sterling work on 6 June.

The instructions now were for *Empire Javelin* to continue her role as an infantry transport ship. It is hard to know whether any of the thousands of troops that she was to ferry across the English Channel and into battle – first in Normandy and then deep into Germany – ever knew what her role had been on D-Day. Possibly her crew of Royal Navy gunners and their commanding officer Lieutenant Gilmour, passed the time chatting about what she had done on that epic day and the men of the 116th who had been the first, the very first, to travel on her decks. More likely, they had no time to dwell on the past, and they locked these memories away – the speed of events in war make nostalgia a luxury of survival when hostilities are over.

Chapter 18

September to December, 1944

After D-Day the *Empire Javelin* was needed everywhere and made numerous 'runs' across the Channel on into the stormy weather of autumn and carefully staying in lanes cleared by the minesweepers. On every trip, which was on average a 100 mile run to Le Havre or other coastal parts of Brittany, feeding men and supplies into Patton's Third Army. The gunnery officer on board the *Javelin* was still Lieutenant John Gilmour RNVR and he and most of the gunnery crew stayed on the *Javelin* from the start of her service right to the end.

'Sometimes the weather was fine, but often it was foul, wet and windy, and unpleasant to be on the open bridge, or like my gunmen who were on watch. The marker buoys were lit but very low-powered, and about five miles apart. The journey was about one hundred miles each way.'

Lt John Gilmour[119]

Shortly after D-Day, the *Empire Javelin* was tasked with a special mission. A long forgotten diversionary tactic as part of OVERLORD was the landing of 1,200 American troops on the west coast of Brittany. Few people seem to have known about this, and research is needed to clarify the details, but Sub-Lieutenant Green was certain that the *Empire Javelin* was ordered to sail around the north coast of Brittany, down through the Channel Islands and onto a small inlet off the Brittany coastline. The intention was to pick up these men from the beach, by the use of landing craft, and then ferry them back through the Channel Islands and drop them – on OMAHA beach. It is hardly surprising that these troops needed rescuing as the Germans had overwhelming superiority in numbers. Sailing in at action stations, Lieutenant Gilmour recalled how he expected to be either fired at or have to deal with E-Boats from Guernsey or Jersey but they were lucky, collected the troops and made a speedy exit. Whether the *Empire Javelin* carried out this mission alone or with an escort, Gilmour did not elaborate.

Occasionally the weather was so bad that entire convoys were prevented from crossing the channel, leaving large numbers of ships packed with troops having to drop anchor and ride out the storm. The decks could be awash with vomit and sea sick men. The *Empire Javelin* could still carry around 1,500 men per trip but this was a heavy cargo and added to her heaving in the swells. On one occasion, the *Javelin* was part of a convoy of thirty ships, including small frigate or destroyer escorts, but the weather was so bad that the convoy commander ordered them all to drop anchor just in the lee of the Isle of Wight to try to shelter from the storm. Dropping both anchors to try to hold her in place, the waves were such that even these huge steel chains could not hold and they broke. The captain could see no way of stopping the ship being wrecked on the rocks – there were no brakes on ships like the *Javelin* so he started the engines and determined to sail around a buoy overnight until the morning. At daylight they were not alone and according to Lieutenant Gilmour, there were twenty-seven ships' anchors and chains on the bottom of the sea. The whole convoy, together with a very unwell complement of American soldiers, sailed for Southampton and new anchors and chains.

Apart from bad weather there was always the silent enemy of fog and the magnetic mines that littered the Channel coastlines. These mines were nasty. They were designed to lay on the sea bed and were activated by the noise of a ship's engines and propellers or by detecting the magnetic signature that a ship generates as it moves through the water. The British had been experts at anti-mine warfare since 1940 and degaussing – cables fitted around the hull to negate the magnetic field – had been fitted to most ships but contact mines were still out there and in large numbers. If a ship was lucky then it passed over the mine before it could hit the hull, if not then a huge explosion would result and normally towards the aft as the ship moved forward. Often the back of the ship would break by the pressure of a magnetic mine exploding many metres below the surface.

By November 1944, and with the ports of Le Havre and Cherbourg in allied hands, LCA Flotilla 551 was no longer needed, as troops could be disembarked straight onto the quayside and so the *Empire Javelin* received orders to sail for Fowey in Cornwall to drop her boats off permanently:

'We arrived there in the morning and the landing craft were dropped and tied up at the far end of the harbour. 'Father' (the captain) decided to have a party for all the flotilla officers and it duly took place. The doctor and I were invited. As we were not due to depart til the next morning, it was decided that we would go ashore after dinner. There was only one sailor who was teetotal, so he was left on board to look after the ship, which was moored fore and aft so [she] could come to no harm. A naval liberty boat took us all ashore, and it was quite a night. Never had the pubs and hotels done such business. In the end, we were

ferried back. How we all got up the side of the ship safely, I will never know. I
suppose in a way it helped to break the tension. There was no damage ashore,
and when we left, most of the natives lined the shore to cheer us out.'

Lt J.A. Gilmour[120]

As the *Empire Javelin* unloaded her LCAs for the final time and they were
moored in the river there, Jimmy Green departed the *Empire Javelin* after
such an intense and moving year of his life on board. Those LCAs sat there
for some time, they had been built for a single purpose and had done their job
well. LCA911, the boat that had carried the Bedford Boys into battle, was one
of them.

As a postscript to this phase of the *Empire Javelin*'s life, it is well worth
recording that Jimmy Green was determined to record his memories of D-Day
and to correct the flamboyant disregard for the facts shown in certain history
books – he named 'Ambrose' (presumably Stephen Ambrose in his book D-Day)
as the worst offender when he stated that Captain Fellers and his men were
struck by a German weapon which 'vaporised' the LCA and all of the men on
board. These fantasies hurt him and Jimmy Green's personal and participant
evidence has put that theory down as a complete fantasy. He never forgot his
conversations with, or the bravery of, Captain Taylor Fellers and his men as he
landed them on that grey and misty June morning when the world changed
for them all.

Christmas 1944 was spent at anchor off Cowes on the Isle of Wight. They
had no troops on board at this moment and the Chief Steward laid on a superb
lunch for all hands – still in the freezers were stores that had been loaded on
board back in the United States over a year previously and never been used.
Turkey, York Hams, asparagus and smoked salmon all made for a bizarre but well
overdue party after the stress of each channel crossing – so far without incident.

A sister ship of the *Empire Javelin* was the *Empire Broadsword* – she had been
built in Wilmington too and named the *Cape Marshall*, and been doing exactly
the same job as the *Empire Javelin*. In his memoirs Lieutenant Gilmour stated
that it was the *Empire Battleaxe* that sank but in fact the Mitchell & Sawyer
directory on the Empire class of ships tells that *Battleaxe* completed the war
unscathed whereas the *Empire Broadsword* was sunk by a mine on 2 July 1944
off Normandy.[121] A point to note here is that all the Empire class of ships sailed
without enough lifeboats – this was to allow the maximum amount of room
for the storage of men and LCAs on board. Gilmour was right to say that, at
the time, the crew was very concerned as the *Broadsword* sank quickly and with
many hands lost – of the crew of 200, only seventy survivors were picked up and
she now lies in 27 metres of water just off the Normandy coastline.

Christmas Day and the Battle of the Bulge, December 1944

But the good cheer of the Christmas Day 1944 dinner just off Cowes would not last long. On the Franco-German border, Hitler had launched his offensive designed to win the war for Germany in the west. The initial advances were rapid and frightening, catching the allies by surprise; reinforcements were needed, and fast. The new United States Fifteenth Army, which had been created in August 1944 in Texas had also arrived at Greenock in Scotland, on board the *Queen Mary*, just as their forebears of the 29th Division had done, and the *Aquitania* and the temporary headquarters was quartered at Doddington Hall in Cheshire. The Battle of the Bulge necessitated the immediate relocation of the Army Headquarters to France and both officers and men moved immediately southwards on 24 December 1944, arriving in Southampton on the 25th to be met by a series of ships, including the *Empire Javelin* which arrived from Cowes on the 26th. 208 officers and 624 enlisted men of the Fifteenth Army Headquarters boarded the *Empire Javelin* which already had 650 United States troops on board plus the crew – the ship was packed to the gunnels as she slipped anchor on 28 December and made for France.

Major Joe Hazen

Major Joseph C. Hazen Jr was one of the American officers on board the *Empire Javelin* as she left Southampton. Born in Janesville, Wisconsin but raised in Illinois and New Jersey, Joseph Hazen majored in architecture at Princeton, was a talented artist and spent his spare time jotting down sketches on any spare pieces of paper he could find. Major Hazen was part of the command structure for the artillery units in Fifteenth Army. Recording his thoughts in January 1945, he recalled how, while at Doddington Hall near Manchester in Cheshire, he received an urgent movement order to move south. Wary of the wartime censorship, he was cautious with details but there is more than enough to get factually close to the events of that last week of December in 1944:

> '...*we said goodbye to our palatial "estate" camp not far from Manchester, England. I was a member of the advance party comprised of some two dozen officers and two hundred enlisted men. Col. Sisson was in charge of the party as a whole; I was in command of the troops. We were on our way to France! First by bus to the station in the nearest town; then by train to a port in Southern England* [we know this was Southampton] *– about a 12-hour ride which was completely uneventful. Here we were met by trucks which took us, not to the pier, but to a tent camp – a miserable place which I believe I described in my Christmas letters.*'
>
> *Major Joseph C. Hazen Jr*[122]

For virtually all soldiers throughout the history of warfare, army life was and is composed of long periods of training, movement and boredom, punctuated by sudden conflict and occasionally death. This is especially true of the 'poor bloody infantry' who are often the worst fed, have the worst beds and sometimes poorly led. Major Hazen's view of Christmas 1944 fits with this generally held view of the depression of the infantry soldier:

> *'The features most vivid in my mind were the cold nights spent on a canvass cot trying to sleep completely clothed and under three army blankets, the lack of light, the series of meals of C rations, the turkey dinner on Christmas [Day] which was excellent but which made 60% of my men sick with the 'trots'.'*
>
> *Major Joseph C. Hazen Jr*[123]

The unit then moved to Camp Eastleigh, a holding camp and former 'sausage' just to the north of Southampton. In a post war description of his detailed drawings, Major Joe Hazen described how he had drawn what he referred to as 'Camp Beastly':

"CAMP BEASTLY" SOUTHAMPTON ENGLAND CHRISTMAS 1944

Camp Eastleigh in Cheshire drawn by Major Joseph Hazen Jr and ironically re-named 'Camp Beastly'. Note the many footprints in the snow from men hurrying to the latrines in the bottom right of the drawing – a gift from the Christmas Turkey of 1944.

'Something was wrong with the Christmas Turkey, and about 75% of the population had the "trots" that night – the sketch shows one of the poor fellows running to the latrine. You'll note that several others left footprints in the snow as they cut corners in their hasty trips to this popular installation. This was a truly miserable place – zero weather, two blankets and very little fuel, worst of all, nothing but canned C rations.'[124]

Two days later, the unit was ordered to break camp and get moving by a foot march the four-miles into Southampton, in full field packs and weapons and then board the *Empire Javelin*. Moving off at 14.00, they arrived late in the afternoon of 27 December. On the way there, Sergeant Frank Mueller described what he saw:

'Southampton was the worst bombed English city I saw. Block after block of houses were levelled especially around the docks. There was hardly a part of Southampton that was not touched by the blitz.'

Sgt Mueller[125]

Also on 27 December, Eisenhower and Montgomery were arriving for a meeting the next day to discuss how best to deal with the German offensive – they had surrounded Bastogne only three days earlier and were now set to advance towards Antwerp so there was a certain urgency to get this Headquarters unit over to Le Havre and on into Belgium.

'After boarding the ship, we ate a late but hot and comparatively excellent meal and went to bed in the well heated hold. That night, the rest of the outfit caught up with us and also boarded the transport – so did five other smaller units which were going our way. The next morning, we were still tied up to the pier, it being too foggy to set sail. Early that morning I made an announcement over the ship's public address equipment to my men who were quartered in two different parts of the ship.'

Major J. C. Hazen Jr.[126]

Naturally no one on board had time or the knowledge to recall that this was the same public address system that had ordered the men of the 1st Battalion, 116th Infantry to board their boats on the morning of 6 June, only some six months previously. Equally, the bunks and beds they had slept in, the desk that Major Hazen was using as he continued to give out instructions over the Tannoy system, had once been there for Captain Taylor Fellers for him to plan out the landing on DOG GREEN beach. Nobody knew what the *Empire Javelin* had already done and where she had been in her short but important life.

When Major Hazen, Sergeant Mueller and their men joined the *Empire Javelin* they were not the first on board. Already there were over 800 men crammed into the aft of the ship. Thanks to Philip Newson, the Maritime Quest archives display the SHAEF signals for the events that followed including a detailed breakdown of the United States units on board the *Empire Javelin* for the coming voyage. A total of 268 officers and 1,215 enlisted men composed of:

56 Hospital Train
HQ 3188 Sig Serv. Bn
473 Medical Company
3188 Sig Service Bn, Company C
360 Harbour Craft Company
Advance Platoon 16th Medical Depot Company and
HQ and HQ Special Troops Fifteenth Army

Sergeant Mueller and his fellow infantrymen had already been on board for a day having arrived on the 26th. For him, the lower decks were just a mass of slowly moving men. Corridors were hot and stuffy with men waiting for the queues to move so they could find a berth for the journey. Officers and NCOs could shout orders as much as they wished, there was just so little room in the holds to move around with full packs, helmets, rifles and bags. The only place Schoichet and his compatriots could find that wasn't crammed was the cafeteria so they just each claimed a steel table and shoved their gear underneath aiming to sleep there that night – better than the three high cots well down in the holds and also better than the tents they had been used to. While Major Hazen gave out his last announcements for eating rotas that evening of the 27th and then bedded down in his quarters as an officer, Schoichet bedded down on his steel table in the mess:

'*We slept like pigs that first night aboard the Empire Javelin* [the 26th]. *When morning came, we discovered that we were still tied up to the pier. Time moved lazily along all that day and that evening.* [Major Hazen and the 15th Army HQ troops arrived that day]. *We had nothing to do and were enjoying ourselves at it. There were countless card games in progress everywhere aboard, and the clarion call of the clinking cubes* [dice] *were plentifully audible. We were having one hellava time. That night we bunked in the cafeteria again. We began to wonder when we were to leave. The suspense became slightly annoying. So, no one felt sorry when the next morning brought the noises of preparations to cast off. There was a general exodus to the open decks and many of us watched the slowly retreating outlines of England with more than a tinge of regret. We had missed a good many of the comforts of life there, but nevertheless our immediate future was at least uncertain and bound to bring with it much more pronounced discomforts than we had already experienced.'*

Schoichet[127]

The *Empire Javelin* was able to start her engines and cast off in a late morning mist at 11.20 on 28 December 1944 and started her way out of Southampton bound for Le Havre with her crew of merchant seamen and nearly 1,500 American troops. Captain McLean was still the master of the ship and, in convoy with the *Javelin*, was the merchant ship SS *Monowai* and an escorting French frigate named the *L'Escarmouche* with Captain de Lesquen du Plessis-Easso in command. The French frigate was originally a River Class frigate in the Royal Navy named HMS *Frome* before being transferred to the Free French Navy on 3 March 1944. By 14.20 the *Empire Javelin* was making good progress and

S.S. EMPIRE JAVELIN   28 DECEMBER 1944

From the stable deck of the French frigate the *L'Escarmouche*, Major Joseph Hazen Jr. was able to sketch the dying *Empire Javelin* from close by. Note that she is sinking by the stern, after the first explosion, and the many swinging ropes over her side down which the 1,400 American soldiers and the Merchant and Royal Navy crews had escaped. Note also the *Empire Javelin's* identification flags still on her masts.

was making 12 knots on a zig zag course as usual to avoid torpedo attacks. The *Javelin* had just passed the half way mark on her journey to France.

'I was in the operations room, sitting at my desk, finishing a wedding day letter to Mary and Bob which had started the night before. I had just finished a sentence commenting on the many good fortunes of us Hazens when WHAM! and I was bounced out of my chair into the air and onto the floor about eight feet away from my starting position. The two other officers and one enlisted man in the room and I all picked ourselves up – our knees a bit wobbly, our ears ringing and our noses smelling cordite fumes. By that time the stern of the ship was no longer level – and all of us knew that we had run afoul of either a mine or a torpedo. I remember that one of the boys said "this is it", another, "what do we do now", and I thought and said out loud "thank god we are where we are and not back there in the stern.'

Major Joseph Hazen[128]

All those unannounced abandon ship practices, all those alarm bell warning sounds and now, within seconds, it was for real. Confusion but not panic simmered across the ship – the men with Schoichet were shaving out of their helmets and relaxing when they too were felled like rows of trees across the entire deck. According to the official accounts of the *History of the 15th Army*, the explosion was on the starboard side and just back from the middle of the ship, so not quite in the stern area. In his Action Report, Lieutenant John Gilmour noted how the crew responded just as they had been trained and lookouts were asked to report any torpedo tracks in order to see where the submarine might be. In the event, the lookouts saw no tracks anywhere around the ship – but that did not mean for certain that a U-boat was not there. The other possibility was that the *Empire Javelin* had hit either a loose mine that had drifted into their channel or a magnetic mine below them had picked up the ship's magnetic signature and had exploded.

Below deck was Staff Sergeant Joe Bein. He had been leaving the toilet and was on his way to his bunk when the explosion occurred. Being in the rear of the ship, Sergeant Bein was right next to the plates where the explosion ripped into the ship.

'I felt a terrific jar and heard the crashing of timber as well as the rushing of water. I steadied myself against the nearby bunks and put my hand over my face for a second as things were flying around. The lights went out and there was the smell of burnt cordite – all was quiet. It seemed that everyone else was up on deck so I decided to make my way back to my bunk, get my life-preserver,

and go on deck. As I passed the opening to the hold, the sound of rushing water became more distinct. The explosion had moved heavy timbers so they had completely closed the opening, but above the noise of the water I heard a voice that will be with me the rest of my life. It was the voice of a pleading, hurt man, dying man realizing that his time had come, and fighting his best to survive. He yelled "Save me, help me, save me" and then yelled for his mother. I tried to see if there was any way to raise the timbers, but couldn't budge them.'

Staff Sgt. Joe Bein
U.S.Army[129]

A working party did rush down to help, but it was too late and the hold was already full of water.

The first thing Captain McLean needed to know was the extent of the damage. Was the ship sinking and how long did they have? At the back of his mind was also the very large quantity of whiskey that had been taken on board at Plymouth and how to grab a bottle before the ship sank – if indeed that was likely. If it was a torpedo, then they wouldn't have long before another would slam into them and then they clearly would be going down very fast. Back in the stern area of the ship where the explosion had ripped into the engine room, there were already some terrible injuries and fatalities.

In the radio room, Arthur Coxhead was at his station and began sending out a morse message that they had been hit. Powered by batteries, the morse signal was the only way they could attempt to get a communication out. Arthur was an experienced sailor. He had voyaged to New Zealand and Australia and, during wartime, he had served in the Mediterranean theatre which was a brutal campaign with many losses in ships and men in the Malta convoys. So Arthur had already seen a lot of action before he signed on as radio operator for the *Empire Javelin* at Southampton on 26 November 1944.

Below decks Sergeant Frank Mueller recorded the scenes he saw when the explosion occurred:

'The lights went out! We were all knocked off our feet: duffle bags, bunks, barracks bags, rifles – everything came tumbling down in our path. The whole ship shook like a giant had it in his hands. Finally after what seemed like an eternity we regained our feet, felt to see if our lifebelts were on and waited for the second explosion – none came.

Somebody lit a match. Somebody else yelled "put that out". It was dangerous as we could smell the powder and gas and it might have started a fire. The first thing we saw when coming up on deck were three fellows sprawled out, their heads split open and blood gushing out. The medics and first aid men were working on them, but it looked hopeless for one of the fellows. They had been standing under some steel beams when the explosion had occurred and were thrown up and their heads hit the beams.'

Sgt Frank Mueller[130]

These three men were not the only casualties. Below decks, seven of Captain McLean's crewmen were dead, dying or trapped – they had been working in the engine room when the explosion tore a hole straight through the side and sent massive steel plates through to the inside of the hull where water was now gushing in. Only shutting one of the five compartments off completely was stopping the ship sinking straight away, but if another explosion occurred then the *Javelin* was doomed. As it was, the stern had settled already quite some way and the bows were lifting up out of the water.

On the bridge, the gunnery officer Lieutenant John Gilmour reacted quickly as the captain had not yet arrived as he struggled in the dark from his cabin. Unable to use the Tannoy system as all power had failed, Glimour shouted through a loudhailer 'Close all watertight doors and scuttles.' 'Troops to boat stations.' 'Guns crews and ship's company to action stations.' There was a deathly silence throughout the ship as 1,500 men waited for a second explosion or for the ship to start sliding under the water. It is of tremendous credit to the United States Army that the men grabbed what they could and filed quietly around the ship to line up near their boat stations – many eye witness accounts testify to the calmness in the face of imminent doom that was shown on the *Javelin* that afternoon. The only problem was that there were no boats. All the davits were empty and there were only a few stacks of rubber life rafts, if the *Empire Javelin* sank quickly at that moment, they would all be in the water, with heavy boots and helmets and undoubtedly hundreds would be dragged beneath the water by the sinking ship.

The engines had stopped and the *Empire Javelin* slowly came to a standstill and was dropping by the stern. Following wartime directives, the SS *Monowai* had immediately picked up speed and carried on, away from what might be a roaming submarine, and sailed into the distance – the frigate also doubled its speed to seemingly get away which was not a very encouraging sign to everyone on board the *Empire Javelin*. The *Empire Javelin* was on her own – without any form of rescue nearby, without lifeboats and without power. There was an eery silence across the whole ship.

Having been thrown from his settee in his cabin, Captain John McLean did the next two most important things by instinct – he grabbed his cap and a half empty bottle of whiskey. Pushing the bottle into the pocket of his large blue serge navy jacket, Captain McLean ran down the stairs to inspect the damage in the engine room and find out the state of his injured crewmen. McLean next sent word to Lieutenant Gilmour, who stood alone on the bridge, that the bulkheads were under great strain and that the sea was breaking though – in fact the *Empire Javelin* was on the way to breaking in half, unable to take the strain of holding the forward part and bows of the ship out of the water.

Gilmour stood and wondered what to do – time seemed to stand still – but it only seemed like that. What felt like hours were in fact seconds. The entire fate of 1,500 men depended on what Gilmour chose to do next – and he had minutes to decide.

Major Hazen recalled running down to his cabin more than once to collect items of value to him. A picture of his wife was in his wallet and he wanted that with him if he was in the water and going to die. The Headquarters unit of 15th Army stood on deck, colonels, majors, captains, lieutenants all equally helpless alongside nearly 1,000 enlisted men, green helmets everywhere but no one to fight except the sea. As Gilmour and the Captain now met on the bridge and discussed what could be done, and as they knew full well that another torpedo might slam into them at any time, a lookout shouted that a ship was now approaching. Indeed, it was, and in its wake were occasional explosions – it was the *L'Escarmouche* and behind her the LST 325. The frigate, K267, had turned around once the SS *Monowai* was out of sight and the huge American LST had picked up the signal. LST 325 was a substantial ship and if she could help then a solution was possible. Also closing in on the far horizon to help was the British ship HMS *Hargood*.

On her return to the *Empire Javelin*, *L'Escarmouche* was dropping depth charges to frighten away any U-boat in the area and as she got closer, Captain McLean agreed that they should try to get the French ship to take at least some of the men off the *Empire Javelin* – but how to communicate with the French ship? Sometimes frustrating, sometimes making the most glaring of errors but never doubt the ability of the British to plan and carry out bureaucracy to the highest levels. In its wisdom, the British Admiralty had placed on board all 'foreign' vessels that now were under its command whether they be Poles, Norwegians, French or Dutch, an RNVR officer was on board to act as liaison with the British fleets and they, as part of their training, understood semaphore – messaging by flags.

On board the *Empire Javelin* Lieutenant Gilmour noted that he had six 'bunting tossers' – naval signallers whose job it was to run up flags and communicate with other ships by semaphore. They had been left on the *Empire Javelin* after D-Day and no one seemed to take responsibility for them so they had just stayed on board living quite comfortably. Gilmour shouted for them to come to the bridge and to start sending a signal to the French ship to come alongside and start taking off some of the troops. Hearing that there were 1,500 men on board, Captain Du Plessis-Easso responded that he could not possibly take that number but he would take as many as he could and came alongside.

Requesting five officers come aboard first to order the troops where to go on board his ship, Captain Du Plessis-Easso then ordered slip ropes to be fitted to hold the two ships together – right on cue, the English Channel was starting to heave a little stronger and the light was failing fast – if the *Javelin* suddenly sank, they would need to slip the ropes and let her go.

It should come as no surprise that there were real problems holding two large steel ships together in a heaving sea. Both hulls screamed and shrieked like banshees as steel rubbed against steel. To make matters even more chaotic, the huge steel davits of the *Empire Javelin*, now dangling quite high in the air, started to swing out towards the French ship – two smashed into the bridge of the *L'Escarmouche* causing a lot of broken armoured glass and tearing into steel frames. The main problem was that the *Empire Javelin* was a lot higher than the French ship so the first transfer of men started from the lower decks while the scrambling nets – the same nets that had put American troops into their boats in Normandy after D-Day – were thrown down the sides of the ship and men had to simply jump from one to the other. French sailors tried to catch the dozens of men as they transferred over – each man was a man certainly saved from the sea and no-one knew how long they had to go. The *Empire Javelin* held together, her bulkheads creaking and buckling and almost seeming to know that they needed to hold on for as long as they could, taking the strain and not giving way, holding the cracks in her steel side for as long as she could possibly do so.

'As the French frigate came alongside of us, it necessarily rammed into several steel beams that projected out from out ship. This made a lot of noise and considerably damaged the French ship's superstructure, and they kept hammering the frigate as she bobbed up and down beside us in the increasingly rough seas.'

Major Joseph Hazen[131]

Had there been a large-scale panic amongst the men, for example if another torpedo had slammed into the *Empire Javelin* or indeed into *L'Escarmouche* then this would be a story of another tragedy at sea with a huge loss of life. As it was, the American troops stood and did exactly as they were told by their officers and the Royal Navy under Lieutenant John Gilmour took command and did what it was trained to do:

'Looking back on the incident over 40 years, I have come to the conclusion that as Captain McLean was Merchant Navy and I was Royal Navy, he expected me to take command of the situation. In times of crisis the Royal Navy is in complete control and is trusted to do the job properly. This must have affected the US troops also. At the time, I would gladly have been the first overboard, but I was trained not only to fight but to defend those in my care. My trust was in God and my prayer that I would be equal to the task.'

Lt. John Gilmour R.N.[132]

The lifeboat, the French and the depth charge

All along the join between the two ships – the *Empire Javelin* dead in the water and swaying like a lifeless whale while alongside her pup was bobbing up and down in the water as a mass of green uniformed men jumped onto the canvass of French lifeboats or wobbled across wooden planks or simply jumped when the French ship came up to meet them. In any episode of concentrated human activity in wartime, there are always many moving parts, moving stories and men who were moved by events. Often, most likely nearly always, so much that took place is either not recorded or the personalities involved are themselves lost in the action. The same is very true on board this single, short period of time on board the *Empire Javelin* where, without realising it at the time, numerous separate events occurred that, ordinarily, would fade into obscurity. Take, for example, the story recorded by our eponymous friend Schoichet. From his new vantage point on board the *L'Escarmouche* he could see activity all around the *Empire Javelin*.

Major Hazen had taken the initiative and, with Captain McLean's permission, had his men launch the life rafts into the water and scramble nets down the hull of the ship, the rafts were already full and moving away from the dying ship. The sole lifeboat left on board had been filled with the wounded, some of whom were simply too badly injured to be transferred easily or quickly enough over to the *L'Escarmouche*, and this was gently lowered away with the critically injured which included one of the comrades of Schoichet:

'...the life boat which contained the most seriously injured men attended by a surgeon had pulled a considerable distance from the ship and the men in it were fondly waving to us. One who could not wave to us and nevermore to be seen was one of the boys of the Medical Section – Bob France – who lay unconscious in the boat. He had been struck by the fall of a large searchlight at the time of the explosion and had suffered a severe injury at the base of his skull.'[133]

Although Schoichet was not to find out until long after the war, Bob France did not survive his injuries. Taken on board another vessel, he was operated on at the main US military hospital in Cambridge in the United Kingdom but there he died of his wounds.

Another small but important event involved Harold Crompton, the engineer officer on board the *Empire Javelin*. He had just completed washing two of his detachable collars from his shirts in his cabin when the first explosion rocked the ship. Hit by a falling wooden wardrobe from behind, he had fallen forward and knocked himself unconscious on the ceramic sink and, after some minutes when he woke, he was on his knees and trapped. After pushing it away and opening the porthole, Harold was able to clear the smoke in his room, dress and run out on deck where he saw a corvette – it was in fact the frigate *L'Escarmouche* heading towards them. Next to him he could hear American voices coming up through the ventilation pipes shouting that they were trapped. With a steadily increasing headache, and probably a serious case of concussion, Harold's step brother, Dennis Crompton, takes up the story:

'..*made his way down to an inspection plate over the shaft which was only large enough for a man's head, Harold shone his torch into the shaft and saw three or four soldiers there. He told them he'd do his best to get them out and made his way back on deck by which time the Free French L'Escarmouche was alongside and he called out to some Americans on board that some of their guys were trapped below and needed cutting gear to free them. Some French sailors went below and came back with huge coils of piping and metal cutting gear which they took below, and after explaining to the trapped soldiers that they needed to keep back a little, commenced cutting the deck plating to enlarge the hole.*'[134]

At this point Harold seems to have been overcome by his head injury, was helped over to the *L'Escarmouche* and taken into sick bay where he fell unconscious. He learnt later that the American troops had managed to get out and off the *Empire Javelin* before she exploded and sank, thanks to him and the bravery of those French sailors. In his memoirs, radio operator Arthur Coxhead recorded the names of the two French sailors who jumped over onto the *Empire Javelin* with their oxyacetylene torch – Goarant and Iaffont – one can only hope that they received the recognition that they deserved.

One incident could have seen both ships sink together. Private Ellis Titche from Louisiana was another member of the 15th Army advance party and also the artillery support unit with Major Joseph Hazen. With a memory for detail as shown by his recollections, Ellis was standing on the side of the *Empire Javelin* waiting to get over to the *L'Escarmouche* when he and his friends saw a quite unbelievable sight. With the decks of both ships heaving up and down as the sailors of both ships tried to rope them together, a depth charge – fully armed and ready to drop as they had been chasing a supposed submarine – broke free and started rolling down the aft deck of the frigate. It was heading for some heavy steel casings and, if it had hit them, it would most likely have exploded and blown the rear of the ship apart. A French sailor, without thinking, threw his body under the rolling drum and took the full impact, acting like a soft buffer to hold the depth charge in place and they were able to put it back into its rack and make it secure.

Within fifteen minutes, hundreds of men had used the entire length of the French ship and crawled, jumped or walked over the gap between the two ships – like ants leaving a disturbed nest, they went in every direction they could. Some tragically fell into the water between the two ships and were lost – estimated at the time to be thirteen – one of which was Private First Class Robert Guyser. In 2012 Lili Marlene Golden enclosed a picture to Maritime Quest of both her father Peter A. Golden and Robert Guyser sitting on the *Empire Javelin* on the day she sank. An incredibly rare photograph of both ship and two American soldiers – one who survived and one who did not.

Major Hazen assisted his men in getting off the *Empire Javelin* by finding a rope cargo sling and had it thrown over to the French ship commenting:

> *'Many of the men would never have been able to make the jumps and do the other athletic feats they did had it been a rehearsal. But this was the real thing and they needed no coaxing. Only a few landed in the water. After boosting about one hundred and fifty fellows over the rail and into the net, I boosted myself over and climbed up the net to the frigate's bridge. I was the last one off the bow of the ship, and by the time I climbed down to the frigate's deck, our sinking ship had been abandoned by everyone except the captain and a dozen other members of her crew.'*[135]

Back on the bridge of the stricken *Empire Javelin*, the captain told Lieutenant Gilmour that the bulkheads were breaking up and that she could not last much longer. Knowing that the end was nigh, Gilmour gave the order to 'abandon ship; Stand fast gun crews' – still aware that she could be attacked by German aircraft even at this late stage. Over the side went the 200 crew of the *Empire Javelin* and, following them down the scrambling nets were, at last, the gun crews.

'Captain McLean was standing on the bridge with the Chief Engineer. I reported to the captain, who said 'We want no bloody heroes here; off you go and that is an order, but please ask their captain to stand off for a little in case anything happens.' He expected a quick breakup of the *Javelin*, and he and the chief engineer elected to remain on board.'

Lieutenant Gilmour saluted and made his way off the *Empire Javelin* for the final time and into the hands of his sailors at the bottom of a rope.

> *'How L'Escarmouche was able to take so many extra men on board is nothing short of a miracle.'*

Slipping the ropes as quickly as possible, the French ship now moved away to about 100 yards or so from the *Empire Javelin* and dropped a small boat in the water to pick up the captain and chief engineer from the *Empire Javelin* but also the signal operator Arthur Coxhead who had remained at his post throughout and the engineering officer Harold Crompton. All along the decks of the *L'Escarmouche* and in almost every conceivable place, stood relieved and grateful US troops and crewmen as they watched the *Empire Javelin*, the ship that had kept in one piece while they had escaped as she sat crippled in the water. Suddenly and unexpectedly another massive explosion rang out.

> *'Another explosion. It was so loud, so shocking we all thought that the frigate or the LST had been hit. But an instant later when we looked toward the ill-fated transport, we were reassured by the awful sight we saw. What appeared to be about half of the transport was sailing sky high in thousands of pieces – everything that had been on the deck was tumbling over and over through the air.'*
>
> Lt. James Gilmour[136]

The thump was below the water line but the noise and water hurled into the air shook the small French ship tipping her over to port and, for a moment, she rocked. The entire centre of the *Empire Javelin* exploded into the air and the ship visibly broke into two parts. The captain and chief engineer could be seen jumping into the water at the very last second and the small French rowing boat set off immediately to pick them up. By now the winds were reaching into gale force and it was touch and go collecting Captain McLean from the high swells. Over his shoulder the *Empire Javelin* was making her final dive and her captain watched as she went slowly down. From the sound of the second explosion to her disappearing from view there were only three and a half minutes. It had only been thirty minutes since the sound of the first explosion.

Postscript

On board the *L'Escarmouche*, the main concern was tipping over. There was no way that this little ship should have been able to fit every one of the passengers from the already crammed *Empire Javelin* into her small spaces – but they did. Ordered to stand in particular places on the ship to try to balance her out, crammed in the holds and even on the bridge, the French ship heaved in the now gale force winds – it was not a storm but it was bad enough and the sea sickness began again. Within half an hour the waiting LST 325 came alongside her to reduce the burden and threw down scramble nets from her far higher decks – over 700 men climbed aboard LST 325 for which her captain, Lieutenant Commander Mosier, was awarded the Bronze Star. The *L'Escarmouche* was initially ordered to head back to Portsmouth and she started back at 17.25 that day only to be turned around again and sent to Le Havre where she arrived at 03.50 the following morning and landed her remaining 700 men – it had been some 24 hours.

One of the soldiers attached to 15th Army Headquarters was Lewis D. Rindone. Aged 25 at the time, Lewis was in the signal corps and also a photographer. Before he left the *Empire Javelin* he had run back down into the ship and retrieved his camera and it is thanks to him that we have preserved for posterity the images of the *Empire Javelin* in her final moments before she slipped beneath the waves along with those of Paul Beltz.

'It was just like in the movies', remarked one soldier in a letter home and no doubt it was, but who on board watching the bows of the ship say goodbye to the world could know anything about her brief but eventful life. *The Empire Javelin* began life as an idea for a class of cargo ships and then became claimed as part of the negotiations for lend lease and was built with the D-Day landings in mind. From her conception through to her building and role in being the foremost landing ship on OMAHA beach and then her subsequent sinking there had only been four years, but what a four years it was. Ships have a special and emotional place in the hearts of people and the SS *Empire Javelin*, though not a famous ship or even a special ship, did what she was asked to do and now lies not far from the cemetery at OMAHA beach where her first passengers also lie looking back at her.

Recalling what happened next, Lieutenant Gilmour RNVR was grateful not only for the bravery shown by the French crew but also their hospitality – as best they could provide – on their journey on to Le Havre. With so many men now on LST 325, conditions on board the *L'Escarmouche* had improved considerably. Once in Le Havre, Gilmour and the rest of his complement of naval ratings were put on board a British frigate, HMS *Hargood* and, on the

29th, taken back again to Portsmouth. Following the same route, they passed the site where the *Javelin* had sunk and saw a number of ships dropping charges and still looking for the supposed U-boat.

Landing at noon the next day, 30 December, Gilmour saw to it that his crew received new clothing from the stores in Portsmouth and seven days survivors' leave before himself settling down to write his action report which he was ordered to hand into the Admiralty Headquarters the next day. In this report to the Admiralty, Gilmour wrote the following:

> *'It is my opinion that the first explosion was caused by a mine. My opinion is based on the location of the damage which was at the Engine Room and No. 4 Hold. The SS Empire Cutlass, as sister ship to the SS Empire Javelin sustained damage to a similar part of her hull and I have seen other ships with damage at that part. The second explosion I think might have been caused by a mine, magnetic or otherwise as due to the lack of power the degaussing gear would be out of action. It appeared to take place about No.5 Hold in the region of the 4-inch gun magazine. Some of this ammunition and ammunition in adjoining lockers may have been detonated at the same time.'*[137]

Several hours were expended looking for the German submarine, but it was never discovered. Many years have passed and still numerous accounts claim that the *Empire Javelin* was torpedoed by *U-772* but the claim was never verified either by the Germans or by the U-boat itself, and it is almost certain that John Gilmour was right. There were no torpedo tracks – not even for the second explosion when the *Empire Javelin* was surrounded by ships overlooking her sad state, they would certainly have been seen by someone. Why was there such a delay between the torpedoes if in fact there was a submarine in the area and why did she not shoot at the many other ships gathering around? No, the *Empire Javelin* sailed over a magnetic mine or into mines that had strayed into her channel.

Epilogue

'Immortality is to live your life doing good things, and leaving your mark behind.'
Brandon Lee

The loss of the SS *Empire Javelin* that December of 1944 went unrecorded in Bedford Virginia – and quite rightly so. Apart from the fact that secrecy meant that no one even knew what ship the boys had travelled on, no one cared anyway. The families and friends of the men in unform had far more grieving to do and some still harboured thoughts that the Army was wrong and their sons, brothers or husbands might still be alive and might walk through their door at any moment. But, over time, along with millions of other families in loss, very slowly acceptance overcame hope. Bedrooms were re-arranged, treasured possessions reminding them of their loved ones were put away, insurance money was received, prayers of hope were replaced by sermons of thanks and wardrobes of clothes and shoes given to friends and family.

The men may have gone but their memory and sacrifice lived on. As the 1940s turned into the 1950s, it was possible to focus on the future and how the past should be recorded. For the town, which had lost nineteen men on D-Day and another three shortly after and a total of thirty-eight in all theatres, it was clear that a memorial was needed and fitting and what was felt in Bedford was replicated elsewhere – in the halls of the Headquarters of the 29th Division, in Ivybridge in Devon and in Normandy itself. Before that however, some of the boys returned and had their say too.

In Normandy the United States and French governments agreed on a permanent cemetery to commemorate the American military dead and, from 1947 onwards, families were given the choice of having their loved ones returned home for burial or leaving them to be reinterred into the new cemetery which was designed and prepared for opening in July 1956. For some, the thought of bringing their son or brother back was too much, maybe just best to leave them with their friends and colleagues. For others, the need to be reunited was overwhelming and the first of the dead to arrive home to Bedford was Sergeant Dickie Abbott who was a mere 22 when he gave his life for freedom on Dog Green beach. Arriving back in Bedford on 7 December 1947 – six years after that 'day that would live in infamy' the Bedford Firemen's Band was there to welcome him home. Most of the bandsmen remembered they had played and marched when Dickie Abbott was one of nearly 100 National Guardsmen marching down Main Street on 18 February 1941 – except this time it was not 'The Star-Spangled Banner' but 'Nearer My God To Thee'. The wooden casket, draped with the Stars and Stripes, stood on the steps of the courthouse where Dickie had trained with his friends before the war. According to Alex Kershaw, 2,000 people filed past to pay their respects.

It was Frank Draper Jr who came home next – his mother apparently opening the casket to ensure it was indeed her son. His terrible shoulder and side wounds from the impact of the shell that hit his landing craft were concealed and the impact of being buried in England and then brought home was covered by his infantry uniform – with skin that, 'if you blew on it would just float away.' More were to follow and the majority are today interred in the town's Greenwood Cemetery, where they rest in the Virginian soil that helped to create them.

In Normandy, the world-renowned American Cemetery stands immaculate and reverential in the highest traditions of the American people. It is here, on the cliffs above the daily tides of Omaha beach, that many of the men of Company A can be found. Nick Gillaspie, Bedford Hoback, Clifton Lee, Jack Powers, Weldon Rosazza, John Reynolds, John Schenk, Ray Stevens, John Wilkes, Elmere Wright and Grant Yopp lie in different parts of the cemetery, united in death overlooking the long sandy beach that they had trained so often to run up in Devon. Their journey had begun in Bedford Virginia, continued across the Atlantic Ocean on board the *Queen Mary*, taken them down the length of Britain from Glasgow to Devon where they spent their last days in an English village, the SS *Empire Javelin* then brought them to the start line of that final race and now here they lay having lived a good life and left their mark on history.

They are buried in rows alongside 9,238 white marble crosses and 151 Stars of David. Amongst them are 45 pairs of brothers, a father and son and three generals. There are also 304 unknown soldiers who are 'Known Only to God.' Staff Sergeants Earl Parker and Raymond Hoback are immortalised on the Tablets of the Missing. Earl Parker's younger brother Joseph, who was killed on 27 August 1944, is also buried at the American Cemetery in Normandy as is Charles Fizer who was killed just over a month after surviving D-Day on 11 July 1944.

Captain Taylor Fellers did not stay in Normandy, his was one of those whose bodies were repatriated back to the United States. Taylor Fellers was reburied in Greenwood Cemetery in Bedford where his parents Peter and Annie Fellers, and his siblings Royal, Ellen (Bertie) and Janie were able to visit him during the rest of their lives. Looking quite forgotten now, Fellers' small engraved marker is humble and deteriorating with time, but it marks out the resting place of not only a brave and noble man, but a fine and respected officer of the United States Army. Just to the north west of Bedford, some twelve miles away in the dispersed community of Cifax, once stood the Nazareth Methodist Church. Just behind the pulpit, two stained glass windows were installed and dedicated on 10 June 1945 by his parents – that would have been the date of Taylor Fellers 31st birthday. The church is no longer there, but the stained-glass windows now reside in the hands of the D-Day Memorial in Bedford.

Lieutenant Ray Nance returned home to Bedford and lived the rest of his life in the shadow of what happened on that one morning in June 1944. He regularly spoke and supported efforts to preserve the memories of the men who died that day and he never found the answer as to why he survived and so many did not. Ray Nance passed away in April 2009 and was remembered in the *New York Times* as 'symbolising the sacrifices of all the Americans who fell at Normandy on D-Day.' He once said, 'I never was very good at reading people's hearts. There was a little twinge of guilt that I was allowed to come back.'

Bedford is home to the National D-Day Memorial. Supported by numerous donations and driven on by dedicated volunteers including John Robert 'Bob' Slaughter, the project came to fruition on 6 June 2001 when President George W. Bush joined 15,000 people on the 80-acre plot. It serves today as a national reminder of the sacrifices made for the freedom to decide the future of the nation. A constant range of educational programmes and events make this a vibrant and ever-present testament to the lives freely given that day.

Within the town there are other smaller stone memorials including one created from stone salvaged from Omaha beach itself and taken to Bedford – this is the scene of an annual service of remembrance in the town every year on 6 June. Bedford is also the location of the Bedford Boys Tribute Centre which holds, together with the National D-Day Memorial, many of the personal effects of the men from the town who died in Normandy. Movingly located within the building that was once Green's Drugstore, the memories of the total of thirty-eight men from Bedford that gave their lives in the Second World War are immortalised in a mass of memorabilia and mementos.

A further grey granite stone memorial stands in the centre of the town of Ivybridge in Devon. News of the losses eventually reached the town during the late summer of 1945 and thereafter of the specific role of the 116th infantry on the beaches of Normandy. Like the families of Bedford, many of the townspeople wondered and worried about what had happened to those young men that they met, danced with, and in some cases loved. To discover that they formed the very first wave must have shocked many of the townspeople.

To enshrine the memory of the association of the 1st Battalion of the 116th Infantry with the town, there have been annual gatherings – especially strong in the 1990s before the number of survivors began to fade. A section of Uphill field still remains in the custody of the town and is kept as a small area of parkland where residents and children can walk – it is in fact the portion of the camp that was the actual site of the Company A Nissen huts. Here and there are signs of the former buildings, paths and roads and a careful investigation in the hedges and trees reveals the concrete bases of outhouses and shower blocks. A beautifully designed oak bench sits humbly against a hedgerow, each tall bleached spindle recording the names and the height in years of the men who died – bleached like the bones of the men it commemorates. In the town itself stands a beautiful granite memorial complete with a GI helmet on one side commemorating the men and that time in the town's history. The local historical society dedicate themselves to preserving all aspects of the history of the town and have never allowed the sacrifice of their visitors between 1943 and 1944 to be forgotten.

At nearby Slapton Sands, where fate spared the 1st Battalion of the 116th Infantry the tragedy that struck their comrades as they took part in Operation Tiger, a lone rusting Sherman tank stands to mark the bodies that washed up on that beach or that were lost at sea. It was on that spot too that the men of Company A landed and trained running up a sandy and wet beach when the tide was out – although no record of their being there exists – yet.

Southwards and over the English Channel and along the coastline of OMAHA beach, the remains of the *Wilderstandsnester* stand empty, their concrete shells a distant memory of the men of the 352nd and the 716th Infantry Divisions that manned them. The grass and shrubs may have recovered and now dominate the hillsides, but the thousands of pockmarks from craters still resonate with the massive gunfire from the ships of Force O – though sadly very few of them are from the bombers that once flew over this section of what was to become the new allied front.

On the beach itself, the tide does what it has done for millions of years – the tidal times remain the same regardless of mankind's activity. Here and there rusty pieces of metal protrude from the stones and the bullets of the MG42s lay deep under the sand in their tens of thousands as a silent secret of what happened over a few hours in 1944. The villages that overlook the beach are now towns and have spread outwards onto what were grassy sand hills where men killed each other, bled and died but the basic geography is the same. If you partially shut your eyes and let your imagination go, then you can breathe deeply and almost see the chaos on that beach from 1944 and where the men from Virginia came to die, visualising the SS *Empire Javelin* some six miles offshore watching her cargo bleed to death on the beach.

There are fourteen monuments of one kind or another along Omaha beach. In Vierville-sur-Mer itself proudly stands the 29th Division memorial. The D-1 objective looks very familiar and the section that was once Dog Green is still guarded by the two bunkers that took so many lives within such a short space of time, mowing the men down like grass with a scythe and on odd walls here and there are other plaques to the Rangers and the Combat Engineers who also suffered just as badly as the infantry.

The mortally injured body of Captain Walter O. Schilling of Company D was later recovered from his LCA and he is buried in the American Cemetery in Normandy – as are Captain Robert Ware, the 1st Battalion Medical Officer, who fell as soon as his ramp went down, and Lieutenant Benjamin Rives Kearfott, who arrived to support A Company only five days before D-Day. Back in the United States of America, a cenotaph was built and erected for Lieutenant Kearfott in Oakwood Cemetery in Martinsville, Virginia. His young wife Mary, whom he had married before leaving for overseas, never re-married and died in 1999. They had no time to have children. Remembering Benjamin Kearfott, his first cousin, once removed, recalls being told that *'he was by all accounts an outstanding person. Kind smart, athletic, handsome. When I asked my brother if he remembered anything our mom had told him about Cousin Ben, all he could think of was that Ben had red hair. He has always been a hero of mine.'*

The family of Captain Ettore Zappacosta of B Company wanted their young son and hero brought home and he is buried in the Holy Cross Cemetery in Yeadon, Pennsylvania while Captain Berthier Hawks of Company C, having survived D-Day was killed in action just before the end of the war on 6 April 1945. He too was returned home and is buried in the Emporia Cemetery in Virginia. Lieutenant William Gardner of Company D was also repatriated at the request of his family and he is buried in the national cemetery at Arlington in Virginia.

Lieutenant Colonel John Alfred Metcalfe III, the commanding officer of the 1st Battalion, 16th Infantry, survived D-Day itself and continued to lead the remnants of the battalion until he too was severely wounded later on 29 June. Like the medic from the SS *Empire Javelin*, John Metcalfe was transferred back to the American hospital in Cambridge, England where he sadly died of his wounds on 15 July 1944. He is buried in the American Cemetery in Cambridge, England.

32 year old Second Lieutenant John B. Clements Jr of New York, another young officer sent to Company A in preparation for heavy casualties, had married just before his departure to Lucy Frances Ferraro in August 1942. Having been

killed in action trying to attack the right-hand bunker on Dog Green beach, his body was repatriated to the United States and is buried in Saint Patrick's Cemetery in Yonkers, New York.

The Germans too lost thousands of men in the first days of the Normandy campaign. An hour's drive over to the west coast of Brittany, stands the German Ossuary outside the small village of Huisnes-sur-Mer. Almost blended into the countryside and surrounded by small grass hills, this place is testament to the difficulty the German authorities had in identifying just how many men they lost in Normandy. In the distance, rising out of the sea like a mystical fortress is Mont St Michel, while to the other are the bones of nearly 12,000 German soldiers. The two-storey semi-circular building contains 34 crypts, each with the bones of 180 soldiers and the plaques leading into each crypt contain the names of those that are known to be there – less than 20 per cent of the total.

One of those whose bones are identified and interred in Huisnes-sue-Mer is 53-year-old Lieutenant General Dietrich Kraiss, who commanded the 352nd Infantry Division. Kraiss withdrew what was left of his badly mauled forces from Omaha and continued to fight a withdrawal action near St Lo where, on 2 August he was severely wounded and died four days later. For his determined efforts to hold back the advancing American forces he was posthumously awarded the Knights Cross of the Iron Cross with Oak Leaves on 1 August 1944.

Oberleutnant Hahn of the 5th Companie, 916th Grenadier Regiment was captured at Sanit-Laurant-sur-Mer and survived D-Day as did Lieutenant Colonel (Oberstleutnant) Fritz Ziegalmann who was subsequently transported to the United States for interrogation and later released. The MG 42 machine gunner, Henrik Naube, miraculously survived the D-Day landings and was a prisoner of war in England for the rest of the war.

Back in England, as one walks along the north bank of the River Thames at Tower Hill, the large and imposing Tower Hill Memorial appears with its large brass plaques carefully engraved. Often ignored as part of the infrastructure of the area, do not be fooled into thinking this is just a one-sided one-dimensional piece. A little investigation will reveal that it is actually one side of the vaulted colonnade that reaches back into the gardens behind it. This is the only way that Lutyens, who was commissioned to design the memorial, could foresee holding the 12,000 names of merchant seaman who lost their lives in the First World War. When the names of the lost at sea from the Second World War were added, this memorial alone contains twenty-thousand names. Listed with the ships on which they died, it is possible to locate the SS *Empire Javelin* and the seven members of her crew who were killed in the first explosion towards the rear half of the ship:

Davies J.H.D was aged 33 and was an electrician on board the *Empire Javelin*.

Hooper R., Robert was engaged as a Donkeyman on board the ship (engineer).

Jones C., Cyril was only 23 years old and from Wales. He had served on the *Empire Javelin* throughout her life with the Merchant Navy.

Robinson D., David Robinson was the Third Officer on board and aged 21.

Scrymgeour G.K., Gordon was aged 27 and was the Third Engineer Officer and was from Cheshire.

Shaw C.J.P., Charles was aged 27 and an Able Seaman.

Southgate D.W.J., Douglas was aged 21 and was also an Able Seaman.

In a post on the Maritime Quest website, Alan Slater tells of how Captain John McLean, his grandfather and the master of the *Empire Javelin*, survived the sinking and settled peacefully in the north-east of England after the war.

Arthur John Coxhead, the radio operator on board the *Empire Javelin* who stayed on board until the end sending out his signals was one of many heroes that day and survived into old age.

Lieutenant John Anderson Gilmour RNVR (1904–1992) wrote down all his memories in old school notebooks and his daughter Margaret set out to preserve and tell his story and achieved both brilliantly.

Lieutenant Jimmy 'Jimmy the One' Green RNVR survived the war. His many experiences served him well and his on-line recollections provide a penetrating and comprehensive view of the work of some of the forgotten heroes of the Normandy landings – the British Royal Navy crews of the landing craft on OMAHA beach. His family, especially Kevan Elsby, have dedicated a large part of their lives to researching the details of 6 June and Jimmy Green's desire that the role of the Royal Navy should not be forgotten.

The Royal Navy surgeon on board the *Empire Javelin* for the duration of her service was Surgeon Lieutenant W. J. Naunton RNVR. His medical team were often complimented for their high standard of efficiency and no doubt Naunton played a key role in attending to the first US casualties as they were brought back on board some two hours after H-Hour on the morning of 6 June. He would have tended to Lieutenant Ray Nance and his painful and bleeding ankle and did what he could for the mortally wounded Sergeant Frank Draper. In 1947, Naunton decided to paint an oil painting of the SS *Empire Javelin* and it was the chance discovery of this painting by the author, jumbled up with many others, that was the genesis of the idea for this book.

The First Lieutenant on LST 325, which came to the rescue of the *Empire Javelin* was Edward Dunning and he recorded how they received a distress call and took off 700 troops by rope ladders from the frigate *L'Escarmouche* and then watched as *Empire Javelin* slipped beneath the waves. LST 325 served in the landings at Gela, Sicily, Salerno and Normandy and survived the war and was immortalised itself in a 2004 book entitled *'Mosiers Raiders'* by David Bronson. Now moored in Evansville, Indiana, LST 325 is a visitor attraction and her engines can still move her from port to port. A remarkable ship.

Lewis D. Rindone, who had the presence of mind to take photographs of the *Empire Javelin* as she sank, survived the war and passed away on 1 September 2010.

The SHAEF report for 1 January 1945 lists one man as dead – T/4 Paul Mayer of the 16th Medical Depot Company who died in Le Havre from his injuries. However, it also goes on to list thirteen other men who were missing, presumed dead:

M/Sgt Charles C Hiltabidle	PFC Curtis B Hill
T/4 Anthony Costa	PFC Stanley J Janusgezak
Cpl John P Robertson	Pte Ottis C Bray
Cpl Christian F Wanner	Pte Michael Dime
T/5 David Cochran	Pte Lonnie C Hand
T/5 Myer D Saucerman	Pte Edward F Walsh
PFC Robert Guyser	

Major General Norman 'Dutch' Cota went on to receive the Distinguished Service Cross for his actions on D-Day. Later he took command of 28th Infantry Division and ended the war near Cologne. Hoping to remain in the US Army, his requests were all denied and he left the Army on 30 June, 1946. He died on 4 October 1971 and is buried with his wife Connie at the West Point Cemetery.

Lieutenant Edward Marcellus Gearing, the only officer of Company A to survive unscathed from Dog Green beach, was awarded the Distinguished Service Cross for his courageous activities clearing the cliffs later during the day of 6 June 1944. Gearing was a regular officer from Woodstock Virginia and had attended Fort Benning Officer School before joining the 29th Division. He arrived into Company A on 1 June 1944 as a second lieutenant and, having survived D-Day, was wounded on 7 June and spent the summer of 1944 either in hospital or back with Company C and then Company A where he was promoted to captain at some point late in 1944. Edward Gearing's parents must have been so relieved that their son survived the war but the harrowing experience that he endured must have lived with him heavily. He was hospitalised again on returning home which is where he met his wife, Betty Zucca, and they were married on 18 May 1946 in Danbury, Connecticut. Betty and Edward had five children but Edward developed a very aggressive form of cancer and died very young at the age of 38 on 13 April 1962 and is buried at the Arlington National

Cemetery in Virginia alongside Betty. His father Frank passed away in 1978 and his mother Bertha died in 1966.

Colonel Charles Canham was awarded the Distinguished Service Cross for his actions on D-Day and later in the fighting for St Lô and the Distinguished Service Order by the British government. Before his service ended in 1960, Canham had been commanding general of the 82nd Airborne Division and 3rd Infantry Division and retired with the rank of Major General. He died aged 62 on 21 August 1963 and is buried at Arlington National Cemetery.

Sergeant Roy Stevens lived to the age of 87 and died in Bedford on 1 January 2007. He never got to grow old with his brother Ray and he is buried at Thaxton Baptist Church Cemetery. Roy was a founding member of the Board of Directors of the National D-Day Memorial and a lifelong member of the 29th Division Association and gave his life to good causes in and around the community.

The final resting place of the SS *Empire Javelin* is almost exactly halfway across the English Channel at 50°5′ N 1°0′ W – sitting as it were, between the two countries she was built to serve on a line between Portsmouth and Barfleur. She had sailed a long way from Wilmington, California and served her country well – the men and women that built her can feel very proud of the brave men she carried and the work that she did. On 14 December 2019 the United States flag which flew from one of the signal lines on board the *Empire Javelin*, came up for auction. Frayed and with a small square piece missing, no doubt cut as a souvenir by a survivor of her sinking, the flag must have been taken down before she sank. Once in the possession of a Dr Clarence Rungee, the worn, soiled and frayed flag had overseen the entire life of the ship and now rests somewhere in the hands of a collector.

Most recently, the Bible belonging to Raymond Hoback found on OMAHA beach on 7 June was given by his sister Lucille to the D-Day Memorial and Museum in Bedford VA. It had travelled to the beaches of Normandy and back home again where it will now remain along with the memory of that fateful day in history.

Amongst all the individual stories that make up this book there is one final tale to tell. In 1938 after all the prototypes of a new British Landing Craft Assault proposals had been assessed, there were two finalists – one from Thornycroft and the other designed by Mr Fleming of Liverpool. Each had failings but the Royal Marines, who tested landing quickly from each of the boats with a platoon of men, reported that they could exit the Fleming boat in a quarter of the time it took to get out of the Thornycroft. It was the fact that the Thornycroft was quieter and that the silhouette was lower that won the day – both were thought to be vital in landing Marines under stealth conditions. The one thing that was not needed on Omaha beach on 6 June 1944 was stealth.

Notes

PART I

1. Britain was perhaps the most advanced nation, in the world in terms of aeronautical research and could boast of great advances in aircraft design and engineering not least with the Supermarine Spitfire developments at the Vickers yards in Southampton and the work of Reginald Mitchell.
2. Baxter, J.P., *Scientists Against Time*, Little Brown, 1946.
3. The acronym MAUD stood for Military Application of Uranium Detonation and was the name of a secret committee formed by G.P. Thompson in June 1940.
4. Kershaw, A., *The Bedford Boys*, Da Capo Press, 2003, p.27

PART II

5. *Virginia National Guard Review*, Published 1940.
6. Kershaw, p.15
7. The one-eyed Kichisburo Nomura was a former Admiral in the Imperial Japanese Navy and, no matter how future films may have portrayed his anguish and disappointment with the failure of negotiations between Japan and America, he was well aware of the Naval position and no doubt supportive of the military solution sought by Japan.
8. Kershaw, p.21
9. This division is often overlooked in the annals of American military history. It was formed outside the United States under the threat of an attack on New Caledonia by the Japanese – the name 'Americal' came from the 'American, New Caledonian Division.'
10. Kershaw, p.25
11. Leonard T. Gerow was an outstanding soldier and attended the Virginia Military Institute and entered the United States Army direct from there as their top student. Gerow was selected for the command of the 29th Division as, not only was he highly experienced, but also because of his knowledge of the type of men from Virginia that made up the division. He would be a Corps commander by D-Day, 1944.
12. Charles Draper William Canham was a career soldier. From Mississippi, Canham was appointed as colonel of the 116th Infantry and was both feared and respected by the men under his command. By the end of his career, Charles Canham would rise to the rank of major general.

PART III

13. The Germans broadcast many clams that the *Queen Mary* had been sunk but these were mostly for propaganda purposes, while numerous U-boat captains hoped to claim the reward and also reported her sunk.
14. Churchill travelled three times on the *Queen Mary* and had a great affinity with the ship, seeing it as symbolic of the British nation in its steadfast fight against Nazism.
15. Prior to the Second World War, much of the United States Army had remained unchanged since 1918 but Pearl Harbor necessitated a widescale re-think and refitting

of the entire army. Much of this, often unpopular, work was led by General Lesley J. McNair who, as commander of Army Ground Forces, had a simple overriding objective which was to create units with the maximum of men and materials in offensive striking units to destroy the enemy. For an excellent analysis of this aspect read *The Evolution of the US Army Infantry Battalion, 1939–1968* by Virgil Ney published in 1968 by HQ United States Army Combat Development Command.

16. Kershaw, p.48
17. *History of COSSAC, (Chief of staff to Supreme Allied Commander) 1943–1944* prepared by The Historical Sub-Section. Supreme Headquarters, Allied Expeditionary Force.
18. Kershaw, p.57–8
19. McCarthy, D., papers of the Ivybridge Research Society
20. Kershaw, p.57
21. Figures here are quoted from the *American Historical Association*, EM13, on how the Lend-Lease accounts were calculated.
22. BBC, *The Peoples War Archives*, Lt. J. Green RN
23. Ladd, J.D., *Assault from the Sea, 1939–1945*, p.36
24. In training exercises, which were mostly carried out in stable weather, the bilge pumps on the Duplex Drive tanks were easily overwhelmed if sufficient water came over the top of the waterproof skirting. This fact was well known and to launch in difficult weather would almost certainly create losses amongst the tank crews – another fact that was well known by commanders.
25. Fraser, D., *A Life of Field Marshal Erwin Rommel* (1994) p.212
26. Ibid. p.213
27. Bryant, Stewart, Jewish Virtual Library translations, 2002.
28. Ibid.
29. Eckhertz, H., *D-Day Through German Eyes* (2016) p.42
30. Ibid. p.149–50
31. Ibid. p.43
32. Ibid. p.44
33. Ibid. p.47
34. Ibid. p.68
35. Murray, Williamson, *Field Marshal Erwin Rommel's Defence of Normandy During World War Two*, History Net (2006)
36. Bryant, Stewart, Jewish Virtual Library translations.

PART IV
37. Extract from and courtesy of Ivybridge Research Group (IRG) archives
38. Ibid.
39. Ibid.
40. Ibid.
41. Kershaw, p.64
42. Ibid., p.65
43. Ibid., IRG archives
44. Ibid. IRG archives
45. Ibid., IRG archives
46. Ibid., IRG archives
47. Ibid., IRG archives
48. Ibid., IRG archives
49. Ibid., IRG archives

50. Ibid., IRG archives and in Slaughter, R., *Omaha Beach and Beyond: The Long March of Sergeant Bob Slaughter* (2007)

51. Kershaw, p.83–8

52. For short biographies, and in most cases a photograph, look at the 11th Infantry Roll of Honor.

53. For a greater examination of the disaster at Slapton Sands see Lawrence., W.S., *Exercise Tiger: The Forgotten Sacrifice of the Silent Few*, Fonthill Media, 2015.

54. Ambrose., Stephen E., *D-Day: The Battle of the Normandy Beaches*, p.86

55. Kershaw, p.91

56. I am indebted to Mrs Mary Kay Washington for her memories of and comments on Lieutenant Kearfott and to Truman Adkins for responding to my random letter in the local newspaper.

57. BBC *The Peoples' War Archive*, Lt. J. Green RN

58. The archive that forms the Maritime Quest website has been steadfastly created over many years and I am indebted to Michael Pocock not only for permission to access and use these resources but also for his support and encouragement to finish the job. The Schoicet account remains almost anonymous and perhaps one day the author will be revealed.

59. Eisenhower Presidential Library (EPL) archives.

60. Ibid.

61. Ibid.

62. Ibid.

63. The role of the Combat Engineers in their fight on Omaha beach has been overshadowed by the focus on the losses sustained amongst the infantry. However, the engineers suffered just as much as any other unit on 6 June, their men performed equally heroic feats of courage in and around those early hours and many lost their lives trying to do an incredibly dangerous job under constant fire.

64. Heiber, H., & Glantz., *Hitler and His Generals: Military Conferences 1942–1945*, Enigma Books (2003) p.434

65. Eckhertz., p.275

66. The USS *Charles Carroll* is one of the iconic ships of the D-Day story – at least from the American perspective. Another product of MARCOM and laid down in October 1941, the *Carroll* had already attended a number of allied landings in Morocco, Sicily and Salerno.

67. Cornlius Ryan Bequest, Ohio University, 29th Division, File 06/15

PART V

68. 116th Infantry, Roll of Honor

69. Cornelius Ryan Bequest, Ohio University, 29th Division, Dallas File 06/16

70. Cornelius Ryan Bequest, Ohio University, 29th Division, Welsch File 07/18

71. Kershaw, p.118

72. Ibid., p.118

73. 116th Infantry, Roll of Honor

74. Eckhertz, p.47

75. Ibid. p.158–9

76. Cornelius Ryan Bequest, Ohio University, 29th Division, Dallas 06/16

77. Eckhertz, p.48–9

78. Maritime Quest, Lt. J. Green RN archives.

79. There are numerous Facebook groups dedicated to various aspects of the Normandy beaches and especially Omaha and these dedicated researchers have turned up many new photographs taken by local people and American forces that show a large number of French artillery guns were also part of the defences.

80. Eckhertz, p.49–50

81. Ibid.

82. BBC *The People's War Archive*, Lt. J. Green RN

83. Ibid.

84. Eckhertz, p.50–1

85. Kershaw, p.129

86. Ibid. p.130

87. The Peter S. Kalikow Oral History Archive is based in the University of New Orleans and contains a large quantity of materials relating to both D-Day and The Battle of the Bulge.

88. A Company, 1st Battalion, 116th Infantry Regiment, 29th Division After-Action Report – June 1944, Battle of Normandy.

89. Ibid.

90. 116th Infantry, Roll of Honor

91. A Company, 1st Battalion, 116th Infantry Regiment, 29th Division After-Action Report – June 1944, Battle of Normandy.

92. Kershaw, p.142

93. D Company, 1st Battalion, 116th Infantry Regiment, 29th Division After-Action Report – June 1944, Battle of Normandy.

94. More information on 1st Lt. William Gardner can be found in Volume X, July 1951 West Point Alumni Foundation for 1951.

95. Cornelius Ryan Bequest, Ohio University, 29th Division Nance 06/23/22.

96. Ibid. Gearing 06/3/30

97. Ibid. Gearing 06/3/30

98. BBC *The Peoples War Archive*, Lt. J. Green RN

99. Article in La Pine, 'Survival Common Sense' by Leon Pantenburg.

100. Ibid.

101. Cornelius Ryan Bequest. University of Ohio. 29th Division, Haynie 06/26/03

102. Eckhertz, p.54–5

103. Cornelius Ryan Bequest. University of Ohio, 29th Division, Welsch 07/18/04

104. 116th Infantry, 1st Battalion, 116th Infantry Regiment, Command Group After-Action Report – June 1944, Battle of Normandy.

105. Eckhertz, p.57

106. Cornelius Ryan Bequest. University of Ohio, 29th Division, De Pace 06/17/03

107. Kershaw, p.141

108. McCarthy, Donald A., 'The War Years', History Blog.

109. Cornelius Ryan Bequest, Ohio University, 29th Division, Purnell 06/46/04

110. Ibid.

111. Ibid., 06/11/10

112. Kershaw, p.155

113. Ibid. p.152

114. Ibid. p.163

115. *Smithsonian Magazine*, 4 June 2014.

116. Kershaw, p.166

117. Ibid. p.199

PART VI

118. Maritime Quest Archive, memoirs of Major Joseph C. Hazen Jr., 15th Army.
119. Maritime Quest Archive. Memoirs of Lt. John Gilmour RNVR
120. Ibid.
121. Mitchell, W.H., & Sawyer, L.A., *The Empire Ships* 2nd Edn., Lloyds of London Press Ltd., (1990). P.426
122. Maritime Quest Archive, Major J.C. Hazen Jr.
123. Ibid.
124. Ibid.
125. Ibid.
126. Ibid.
127. Ibid. Schoichet Letters
128. Ibid. Major J.C. Hazen Jr.
129. Maritime Quest Archive, S/Sgt. Joseph Bein, 15th Army.
130. Maritime Quest Archive, Sgt. Frank Mueller, 15th Army.
131. Maritime Quest Archive, Major J.C. Hazen.
132. Ibid. Lt. J. Gilmour
133. Ibid. Schoichet letters
134. Maritime Quest Archive, memoirs of Harold Crompton, Engineer Officer
135. Maritime Quest Archive, Major J.C. Hazen Jr.
136. Ibid. Lt. J. Gilmour
137. Ibid. The power failure meant that the copper cables wrapped around the ship to distort the magnetic signature would have failed leaving the ship open to drifting over another magnetic mine or perhaps it simply hit another floating mine under the surface.

Bibliography

Ambrose, Stephen. E., *D-Day: June 6, 1944 – The Battle for the Normandy Beaches*, Simon & Schuster, 1994.

Beevor, A., *D-Day: The Battle for Normandy*, Viking, 2009.

Buderi, R., *The Invention that Changed the World: How a small group of radar pioneers won the Second World War and launched a technological revolution*, Simon & Schuster, 1996.

Eckhertz, H., *D-Day Through German Eyes*, DTZ History Publications, 2016.

Ewing, Joseph., *Let's Go!: A History of the 29th Infantry Division in World War II*, Battery Press, 1986.

Flokstead, Willim B., *The View from the Turret – The 743rd Tank Battalion During World War Two*, Burd Street Press, 1996.

Fraser, D., *A Life of Field Marshal Erwin Rommel*, Harper Collins Publishers, 1994

Keegan, John., *Six Armies in Normandy*, Viking, 1982.

Kershaw, A., *The Bedford Boys – One American Town's Ultimate D-Day Sacrifice*, Da Capo Press, 2003.

Ladd, J.D., *Assault from the Sea, 1939–1945*, David & Charles, 1976.

Lawrence, Wendy S., *Exercise Tiger: The Forgotten Sacrifice of the Silent Few*, Fonthill Media, 2015.

McManus, John C., *The Dead and Those About to Die: D-Day The Big Red One at Omaha Beach*, New American Library, 2015.

Mitchell, W.H., & Sawyer, L.A. *The Empire Ships*, Lloyds of London Press Ltd, 1990.

Morrison, James W., *Bedford Goes to War – The Heroic Story Of A Small Virginia Community In World War II*, Self published, 2013.

Ryan, C., *The Longest Day: The D-Day Story June 6th, 1944*, Taurus Parke, 2019.

Schildt, John W., *The Long Line of Splendour, 1742–1992*, Antietam Publications, 1993.

Stillwell, Paul., *Assault on Normandy: First-Person Accounts from the Sea Services*, Annapolis, MD; Naval Institute Press, 1994.

Slaughter, R., *Omaha Beach and Beyond: The Long March of Sergeant Bob Slaughter*, Zenith Press, 2007.

Small, Ken., *The Forgotten Dead: The True Story of Exercise Tiger, the disastrous rehearsal for D-Day.* Osprey Publishing, 2018.

Whitmarsh, Andrew., *D-Day Landing Craft: How 4,126 'ugly and unorthodox' Allied Craft Made The Normandy Landings Possible*, The History Press, 2024.

Index